ROCKY MOUNTAIN ADVENTURE COLLECTION

Rocky Mountain Adventure Collection

The Adventures of a Colorado Mountaineer

TJ BURR

Illustrated by Andrew Triemer

FITHIAN PRESS

SANTA BARBARA · 1992

To the preservation of the Rocky Mountains
so that future generations
may experience their
majestic splendor.

Design and typography by Jim Cook
Cover design and illustrations by Andrew Triemer
Author photograph by Brent Wessel

LIBRARY OF CONGRESS CATALOGING IN PUBLICATION DATA
Burr, T.J., 1964–
   Rocky Mountain adventure collection: adventures of a Colorado
mountaineer / T.J. Burr
      p.   cm.
   1. Outdoor recreation—Rocky Mountains. 2. Mountains—Rocky
Mountains—Recreational use. 3. Rocky Mountains—Description and
travel. I. Title.
GV191.42.R63B87   1991   91-23499
790'.0978—dc20   CIP
ISBN 1-56474-003-X

Table of Contents

PREFACE

T HIS IS A BOOK of adventure for adventurous readers of all ages and backgrounds. For the last twenty years I've been adventuring in the Rocky Mountains of Colorado and Wyoming. I enjoyed those adventures so much that I felt compelled to share them with somebody. Therefore I compiled a collection of my most memorable adventures to share with you. I wrote this book to share, communicate and to touch a wide range of readers. It is for anyone interested in learning more about the mountains, high adventure, recreation or all three. Regardless of your personal experience with the mountains, if you enjoy reading about mountain adventure, you will enjoy reading this book. You will read about several of my greatest experiences in high adventure in the spectacular Rocky Mountains. If you are an adventurer yourself, you may be curious to get another person's perspective on similar adventures that you have experienced. If you have a passive interest in high adventure, you will enjoy being able to read about my experiences from the comfort of your favorite reading chair. If you are just getting interested in high adventure, I will introduce numerous recreational mountain activities for you to consider. If you are just shopping for adventure activities, this is the book for you.

My adventure stories go beyond the realm of purely physical, nonstop action. At times, I hope to put you on the edge of your seat; other times I hope to convey a deeper, intellectual message about the mountains, life, nature and our environment. Through my collection of personal experiences, I intend to increase your appreciation of your own recreational time and the importance of having recreational resources like the Rocky Mountains. Also, I want to share my feelings and experiences with those who may or may not have had similar recreational opportunities. While reading my adventure tales, you will share my feelings of fear, joy, triumph, freedom, exhilaration, agony, pain, delight and elation. Throughout my adventure stories I try to convey the settings, actions and feelings as I experienced them.

Additionally, I will provide you with a preview of adventures that you may wish to pursue. I will describe possible challenges that await you in the Rocky Mountain wilderness. After all, my interest in high adventure sprouted from hearing and reading about the experiences of others.

This book is not an instructive book describing techniques of climbing or skiing; nor is it a comprehensive guide describing where to go climbing, skiing, backpacking and so on. However, I will tell you how to get to most of the adventure settings that I have used in the book. There are many other books in print that describe techniques, locations and mountain geology, but you will not find another book in print that matches this adventure collection.

As the title implies, this is a selected collection of contemporary Rocky Mountain adventures. If I included all of my adventures, this book would have to be expanded into five volumes. Therefore, I selected a special collection of adventures based on their quality, entertainment value, meaningfulness and ability to broaden your perspective of the incredible Rocky Mountain environment. If, after reading this book, you feel that the Rocky Mountains are recreational resources worth preserving forever, you will have gained the same feeling that I have for them. I hope that human-kind has the foresight to preserve all of our recreationally and ecologically vital areas.

ACKNOWLEDGMENTS

I WOULD LIKE TO THANK and acknowledge my wonderful family, friends and fellow adventurers who made these Rocky Mountain adventures so memorable. I would also like to introduce briefly my fellow adventurers who will appear later in the context of the adventures. First, I want to thank my wife, Roni, my parents, Dixie and Merlyn, and my sister, Aisa, for being so patient with me during the hundreds of hours that I spent writing and rewriting this book. Second, I want to thank my adventure companions with whom I shared these great experiences. Thank you Craig McCoy, Brent Wessel, Al Hinman, Sean McHugh and everyone else who has ventured with me.

The following deserve special recognition. Roni Burr, my lovely wife, is a native Wyoming ranch girl who was born and raised in Rocky Mountain territory. During college, when she was trying to win my attention she followed me down a 100-foot rappel on a vertical rock face at Vedauwoo, and later she followed me a quarter mile into the dark, dingy depths of Cave Creek Cave. She definitely got my attention! Three years later we were married at a mountainside chapel in Wyoming's Medicine Bow Mountains in the foreground of the scenic Snowy Range. I especially thank her for her tender loving support during my book-writing endeavors.

Merlyn, my father and a retired school teacher of twenty-six years, was responsible for getting me into and interested in the Rocky Mountains. When I was five he took me on the first climb I can remember. Before I was five, he carried me on his shoulders on hiking, fishing and hunting excursions in the mountains. Later he climbed many mountains with me until my appetite for climbing exceeded his. He made my adventures possible when he moved from St. Francis, Kansas, to Brighton, Colorado, in 1963. Thank you for the cherished memories, Dad.

Dixie Burr, my mother, kept me in balance and watched out for me. She provided me with the motherly support and loving care that I needed throughout my adventurous life. She was always concerned about my safety while climbing, and on many occasions I recalled her words of caution before taking an unnecessary risk. Thank you for taking care of me, Mom.

Aisa Burr, my sister, gave me great encouragement and support throughout my adventurous years while living at home. Although most of my alpine adventures were too strenuous and fast paced for her, we did go on several memorable hikes together. Thank you for being a super sister and friend.

Andrew Triemer, my friend and illustrator, did an excellent job of portraying the adventure spirit through his illustrations. He is from Gulf Breeze, Florida, and enjoys being near the ocean. Andrew and I worked together for four and a half years in Atlanta, Georgia.

Craig McCoy and I have logged many, many backcountry miles together. Consequently his name will appear more than any other in the following pages. Craig is an Oklahoma native, part Cherokee and adopted Coloradoan. Craig's most outstanding adventure quality is his endurance. Once he sets his mind to achieving an objective, he always reaches it. During an extremely strenuous portion of our five days in the backcountry, his pulse skyrocketed to 180 (three heartbeats per second)! Our physical size, strengths, attitudes and intellects are well matched, and if anyone can outlast me in the high country it is Craig. We shared many momentous adventures together in the Rocky Mountains.

Brent Wessel and I first met as neighbors in a residence hall at the University of Wyoming. He is a Wyoming native (I don't hold that against him) of Encampment, a peaceful small town nestled against the Medicine Bow Mountains. We first teamed up to help each other through the rigors of engineering. Later, when we found some free time, we teamed up to experience many enjoyable adventures. Brent is a gung-ho caver, a fearless motorcycle rider (hogger), and a rock scrambling maniac.

Gayle Wessel is a very supportive friend whom I thank for allowing Brent to go adventuring with me.

Al Hinman is another Wyoming native whom I met at the university. He is from Greybull, Wyoming, a small town near the base of the Bighorn Mountains. Although he is very capable in many outdoor areas, he is an adept spelunker. He possesses all of the skills required in subterranean exploration, and he is an active member of the National Speleological Society. Al and I have caved, hiked and rappelled together on several occasions.

Like many good friends of mine, I also met Sean McHugh at the university. Like myself, he is also a Coloradoan who crossed the state border to go to college in Wyoming. We have caved, climbed, hiked, camped and explored together in the Rockies. He loves the high country as much as I do and is adept in backcountry survival. He has a positive personality and is an asset to any mountain-climbing team. He has also led backpacking trips into Banff National Park in the Canadian Rockies and other wilderness areas.

Now pursuing our careers, most of us have radiated from our Rocky Mountain origins. However, I'm sure that the allure of the Rocky Mountains will bring us all back together some day to share once again high adventure.

ROCKY MOUNTAIN ADVENTURE COLLECTION

Introduction

*To be an adventurer is to be engrossed
with the spirit of adventure!*

DWARFED BY THE towering 14,197-foot peak, the three of us appeared as spots on the side of one mountain within a sea of mountains. Our lives literally rested on the mercy of the mountain's powerful grasp. Nobody knew where we were; and nobody shared in the death-defying ordeal that we faced that afternoon.

On our descent of the fourteener, we wrongfully took a shortcut down a mountainside of dangerously loose rubble (talus). The entire mountainside was extremely unstable; with every step we dislodged a few rocks that, in turn, dislodged a few more, threatening to bring the entire mountainside down upon us. I took every cautious step as if it were my last. In a staggered formation, each separated by twenty vertical feet, the three of us zigzagged precariously down the mountainside.

Two hundred feet into our descent we were committed to continuing down the unforgiving mountainside. Backtracking back up the unstable slope would be more dangerous than continuing downward. From back up on the ridgetop, the mountainside had looked like a dozen other rocky mountainsides that I had safely descended. That was a dangerously misleading perception. Once committed to the route, we discovered that the rocky mountainside was dangerously unstable. It was like walking on a booby-trapped mountainside armed with several thousand tons of loose granite.

That afternoon was the longest of my life. Our progress was dreadfully slow, and the mountain before us seemed to stretch on forever. I truly thought that my days of high country adventure were over. There was no turning back, and no easy way to get off that mountainside. My eyes burned, and my vision was blurred from sweat dripping off my forehead. My heart pulsated rapidly. I focused my full attention on making each consecutive step.

Life began to reveal itself to me like never before. It seemed as if I would die before ever making a significant contribution to society: before starting a family; before telling my parents how much I loved them; before doing any of the other things that I hoped to do. As I treaded across the surface of that mountainside, my appreciation for life grew immensely. My will to live was stronger than ever. I began longing just to see the sun rise in the morning. But why did my appreciation for life blossom on this mountainside?

Like many important things in our lives, we seldom realize how important many things in life are until they are gone, or until the threat of losing them is realized. On that afternoon in the Colorado Rockies, I realized the value of my precious investment in life. I wanted to invest more time in living a quality life. I wanted to live so much that I asked God to help me safely to the bottom with every step. During that day on the mountain I had plenty of time to think about life and death.

Our predicament that afternoon continued to worsen. At one point, while traversing a steep snowfield, my life was held by the compacted snow beneath my feet. If the snow had broken away, I would have slid 200 feet to the rocky bottom. Regretably, I didn't have a safety rope, crampons or an ice axe to help break a fall. If I slipped, I would slide to my death.

Besides saying many silent prayers that afternoon, I also made several promises to myself. Writing *Rocky Mountain Adventure Collection* is one of the things that I promised to do. I realized that if we died that afternoon, nobody would ever know about the traumatic experience we had shared on that mountainside. Indeed, nobody would ever know about any of the countless meaningful experiences that I have had during my Rocky Mountain adventures.

However, I didn't write this collection just to tell about my adventures; I also wrote it to share the importance of those adventures and the importance of maintaining our natural recreation areas. Of course, the mountains aren't the only place to spend your recreational time. There are thousands of parks and wilderness areas preserved for our enjoyment. To preserve our national parks and to get even more park acreage, we have to understand the importance of wilderness to our health and to the health of our environment. To compete with economics, we have to put a value on adventurelands, recreational areas, wilderness and our environment. As exemplified by this book, the value of the Rocky Mountains and other wilderness areas is infinite. They are irreplaceable natural resources.

This book is a record of my greatest investments in life; time invested in enjoying an irreplaceable resource, and making the most of my recreation time. Of course, I don't expect everyone to have the great amount of time that I used to have to invest in recreation and adventure. Nor do I expect you to go out and take the same risks that I have taken. If you're not enjoying yourself, you're not participating in recreation. You may find recreation in the city park down the street or in the state parks across town. That is fine. Of course, if you're seeking high adventure, you'll have to go further than the city park to walk the jagged edge of a mountain ridge. I enjoy high-country adventure; it is my kind of recreation. As the prospectors of the gold rush days had gold fever, I have Rocky Mountain fever (not the kind that you get from a tick). The spirit of the Rocky Mountains is in my soul.

As many Colorado natives will attest, once the Rocky Mountain way of life is in your blood it will always be there. It is like a welcome obsession. No matter how far from the mountains I venture, the vitality of my spirit still resides in the Rocky Mountains. As the adventures in this collection will show, the Rocky Mountains have enriched the spiritual, intellectual, emotional and physical quality of my life. While meditating in grassy alpine meadows surrounded by lofty peaks, I find spiritual tranquility (peace of mind). While backpacking through lush evergreen forests, my intellectual energies are rejuvenated by the invigorating environment. The innocence and natural beauty of the wilderness captures my emotions, and the physical challenges that I face cultivate my health.

The mountains and my experiences there have played a significant role in my overall development. When I was a child, the mountains were my fantasy land. When I was a teenager, they were my inspiration to achieve higher goals, and a healthy alternative to the common pitfalls of the teenage years. When I became an adult, the mountains became my adventureland, my symbol of hope, my classroom and my place of solitude. I also go to the mountains to make the best use of my recreation time, and to seek a deeper understanding of the environment and humankind's role in that environment. The mountains are my choice source of recreation. Everyone should have someplace where they can "cut loose" and feel totally free.

As the stresses of a more complicated and overcrowded world increase, the importance of recreation also increases. We need to add more recreation and relaxation to our lifestyles. Statistics indicate that our recreation time is less today than it was during the Dark Ages. Instead of making life easier, computers, automated machinery, data facsimile machines and technology have helped create more work for us. We are in an era in which time and money rules our lives. Now that we have such rapid communications, there is a misconception that everything has to get to its destination today, or tomorrow at the latest. Now, we can handle and process more information than ever before. Information overload is running rampant. By 9:00 A.M. on a typical workday, millions of people around the world are already suffering from information overload. It's easy to understand why more and more people are burning out, turning to drugs and consulting psychologists. The world isn't going to stop spinning if we decrease our information processing by a few hours each week. We aren't going to beat the clock by working ourselves into a cemetery. So don't feel guilty if you leave work at quitting time. Plan your vacations wisely, and enjoy your recreation time. If you're a teenager or younger, use your summers and holidays to learn more about your environment through outdoor recreation. Don't just sit idly fixed to a television screen while the most active years of your life pass by.

Turning the computer on to write this book was the worst thing I did for my recreation time. But, if you can benefit from reading about my Rocky Mountain adventures, my time will have been well spent. I have high expectations for my book; but if they all fall through you will at least receive a few hours of reading entertainment as a minimum return on your investment.

Through the adventures in the following chapters, my primary goal is to entertain you with my tales of high-country adventure. My second goal is to show you the importance of recreational adventure in a person's life. My third goal is to point out the importance of preserving parks and wilderness areas for our health and our environment's health. Our public parks, forests and wilderness areas are the last strongholds for recreation and adventure. We must realize the irreplaceable recreational value of these natural resources. And finally, I want to persuade you to make the most of your recreation time. Whether it's playing Frisbee in the city park, backpacking in a state forest or climbing a mountain, you should strive to make it an experience worth remembering. Invest your recreation time in making quality memories, memories that you would be proud to put in your own adventure collection.

The adventures in this collection span twenty years of my life. Only my most memorable and meaningful adventures are included. All the adventures have, in some way, enhanced the quality of my life. I hope the energy and emotion that I put into sharing my adventures with you will inspire you to make the most of your precious recreation time.

This collection contains several adventures associated with a variety of mountain activities. It is organized around seven main activities: climbing, skiing, running, backpacking, caving, exploring and prospecting. From each of these recreational activities, I have included a few of my best adventure stories. They are stories worthy of repeating at night while sitting around a blazing campfire. Well, at least I've told them to some of my friends while sitting around a campfire deep in the wilderness of the Rocky Mountains.

In these adventures I'll take you with me to the summit of Colorado's highest peak, into high country wilderness during the dead of winter, on a hair-raising summit run, on a five-day trek across fifty miles of Rocky Mountain wilderness, into the dingy depths of a mountain cave, back into Colorado's colorfully rich mining history, prospecting in gold country, and on several other exciting adventures.

To get you into a Rocky Mountain mood for the upcoming adventures I've included a chapter to help you put the Rocky Mountains into perspective. It is a chapter about the mountains, the beautiful setting for all of the adventures in this collection. It is not a detailed description of the physical composition and geology of the mountains; that information is available in numerous other books. The Mountains of Adventure is an ice-breaking chapter to familiarize you with the Colorado Rockies and how they compare with other mountains of the world. Basically, it's an orientation chapter to prepare you for the high adventure that will follow it.

Before you read the last paragraph, I must caution you. The adventures in this collection are all true-life adventures. They start with my first adventures as a child; I wasn't always a responsible adult. You will be reading about many of my adventures as a beginning mountaineer. Unlike a mountain goat, I wasn't born into the natural rhythms of the high country; I learned the ways of the mountains through my own experience. The truth is, I made and continue to make mistakes just like we all do. Some of the things I did during my adventures were foolish, careless and very risky. Since I didn't read much when I was younger, much of my backcountry knowledge came out of trial and error. I made many foolish mistakes; fortunately, I am still alive to write about them. During my upbringing, my mother accused me of "taking unnecessary risks." Among other things, she called me "crazy." My father also had some creative adjectives that he used on me. So, if some of the things that I do in the adventures seem unreasonably risky, it's because they are.

Please turn the page and journey with me on these real-life Rocky Mountain adventures in "The Mountains of Adventure."

1. Mountains of Adventure

The mountains are the spectacular geological formations that harbor the spirits of mountaineers.

L IKE A SCENE from a fairytale land, lofty, snow-capped peaks rise up from the great plains. To the east and west, vast expanses of rolling hills, grasslands, and farmland extend for hundreds of miles. Mysteriously, the great Continental Divide, the spinal cord of the Rocky Mountains, splits the continent into two distinct parts. All of the precipitation falling on the west side flows toward the Pacific Ocean, and all of the precipitation falling on the east side flows toward the Gulf of Mexico. The Rocky Mountains stretch north and south across the United States from Mexico to Canada. The Rocky Mountains "peak-out" midway between the two borders in the highest state in the nation, Colorado, where they reach their highest grandeur.

The Rocky Mountains are an adventurer's paradise. Rugged granite peaks tower to heights over 14,000 feet and contain some of North America's greatest wilderness areas. Here are mountains for adventure and recreational land created for living life to its fullest. The mountains offer a full spectrum of opportunities to match everyone's willful risk level. From the sightseeing tourist to the gung-ho mountaineer, the mountains have the features to satisfy the extremes and the in-betweens. The jagged peaks that tourists like to view from a distance are the same peaks that mountaineers like to climb, a setting for high adventure and alpine beauty.

Beautiful, pyramiding peaks; steep snowfields year-round; glaciers; raging white water rivers; shear granite cliffs; caves that meander beneath the mountaintops; deep canyons; turquoise blue tarns; and evergreen forests that resemble fairytale settings. Thankfully, they aren't imaginary. They provide the places that allow common people, like you and me, to transform into adventurers. They make adventurers crawl out of their tents at sunrise and scream in ecstasy!

The mountains burgeon with life! The Rocky Mountains are dynamic, constantly changing. The topography, the flora and the fauna dance to nature's rhythm. Every day, every hour and every minute is different from the last. The ever-changing mountain environment is integral to its beauty and its magic.

Every time that I am in the mountains I experience a mysterious, magical sensation. My body feels lighter. I seem to draw physical and mental energy from the environment. The mix of thin air, lower atmospheric pressure, less gravity, natural surroundings and evergreen trees gives me a "Rocky Mountain High." I feel exuberant every time I am in the mountains. Many times while my friends and I have been doing something in the mountains I'll laugh or smile for no apparent reason. I've noticed similar expressions on passing hikers, and I've received some of the heartiest greetings ever while hiking in the high country. The mysterious smile that accompanies the sensation is what I call a Rocky Mountain Smile. It's always a welcome expression, an expression of happiness about being in the mountains. A Rocky Mountain Smile is preceded by a euphoric rush of mental energy, a refreshing feeling reflecting the august mountain environment through a happy spirit. A Rocky Mountain Smile is just one of many special sensations that isn't entirely scientifically explainable. You'll read more about Rocky Mountain Highs and Rocky Mountains Smiles in the following chapters.

The Rockies are among the world's most fascinating natural features. They were formed about seventy million years ago, when Colorado was sill covered by a sea, during a period of violent geosynclinal activity. The uplift took place during the period referred to as the Laramide Orogeny. Enormous masses of granite were thrust upward by faulting activity, and the resulting masses of granite formed the base. Like a master sculptor working on a clump of clay, nature carved the granite into a masterpiece, using its dynamic forces to shape the mountains. Physical and chemical weathering hewed the granite mass for millions of years. Glacial activity carved the peaks, ridges and valleys into their rugged forms. Glaciers were, and still are (in some areas) nature's work horses.

The alpine glaciers have retreated from the southern Rocky Mountain regions. Many former glaciers that are now glorified snowfields are still referred to as glaciers, such as Arapaho Glacier. At one time, a much colder time, glaciers dominated the Rocky Mountain landscape. Precipitation, freezing temperatures and gravity created the glaciers; over long periods of time gravity compressed the snow and ice into incredibly massive and heavy ice sheets. Pulled by gravity, the dense glaciers plowed paths (glacial troughs) through the uplifted masses of granite. Glaciers crushed the rock beneath them and plowed through rock in front of them. Rocky debris was pushed aside like dirt from a plow to form moraines on the sides. The glaciers cut away from two or more sides to form peaks, ridges and spurs.

The resulting alpine valleys now contain rivers, waterfalls, lakes and alpine meadows that once supported tons of ice. These ancient glacial troughs have a distinctive U-shaped profile, as opposed to the steeper V-shaped valleys that are carved by rivers. After the glaciers melted, they left remnant features that help give the Rocky Mountains their rugged, beautiful character. Cirques, hanging troughs, tarns, finger lakes, spurs, aretes, horns, cols and knife-edged ridges are some of the most spectacular glacial features. Cirques are the circular depressions (bowls) that once contained the top ends of glaciers. Today, some of them contain picturesque alpine lakes, and some of the higher cirques contain permanent snowfields. The cirque lakes (tarns) are typically filled with scintillating turquoise water. The spectacular color of the tarns is a result of sunlight reflecting off very finely ground soil, or glacial flour, that remains suspended in the water.

Hanging troughs were created when a glacier intersected with a deeper, main glacier. A cliff was formed where the smaller glacier intersected the larger glacier. Today, many of those cliffs (hanging troughs) are sites for beautiful waterfalls. Crater Lake, east of Granby, Colorado, is surrounded by hanging troughs with multiple waterfalls trickling over the edges and into the lake. South of the lake there is a high cirque filled with snow most of the year; the melting snow from that cirque is a primary source of water that feeds the beautiful waterfalls.

Finger lakes are elongated lakes that occupy depressions in lower parts of glacial troughs. Long Lake, in the Indian Peaks Wilderness Area, is a supreme example of a finger lake.

Spurs, aretes, horns and cols are formations that remained between the glaciers, the surviving granite not carved away by the glaciers. These are the formations that give the peaks their character. Spurs are lower, rounded ridges that are often covered with tundra-like vegetation. Niwot Ridge, in the Indian Peaks, is a good example of a spur. An arete is a jagged, knife-like ridge between two cirque walls. Aretes are common Rocky Mountain formations; they give the peaks their rugged appearance. Horns are the most impressive peak formations of all. The Matterhorn of the Swiss Alps is the best-known horn in the world. A horn is the remaining rock left in the middle of three or more cirques. Its characteristic steep sides are a result of the carving action of several glaciers on several sides. A col is a notch or low point in a ridge formed at the intersection of two cirques from opposite sides of the ridge.

Don't be discouraged if you don't remember all of these terms when they reappear later in the adventure stories. There is a glossary in the back of the book for quick reference. Since I am neither qualified nor willing to tell you the complete geologic history of the Rocky Mountains, I won't. Libraries and bookstores contain numerous books covering that. So, if I've whetted your appetite for such information, please pursue it (after you're finished reading this book, of course).

The glaciers were the workhorses that performed the bulk of the carving work. They carved the basic shapes that still remain. The other forces that helped fine-tune the shape of the Rockies are still at work. Every year, the mountains are a little different than the previous year. Unfortunately, nature's forces (namely entropy) will not stop until the Rockies are flattened. Gravity and physical and chemical weathering are continually at work, reshaping the mountains and slowly wearing them down. In another 150 million years the Rockies might look like the Appalachian Mountains do today. In 300 million years they may be reduced to the size of the Ozarks. Weathering processes reshape the mountains by grinding, washing, cracking and breaking apart. Water, acting under the forces of gravity and temperature fluctuations, is a primary weathering agent. Freezing water inside cracks in rock masses expands and breaks the rock masses into smaller masses and the fragmented boulders and rocks tumble down at the mercy of gravity. Flowing water carves valleys and canyons and carries the broken-down granite down toward the plains. Water, plants, animals, wind and sunshine all contribute to the reshaping of the mountains. These dynamic forces will continue to act until the potential energy of the earth is null, and the landforms are all flat (at equilibrium). But for now, it is the process that helps make the mountain environment spectacular and challenging.

It is important to remember that the mountains, like everything else, are part of a changing environment. Anyone who enters the Rocky Mountain domain is subject to all of nature's dynamic forces. The same forces that shape the mountains into attractive adventure paradises also make the mountains hazardous playgrounds for experienced and inexperienced visitors. Nature doesn't cancel a thunderstorm so that you can have a pleasant picnic in the mountains, nor does nature prevent an avalanche from hurtling down the mountainside just because you have a tent set up in its path. Since the dangers, risks and pitfalls of mountain adventure will be thoroughly encountered in the context of the collection, I will not risk sounding didactic to elaborate on them. You have to use the same common sense in the mountains that you use when venturing anywhere else: you must know your limitations and abilities. If you are planning your first backcountry backpacking trip, you should go with an experienced backpacker. My first backpacking trip was on a trek with my junior high outdoor recreation class. Experience and common sense are key aspects of survival in any part of the world. As you will discover in some of my early adventures, I was blessed with neither of those virtues.

Before you get into the adventures, I want you to have a good understanding of how the Rocky Mountains compare with the other mountain ranges of the world. I also want to orient you to the setting for most of my adventures, specifically the Colorado Rockies. We'll start with the global perspective and work toward the specific, state-wide picture.

The greater Rocky Mountains of North America rank third relative to the major mountain ranges of each continent. Table 1 lists the ranking of each continent's major mountain range based upon magnitude, mountainous area and average altitude of the higher peaks. (Although Africa's Kilimanjaro is higher than Europe's Elbrus, Europe's mountains appear to be more impressive as a whole than Africa's.)

The Colorado Rockies are part of North America's Rocky Mountain chain. The Himalayas of Asia are undisputedly the

Continent	Major Mtn. Range	Highest Mtn.	Elev.
1. Asia	Himalayas	Mt. Everest	29,028'
2. South America	Andes	Mt. Aconcagua	22,834'
3. North America	Rocky Mountains	Mt. McKinley	20,320'
4. Europe	Caucasus	Mt. Elbrus	18,510'
	Alps	Mt. Blanc	15,771'
5. Africa	Eastern Africa Range	Mt. Kilimanjaro	19,340'
6. Antarctica	Scattered Ranges	Vinson Massif	16,860'
7. Australia	Great Dividing Range	Mt. Kosciusko	7,310'

TABLE 1—Highest mountains on each continent

highest, most impressive mountains in the world. At 29,028 feet, Mt. Everest is over twice the height of Colorado's Mt. Elbert. The Colorado Rockies probably compare closest, with respect to basic character, with Europe's Swiss Alps, although there are only ten fourteeners in the Swiss Alps compared to fifty-four in Colorado.

In North America, Alaska, Canada, Mexico and California are the only states or countries with peaks higher than Colorado's Mt. Elbert. Mount Elbert is the twenty-ninth highest peak in North America. Of the twenty-eight higher peaks, only one is in the contiguous United States. Characteristically, the mountains of California, Alaska and Canada are closest to the Colorado Rockies. Mexico's Pico de Orizaba towers to an impressive 18,700 feet, but Mexico's big mountains are tightly grouped and much different from the Colorado Rockies. Sheer height and ruggedness are not the only characteristics for measuring the impressiveness of a mountain range. Besides Alaska, California and Colorado, there are many other states that have impressively beautiful mountains, such as north Georgia's Blue Ridge Mountains.

In the contiguous United States, California's Mt. Whitney is the highest. Colorado's Mt. Elbert is the second highest peak, only sixty-one feet below Whitney's summit. In the contiguous United States there are sixty-eight fourteeners: fifty-four in Colorado, thirteen in California and one in Washington (Mt. Ranier). Colorado has over 1,000 peaks above 10,000 feet. The lowest elevation in Colorado is 3,350 feet. That explains why Colorado has the highest average elevation of any state. And surprisingly, only forty percent of Colorado is mountainous. The Colorado Rockies stretch north and south across the state, blending into the Rocky Mountains of New Mexico and Wyoming at each end.

The Colorado Rocky Mountains are grand mountains that contain many natural blessings. However, many other states also have mountains that are grand in their own ways. Thirty-eight other states have at least one mountain or more, or some variation thereof. Even Louisiana claims a mountain: Driskill Mountain (535 feet). To show you how the states with the top twenty-five highest elevations compare, Table 2 lists the rank, state, highest

State	Highest Point	Elev.
1. Alaska	Mt. McKinley	20,320'
2. California	Mt. Whitney	14,494'
3. Colorado	Mt. Elbert	14,433'
4. Washington	Mt. Ranier	14,410'
5. Wyoming	Gannett Peak	13,804'
6. Hawaii	Mauna Kea Peak	13,796'
7. Utah	Kings Peak	13,528'
8. New Mexico	Wheeler Peak	13,161'
9. Nevada	Boundary Peak	13,143'
10. Montana	Granite Peak	12,799'
11. Idaho	Borah Peak	12,662'
12. Arizona	Humphreys Peak	12,633'
13. Oregon	Mt. Hood	11,239'
14. Texas	Guadalupe Peak	8,749'
15. South Dakota	Harney Peak	7,242'
16. North Carolina	Mt. Mitchell	6,684'
17. Tennessee	Clingmans Dome	6,643'
18. New Hampshire	Mt. Washington	6,288'
19. Virginia	Mt. Rogers	5,729'
20. Nebraska	Mt. Constable	5,426'
21. New York	Mt. Marcy	5,344'
22. Maine	Mt. Katahdin	5,268'
23. Oklahoma	Black Mesa	4,973'
24. West Virginia	Spruce Knob	4,863'
25. Georgia	Brasstown Bald	4,784'

TABLE 2—Highest points of top 25 states

point and elevation. Originally I only included the top fifteen states, but since I lived in Georgia for a few years I felt compelled to extend the list to include Brasstown Bald—the first Appalachian mountain that I "climbed."

The Colorado Rockies are composed of hundreds of mountains, each of which has unique characteristics. Some are steep, rocky cones of granite; some are covered with dense forest; some are spotted with snowfields year-round; some have steep rock faces

that attract technical climbers; and some are merely steep hills. Every mountain has its own unique characteristics and history. Some might even say they have their own personalities. And every mountain has some appealing geologic, historic or ecological significance. Colorado has fifty-four officially recognized fourteeners and twelve other questionable summits with high points above 14,000 feet. There are about 740 summits above 13,000 feet. Below 13,000 feet there are so many peaks that I didn't have time to count them all.

The Colorado Rockies are divided into ten subranges. From east to west across the state those subranges are the: Front Range, Sangre de Cristo Range, Ten Mile Range, Mosquito Range, Sawatch Range, Elk Range, San Juan Range, Needle Mountains, Sheffels Range and San Miguel Range. Longs Peak, in the Front Range, is the northernmost fourteener, and Culebra Peak, in the Sangre de Cristo Range, is the southernmost fourteener.

Most of the adventures in this collection took place in Colorado. A few of my adventures were in wonderful Wyoming. The Wyoming adventures took place in the Shirley Mountains, Sherman Mountains and Medicine Bow Mountains, Rocky Mountain subranges in southeastern Wyoming.

Now that you know how the Rocky Mountains rank with the other mountain ranges of the world, let's look at some of the features that attract adventurers and others to the Rocky Mountains.

The Rocky Mountains are an ideal setting for anyone looking for a challenge or something to break the often monotonous work cycle. The invaluable wilderness areas provide adventurers with the wild settings that they need when they feel the driving urge to "cut loose." In a world dictated by an abundance of human-imposed structure, some people have to escape to the wilderness occasionally to keep their sanity intact. In the mountains, you can do almost whatever you want. If you want to run deep into the woods and howl like a wolf, that is your business. If you howled like a wolf in the city, society might lock you up. But guess what? Nature doesn't care whether you act crazy or not. In the wilder-

ness, you are in command of your actions and the results of those actions. You have to decide whether or not you're willing to take the risks associated with your actions. If you're willing to risk your life scrambling to the top of a cliff, that is your choice to make. The freedom to encounter danger and take risks are the principal reasons that adventurers are attracted to the Rocky Mountains. The mountains give the adventurer a setting that allows true freedom of choice. In some cases it is the choice to live or die. For mountaineers, living in the mountains is the only way truly to live.

There are numerous other things that attract people to the mountains. The American Indians came to the mountains to live. The Spaniards came to explore and search for gold. The early explorers came to satisfy their curiosities. The mountainmen came for the valuable furs and the secluded way of life. And the prospectors came for the gold. Today, people visit and live in the mountains for recreation, the lifestyle, vacations and of course, adventure. The Rocky Mountains have something for everyone to enjoy. Mountaineers, tourists, skiers, naturalists, backpackers, campers, spelunkers, rafters, fisherpersons, technical climbers and all categories of adventurers have their own special reasons for entering the Rocky Mountain domain. I enjoy doing anything in the mountains, from a family barbecue to climbing the highest peaks. Even a modern adventurer, like myself, slows down for an occasional picnic or relaxing day of fishing.

Since this is a book of adventure, I will define what I consider to be adventure (as it is used in this book). An adventure is a remarkable experience or an experience that involves exposing yourself to danger and taking risks. So, if you're a Florida native taking a ski trip or other vacation to the Rockies, you're probably embarking on an adventure. Most family vacations would qualify as "remarkable experiences." Of course, that isn't the kind of adventure that I'm referring to in this book. I'm referring to remarkable experiences and dangerous experiences in natural settings. Adventures take place in wilderness areas that are remote from the conveniences that most of us take for granted. An adventure goes beyond the common, everyday experience. To experience an adventure, the adventurer must be mentally and physically involved in the activity. A true adventurer is engrossed in the spirit of the adventure. In fact, in most adventures, survival depends upon being engrossed in the activity; performing the motions in a perfunctory manner is not enough. To experience true adventure you must hold your adventure close to your heart for the duration of the experience. You must be in the spirit of adventure!

The Rocky Mountains contain the necessary ingredients for adventure. The mountains are part of a dynamic environment that is filled with plenty of potential pitfalls for wandering adventurers. Climatic variations, rapidly changing weather conditions, physical obstacles, avalanches and wild animals are all variables in the adventure equation. The mountains aren't always the calm, picturesque paradises that are often portrayed on television and in paintings. If you're nestled by the fireside with your wife in your alpine summer cabin, it probably is paradise. But, if you're caught on a rocky summit without shelter during a thunderstorm, it can be miserable. Or you could be on a slippery mountainside during a torrential downpour being chased by an undernourished mountain lion. Or you could be mauled to death during the night by ravaging grizzly bears. All right, so I got a little carried away with the spirit of things. Those are stories that adventurers like sharing at night around a campfire.

It's always fun to laugh and joke about dangerous experiences and exciting adventures after they are over (and you are still alive to laugh about it). But, when your life is hanging by a nylon rope and you are 100 feet above the ground, it's not a laughing matter. For now, pretend that you are relaxing by the fireside in a mountain hideaway, and I am telling you my adventure stories. The following adventure stories are my actual experiences in "The Mountains of Adventure."

2. Climbing

Mountain climbing reaches beyond the levels of ordinary sports. It tests strength, educes emotions, galvanizes the mind and enlightens the spirit.

F ROM THE TRAILHEADS below we appeared as two spots slowly moving up the mountainside. From our perspective we were two climbers progressing toward the top of an elusive peak. For that day, the climbing experience was ours. Others could speculate what it was like to be climbing the majestic mountain, but only we knew what it was like to be high on the mountainside. Although we lost sight of the summit as it dipped behind other formations in its foreground, we knew how to get to it. Craig and I would continue upward until we achieved our goal of reaching the summit.

Every step offered a different perspective, a different challenge and a different attitude. At the base in the valley below, we saw everything before us: our goal, intermediate objectives and our route to the top. At the base, the challenge was impossible to comprehend; we were optimistic about making it, but our attitudes didn't reflect the difficult reality of the challenges before us. Slowly, everything changed as we ascended close to the top.

Even though we climbed together, we climbed alone; our greatest challenges came from within. We had to carry ourselves to the top, and the inner struggle was as great as the physical struggle up the mountain. Like a central processor, my mind constantly received information from my body and its surroundings: aching muscles sent signals of pain with every step, the blood's oxygen level lowered, bodily energy was burned at ten calories per minute, body temperature rose and sank to adjust to the changing environmental conditions, eyes and ears allowed the mind to react to any environmental hazards that might arise. With every step, my mind analyzed all of the incoming information to make the decision on whether to continue, stop or turn back. The mind supplies the inner-drive that keeps a mountaineer climbing and also supplies the common sense that keeps a mountaineer alive when the body is too exhausted to continue, or when the conditions are too hazardous to continue.

To any onlooker, perhaps someone in the valley watching us with a telescope, we appeared as distant climbers pitting our physical strengths against the challenges of the mountain. To us, it was much more than a matter of endurance. It was a holistic experience with our physical, emotional, intellectual and spiritual selves. Mountain climbing is much more than challenging the elements and obstacles of the mountain.

Climbing is a very personal activity. Even though teamwork is often an important part of a climbing expedition, it is really an individual challenge between the climber and the mountain. Solitary climbers have climbed the world's most challenging mountains many times, including Mt. Everest and the Eiger. But, whether as an individual or as part of a team, the person chooses to climb for personal reasons. Some of the reasons that I climb are common among many climbers and some are unique.

There are several reasons why I love climbing mountains. Probably the most common reason is in the old cliché "because it's there." Although I haven't climbed any mountains that aren't "there," that is not on my list of reasons for climbing mountains. Volcanoes are also "there," but I haven't yet had the urge to thrust myself into the crater of one. I climb for the satisfaction of setting and achieving goals, for the holistic experience that I get from climbing, for the enriched appreciation of life that I get from facing the sometimes life-threatening challenges on mountains, for the summit experience, and because mountaineering is in my blood.

Climbing a mountain, unlike many other goals in life, is a measurable goal that can be accomplished in a relatively short period of time. Reaching the top of a mountain can be accomplished in a matter of hours, days, weeks and, at most, a few months. It is a goal with a definite beginning and end, with progress being measured at each step upward and each foot of elevation gained. When I set my mind to climbing Mt. Elbert, I had a definite goal, a strategy to meet that goal and several objectives leading toward that goal. The goal was to stand upon the summit, the strategy was to follow a route from one objective to the next and the objectives were a number of intermediate landmarks leading toward the summit. Achieving a goal is always a satisfying experience, and, unlike saving money for a dream house, climbing Mt. Elbert is a goal that can be accomplished in one day. However, the climbing experience is more important than the satisfaction of achieving goals.

Another reason that I climb mountains is for the holistic experience: the physical, emotional, intellectual and spiritual aspects of climbing. Physical challenges, feelings, thoughts and a spiritual sense of existence combine to form the holistic experience that we remember as a memory. I am proud to say that my mountain-climbing memories are some of my best memories. The holistic climbing experience (the memory) starts on the physical plane of existence.

The physical challenge of mountain climbing is all that can be observed by a distant spectator. The spectator sees the climbers overcoming the obstacles of the mountain: boulders, avalanche chutes, snowfields, crevices, rockslides, vertical faces and the elements. Indeed, the physical challenge of mountain climbing is certainly a part of the overall experience. Mountain climbing allows the climber to test his or her physical limits and endurance levels; and it is a good way to stay in vigorous physical condition. It is the individual's physical strength and endurance against the mighty mountain. Step-by-step, foot-by-foot, you have to push for the top. Every muscle in the body is used; in nontechnical climbing the legs and lungs get the greatest workout. When the body starts to tire it recruits the assistance of emotions in an effort to coax the mind into stopping.

Pain, freedom, fatigue, aches, satisfaction and jubilation are some of the emotions felt while climbing. As muscles get tired and energy levels get low the mind is bombarded with signals of pain and fatigue. On the positive side, the mind is also treated with feelings of freedom, satisfaction and jubilation. When I am climbing in the mountains I feel that I am free, free to go anywhere that I want, free to make my own decisions whether good or bad. I feel jubilation and satisfaction after reaching the summit. Above all, I feel an emotional sense of concern for the mountains and for nature in general, developed through my many mountain adventures. Emotions work to influence my mind to make decisions and take action.

Mental and intellectual processes are another part of the holistic climbing experience. The mind is the climber's central processing unit during the climb. It provides the willpower that drives a tired body to the summit. It makes the critical decision whether the body can continue, it analyzes environmental conditions to determine whether the body can survive, and it reacts to hazards and steers the body away from taking unnecessary risks. Unfortunately, I haven't perfected the use of my mind, and so I don't always make the best decisions. I have continued when I should have turned back, I have taken shortcuts when I should have stayed on well-known routes, and I have taken unnecessary chances when I should have gone with the sure choices. My climbing decisions haven't been and aren't flawless; but, somehow, I have survived to tell you my stories, although my vitality may be a result of my spirit rather than the result of a conscious decision.

The spiritual plane of existence is the final part of the holistic experience of climbing. If twenty people were asked for the definition of "spiritual" you would get twenty different answers. In this book, the spiritual plane is meant to be the highest level of existence. The spirit is the mysterious part that survives after death. It is your eternal life force, where your morals and deepest beliefs are kept. The spiritual plane is where you communicate with forces or entities that you cannot physically detect. Mountain climbing strengthens my spiritual awareness. Climbing gives me a chance to get in touch with nature and the very forces responsible for my existence, and it is from my experiences in the mountains that I know our existence is integrally tied to the environment.

Another, less profound, reason that I climb mountains is for the enriched appreciation that I get from facing life-threatening situations. I am not the gung-ho sport adventurer who lives for danger. But, occasionally, I do enjoy walking along the narrow ridge between life and death. Obviously, I haven't been killed while climbing mountains, but I have come close to dying three or four times too many. I carried the Grim Reaper on my back down the Chalk Cliffs of Mt. Princeton; fortunately, I shook him off at the end of the terrifying descent. I was close enough to death to think seriously about all the things in life that I cherish. Just thinking about losing all of life's treasures made me appreciate life much more. After surviving my descent from Princeton, I valued everything about life, even the simplest things, such as breathing, feeling wet feet, touching a tree, throwing a rock, feeling the warmth of sunshine, and smelling the air's piney aroma. Realizing that death is a definite possibility makes life seem extremely precious. Although encountering life-threatening challenges is not my aim, I accept it as a natural part of mountaineering. If I wanted to climb just for the thrill of facing death, I could get the same thrill by jaywalking in a large city during rush hour.

Another, more positive, reason that I mountain climb is to enjoy the summit experience. The summit experience is well worth any hardships suffered during the ascent. What is the summit experience? It is a climber's reward for reaching the summit. It isn't ice-cold beer, hotdogs, a reception committee and trophies; summit conditions can be miserable. The temperature could be near freezing, winds may be in excess of forty m.p.h., the sky may be overcast and you may wish that you were back at the base camp in your tent. However, on a clear summer day the summit experience is an ultimately satisfying experience: topping the summit and absorbing the self-rewarding aspects of being on the summit, the climactic moment that the climber steps onto the highest point on the mountain. The panoramic view, the "on top of the world" feeling, the thin-air satisfaction, relaxing on the summit and the feeling of accomplishment make climbing worth every ounce of sweat.

My final, catch-all reason for climbing is that mountaineering is in my blood. The mountains are in my spirit; I think I was sprinkled with mountain magic during my first trip to the mountains as a toddler. Since then, the mountains have held a place close to my heart, because there isn't a mountain recreational activity that I don't like. Everything that the mountains mean to me started with climbing. The earliest climb that I can remember was a climb with my father when I was five. However, according to my father, I was in the mountains for the first time at age three. I grew up climbing mountains. I love the alpine environment: the cool, fresh morning air; cold, clear streams; breathtaking panoramas; and peaceful forests. If I had the time and money, I would love to be a full-time mountaineer.

There are basically two categories of climbing: technical and nontechnical (recreational). Under those two categories there are four types of climbing: (1) free climbing (technical), (2) direct aid climbing (technical), (3) hiking up steep inclines (nontechnical), and (4) scrambling up mountainsides and cliffs without ropes (nontechnical). Most mountaineers are experienced in both technical and nontechnical climbing. I have experience in both types of climbing, but I prefer recreational climbing. Technical climbing requires the assistance of ropes, pitons, carabiners, wedges and other climbing equipment. Nontechnical or recreational climbing is unassisted climbing without ropes and sophisticated climbing devices. Many mountains can't be climbed using purely nontechnical techniques. For instance, the steep face of the Eiger cannot be climbed without using technical climbing techniques. The climbing adventures in this collection are nontechnical. Each type of climbing has its own advantages and disadvantages, challenges and rewards.

Technical climbing gear is cumbersome, expensive and subject to wear and tear. Technical climbers have to rely on their skills and strengths, and the strengths of their climbing gear. Recreational climbers are on their own; their lives are dependent only upon their dexterity, skill and judgment. A recreational climber's gear consists of hiking boots or climbing shoes, crampons, ice axes, an occasional belay rope, face protection and plenty of warm clothing. Recreational climbers are allowed to use belay ropes without crossing into the technical climber's domain; again, the drawback is that many mountains cannot be climbed using purely recreational climbing techniques. Out of necessity, most mountaineers possess technical and nontechnical climbing skills. There were a few difficult climbs where I wished I had some climbing equipment, but I had neglected to pack any. On climbs that require lengthy hikes just to get to the mountain, it is all too tempting to pack lightly, thereby leaving some equipment behind.

A true mountaineer, not just a weekend rock climber, is a mountaineer because his or her spirit is in the mountains. A true mountaineer is born out of love for the alpine environment. Mountaineers feel at home in the mountains, and they are comfortable anywhere in the mountains. Don't consider yourself a mountaineer if the 6,643 foot summit of Tennessee's Clingmans Dome is the only mountain you have climbed, especially if your route was the quarter-mile stroll up the paved trail from the parking lot. Try climbing Clingmans Dome from the Deep Creek Campground in one day. Craig and I made the fifteen-mile plus endurance climb on 22 May 1988.

So someday, when someone asks, "Why did you climb Mt. McKinley?" I will say, "Because it was there," of course. Who will believe all of that other malarkey about achieving goals, holistic experience, life-threatening challenges and the summit experience?

This collection includes a selection of climbing expeditions and experiences from my adventure log. These selected adventure stories and experiences were integral to my development as a mountaineer.

This chapter includes five subchapters. The first subchapter is a collection of my earliest climbing experiences and stories. The second subchapter is a narrative of my first climb of a thirteener. The third subchapter is narrative about Craig's and my first major climb together. The fourth subchapter is a story about my first climb of a fourteener. The final subchapter is a narrative about Sean's and my climb of Colorado's highest peak (the twenty-ninth highest in North America).

The Early Years

WHEN I WAS THE tender age of five, my father took my hand and led me to the top of a small mountain in Boulder Canyon. It was the first mountain that I remember climbing. Although I don't have any vivid memories of earlier climbing excursions, Dad said that during my earlier climbs he did most of the climbing with me perched on his shoulders.

My most vivid memory of that first climb was looking over the rocky edge of a cliff at the top. The cars looked like matchbox cars buzzing up the canyon road below. Dad stood bravely at the cliff's edge, looking into the canyon while I crawled to the edge and peeked over. I was terrified by the sheer height of the cliff! I quickly crawled back from the edge, and I urged Dad to do the same. Knowing that I wanted to be a mountain climber Dad asked, "How are you going to climb mountains if you're afraid of heights?"

"I just won't look over the edges," I said.

I didn't like looking over sheer cliffs, but I enjoyed the feeling of standing atop a mountain. It felt even better knowing that I climbed to the top side by side with Dad. As we sat resting upon a boulder I felt that we had accomplished something special. It was similar to my experience of catching my first fish. It was a father-son activity, a period of time that is now a cherished memory. I enjoyed everything that Dad and I did together, especially mountain climbing, and we share many good memories of times in the mountains and the plains.

During that first climb, Mom sat on the river bank in the canyon bed far below. From our high vantage point, we yelled, "Hello!" and waved at her. She saw us, and waved back at us. She was probably worried that we might fall or get hurt some other way. She always worried about every pitfall conceivable. Rock slides, bears, mountain lions, rivers, storms and mine shafts were at the top of her list of concerns for our safety. I wasn't about to stop hiking and climbing, so I had to reassure her that I would be careful. Although her concerns were understandable motherly ones, I didn't realize that until much later in life.

From that day on, the mountains gradually became more and more a part of my life. The mountains were a childhood dreamland of unlimited adventure. For an introverted child, the mountains provided ideal settings for my fantasy role-playing. My favorite roles were of cowboys and Indians, sheriffs and robbers, mountainmen, soldiers and explorers. Forests, boulders, rivers, streams, cliffs, ledges and canyons made the games really exciting. Since we didn't live in the mountains, trips to the mountains were extra special.

We lived on a small two-and-a-half acre place in the high Colorado plains, thirty miles east of the Front Range of the Rocky Mountains. We lived reasonably close to the mountains, close enough to see the wall of majestic mountains stretching north and south to the horizons, towering up from the rolling hills of eastern Colorado's great plains. From our hillside country home, the mountains looked like a giant, jagged wall, the same view that the early westward settlers saw as they traveled across the great plains toward the Rocky Mountains.

During my early years, prior to age sixteen, my mountain

adventures were limited to family outings to the mountains. I frequently thought about hiking or biking to the mountains, but, at that age, thirty miles seemed incredibly distant. Whenever I became mad at my parents and thought about running away from home, I naturally considered running away to the mountains; but I seldom ran farther than a nearby fishing pond. When Mom and Dad planned a picnic, fishing trip, camping trip or other mountain outing, I was the first one packed and ready to go. The mountains were my favorite place to visit.

I spent many hot summer days around home wishing that I could be hiking or climbing in the cool shade of a mountain forest. Sometimes I just sat on the grass gazing at the peaks trying to imagine what it was like atop their summits. One peak stood apart from the others, rising higher in the northern Front Range. Longs Peak is the northernmost Colorado fourteener. Its prominence is pronounced by the shorter, 12,000 and 13,000 foot peaks that surround it. During my early years I lived in a small world with limited knowledge of the world beyond; Longs Peak seemed to be beyond reach. Back then, Longs Peak seemed as distant and mysterious as Mt. Everest seems today. One day I wanted to climb Longs Peak; I wanted to stand upon its summit and gaze out across the plains. I didn't know how I would get there, but I knew that I eventually would.

The earliest physical evidence of the beginning of my mountain ties is a priceless picture of my mom and I cooking breakfast on a Coleman stove at a campsite in the Shirley Mountains of Wyoming. I was three years old in that photograph. Even at three, I tested my limits by trying to wander away from Mom and Dad's safety radius. As I grew older, I slowly expanded my boundaries, and every time we went to the mountains I made it a challenge to get away from their control. I ventured as far as I dared, learning to recognize and use landmarks to find my way back to camp. As I gained experience and confidence in the backcountry, I hiked farther away from camp, increasing my boundaries. Eventually, my parents gained enough confidence in me that they let me venture off into the mountains for several hours alone. Either that, or they just got tired of trying to stop me. I practiced improving my sense of direction and increased my endurance and dexterity. Throughout my early years, my love for the mountains continued to grow, I learned more about the backcountry, and I started to build the foundation of a mountaineer.

I spent my first fifteen years expanding my limits and learning about nature's incredible facets. My early adventures spawned from hiking, climbing, exploring, fishing, camping and hunting excursions. If I couldn't talk my dad, mom or sister into going with me, I often went on hiking excursions alone. I discovered an extremely comforting environment hidden deep in the forest, away from noisy roadways, cities and campgrounds. I was most relaxed and at ease with the world when I was surrounded by natural sights and sounds of a mountain summit, an alpine brook or a forest. Throughout my first fifteen years of life I grew very comfortable being in the Rocky Mountain backcountry. At times, I found more comfort sitting on a rock in the middle of a mountain creek than I did in my bedroom.

My interests in mountaineering originated from my climbing experiences with Dad, exercising my growing muscles, being in the mountains, and making it to the top. Mountaineering is a self-rewarding activity. Inner rewards make mountaineering appealing to me. Simple enjoyment and self-satisfaction are the greatest rewards that one can achieve upon reaching a mountain summit. The incredible vista, serenity of the summit, the invigorating air and the feeling of accomplishment are some of the reasons that make the "summit experience" special. However, when I was climbing smaller mountains during my early years, there was always a higher mountaintop beyond the one that I climbed. That tempted me to climb the next mountain to see what was beyond it. But because we started our climbs in the foothills, we could conceivably climb dozens of mountains before reaching the highest one.

Dad taught me some of the essentials to backcountry survival. He showed me how to recognize poison oak. He taught me how to tell direction using the sun and tree moss. He showed me how to extract wood ticks. He taught me how to pitch tents, build campfires, catch fish from a river (without a fishing pole) and how to whittle wood.

Our climbing partnership dissolved somewhere between my eleventh and thirteenth birthday. The dreaded time finally came when Dad quit climbing with me; it was a disappointing reminder that all good things eventually come to an end. Dad was slowing down with middle-age, while I was overflowing with the energy of youth. After our climbing partnership dissolved, I became even more determined to climb harder, hike farther and run faster. Dad exchanged his hiking shoes for a fishing pole. Nonetheless, I will always be thankful for the wonderful times that we shared and the mountains that we climbed together.

During my early teens, my mom, dad and sister spent their mountain time fishing while I traipsed about in the backcountry. Fishing was too passive for my energetic metabolism. If I didn't catch a fish within thirty minutes, I lost all patience for the sport. I often started out with a fishing pole in my hands, but shortly thereafter I would be exploring the wilderness. I just couldn't sit waiting to catch a fish when I was at a mountain lake surrounded by majestic peaks and a beckoning unknown.

Hiking into the wilderness alone became an exciting challenge. By age eleven, my appetite for adventure was growing faster than my body. I frequently went on two- and three-mile backcountry adventures. At that age, any backcountry excursion seemed like a daring adventure. I was really naïve; I had no conception of the potential dangers of exploring the mountains alone. As long as I could find my way back to the family car I felt safe. After all, not getting lost was a great challenge. Mom's fading words, as I darted into the woods, were always, "Be careful, and don't get lost." I knew that if I ever got lost (and survived) Mom and Dad would keep me under lock and key for the rest of my boyhood years.

The following is an excerpt from an entry in my hiking journal that I kept when I was eleven years old:

HIKING

When I hike I always find a landmark. When I climb I grab a hold to solid trees. I also watch out for loose rocks.

I went up to Brainard Lake before, in Colorado. They had a few trails that went to lakes. We went on a mile hike.

I went hunting up in Wyoming with my Dad, up by Medicine Bow. There were a few mountains by this one place [Shirley Mountains]. And there were a few mountains by Laramie called Robber's Roost. Dad and I went hiking around there. And we took pictures of each other on big rocks.

I been hiking up in Gledno, Wyo. I hiked about three miles up there. Once I about got lost at these camping grounds up in Glendo there is all kinds of roads going all over. And I took off playing Billy the Kid. Before I left I saw a recreational vehicle. When I wanted to go back I couldn't find my way. Then I saw that recreational vehicle so I knew I was back. That wasn't a very good landmark because it could of drove away.

And sometimes I just hike around our place. I always hike up to the lake by our place. It's about a half mile to it. And I hike a mile to this one tree with a tire swing on it.

Δ

Since I wrote that entry in my hiking journal I have grown a little wiser. I still get confused by "roads going all over," but I quit using movable objects for landmarks. I am more likely to get lost in the city than I am in the wilderness, where I seem to have a natural sense for finding my way. The secret is to recognize key landmarks that are distinctly different from other common surface features. In a forest, trees are not good landmarks; there are thousands of similar looking trees. When off trail hiking in the mountains, I rely on making a mental list of distinct landmarks, and to find my way back, I simply travel from one landmark to the next in reverse order. Navigating through the wilderness was a matter of pride. Mountaineers don't get lost, so as long as I didn't get lost, I didn't care too much what else could happen to me, nor worry much about the other dangers in the mountains. I was so confident in my physical agility, that falling wasn't a concern. I didn't think twice about encountering wild animals, crossing raging rivers and running down steep mountainsides. I refused to let fear and paranoia keep me from enjoying the great Rocky Mountain wilderness.

The first big test of my backwoods skills came when I was thirteen years old. I went with a friend and his family to their cabin in the Rocky Mountains of Eagle County, Colorado. Shortly after getting to the cabin I conjured up a mountain climbing expedition. The allure of a distant mountain, the highest one around (somewhere in the Suicide Mountain topographic quadrangle), captured my attention. Climbing that mountain became an obsession. After I told my friend that we would have to leave at 5:30 in the morning, he lost interest in the expedition. Unfortunately, his younger, bratty cousin, David, was eager and willing to go. Being the healthy, mature and experienced thirteen year old that I was, I didn't want a nine-year-old slowing me down. That night, before the big adventure, I tried to sell him a hardship story to discourage him from tagging along. Unfortunately, David was adamant about going mountain climbing with me. He was as determined as I was when I was his age.

The following is the story about my first big hike:

The last thing I wanted on my great mountain climbing adventure was a tag-along brat who couldn't carry his own weight. David was a nine-year-old, scrawny, squirrely toothpick. He couldn't possibly make it over the first mountain. I neither wanted my progress hindered nor the responsibility of watching out for someone else's welfare.

He was determined to tag along. And I was determined to leave him at the cabin. Somehow, I had to convince him that it would be too dangerous.

The night before, while I was packing some granola bars and sandwiches in a daypack, he asked me what he should pack.

Skirting his question, I told him, "I'll be leaving before sunrise. It is going to be cold, dark and dangerous out there. The wolves and bears will still be prowling around in the woods."

He saw right through my wolf and bear story. He knew that I was just trying to scare him. He wasn't as naïve as I had thought.

I continued, "I'm going to hike at least twenty miles. Can you make it that far?"

David shrugged his shoulders, then said, "Yeah. As long as I have something to eat and drink."

His heart was set on climbing with me. Sympathetically I finally told him to pack his gear.

At dusk on the evening before, we went outside to look at our objective. I pointed to a partly snowcapped mountain peak rising above some shorter mountains in its foreground, the most prominent peak in the area, about five miles away.

"That is where we are going tomorrow."

"How long will it take us?" he asked. "My parents are leaving at three o'clock."

"We'll be back by then if we get an early start."

After nightfall, everyone settled into the cabin for a relaxing evening of light conversation and game playing.

At bedtime everyone crawled into a sleeping nook in the three-room cabin. I had the lower bunk of a bunkbed and was awake most of the night worrying about waking up on time, because I didn't have an alarm clock to rely upon.

Somehow, I woke up right at five o'clock. David was still asleep, and I didn't have any reason to wake him. I quietly slung my pack over my shoulders, strapped my canteen to my army belt and tiptoed out the cabin door.

Without David tagging along I could blaze across the mountains with unhindered speed. I set a direct course for the distant mountain. From the valley I picked an intermediate landmark atop the first ridge on the way, a tall pine tree upon a prominent high point, silhouetted by the moonlight. That tree was my first intermediate objective enroute to the big peak. A meadow of knee-high grass lay between me and the foot of the ridge.

Determined to reach the big peak, I marched out across the grassy meadow in a southeasterly direction. Then, only two hundred feet from the cabin, I heard a door slam—a sound that I didn't want to hear. Without looking back I knew who was coming. The thought of trying to outrun him crossed my mind.

David ran through the dew-covered grass to catch up with me. Some inbred sense of morality forced me to wait for him. After he caught up with me, he angrily asked me why I didn't wake him up. Telling him a white lie, I told him that I was worried about waking his parents or stumbling across someone else in the dark.

He wasn't satisfied with my answer, but we both forgot about it as the challenge before us demanded our attention. He was with me for the duration, and I couldn't do anything about it. I decided to make the best of the situation. I had to slow my pace to match his shorter strides. At our pace, I had early doubts about our ability to reach the big peak before noon, but we would make our best attempt at it.

Startled by the sound of a cracking branch, we froze in mid-stride. My heart momentarily leaped into my throat as I wondered what lurked in the dark wilderness. Our fear subsided after we saw two doe mule deers standing in the twilight of predawn. They stood midway up the ridge, cautiously watching us. They blew breaths of steam through their nostrils. The moment we stepped forward they sprang off into a thick patch of trees and vanished into the dark woods.

After crossing the meadow, our tennis shoes and lower pantlegs were soaked from the morning dew. The dampness made us a little uncomfortable, but we knew that the morning sun would soon drive the dampness away. At the foot of a ridge, we faced our first climb. It was an easy climb; the ridge was steep but relatively clear. The trees were sparse, there wasn't much dead wood on the ground and the footing was solid. The most challenging aspect of the climb was bushwhacking through the tall bristly sage brush.

At the break of dawn, we reached our first intermediate landmark, the lone pine tree standing on the crest of the ridge. The view from atop the ridge was spectacular! The dark mountains, to the east, were outlined by a blazing orange backdrop. In the foreground, the mountains and valleys were still very dark, only discernible by their varying shades.

I was pleased to see the scary darkness of the forest burning away. Although I maintained the intrepid explorer image on the outside, inside I was afraid of the darkness and the creatures that lurked there. As the darkness gave way to daylight, my fears of the forest subsided.

Behind us, the tiny cabin sat in a meadow in the large valley between two mountain ridges. The valley was sparsely dotted with cabins and tiny columns of smoke rose from the chimneys of some. It was a quiet, calm and peaceful setting, nothing like boisterous urban settings.

After relaxing for a few minutes, we turned our attention toward the big peak. We picked the top end of a gulch as our next intermediate landmark. The gulch carved a deep path in the bottom of a valley.

We skipped down the other side of the ridge into the valley. We stopped at the edge of the gaping gulch to get our bearings and quench our thirsts with water from our canteens. The stream-bed in the bottom of the gulch was dry. The valley was covered with thick, impossibly difficult brush. It was bushwhacking territory. The dry stream-bed in the bottom of the gulch provided a clear path up the valley. It was a welcome alternative to tangling with sage brush.

I commented, "In 10,000 years, this will be another Grand Canyon."

The gulch was deep, steepwalled and narrow at the bottom, with no easy way to get in. We hiked along the top edge searching for a safe entry point but found none. After struggling through sage brush for a few minutes, we decided just to slide down the sandy gulch wall. I slid down first, all the way to the stream-bed. Before my dust settled, David dropped to his rear and slid down the sandy embankment. It was easier than it looked from above. We both made it unscathed.

With a clear stream-bed to follow, we quickly settled into a comfortable hiking pace. After I settled into the rhythm of our hiking pace, my mind wandered, as it often does when I am hiking. I imagined a terrifying scenario. I pictured a mountain lion walking down the gulch toward us. There was no way for us to escape the confines of the gulch, and we wouldn't be able to outrun it. At least, if we weren't trapped in the gulch, we could climb a tree to safety. I tried to think of something else, but my imagination ran rampant. For the duration of our hike up the gulch, I wondered what might await up around each consecutive bend, what might pounce on us from the top of the gulch or what might sneak up on us from behind. I desperately wanted to reach the end of the gulch so that we could get out of it.

When we reached the top end of the gulch, the morning sun was edging above the mountaintops. It refreshingly warmed our bodies and the fresh air to a comfortable (short-sleeve shirt) temperature. We welcomed the comfort of a sunny, clear sky.

Climbing out of the gulch was easy. I pulled myself out by using sage brush for handholds, then grabbed David's arm and helped him out. We reached our second landmark.

We sat on a log to rest our legs and eat a snack. I ate a granola bar and washed it down with some water from my canteen. We kept our rest break short; it was getting late in the morning, and the peak was still at least three hours away. We had to reach the summit by eleven o'clock in order to have enough time to get back to the cabin by our three o'clock deadline. We could travel faster on the return descent, but we still had a lengthy ascent before us.

Unfortunately, we couldn't just climb straight toward the summit. We had to circle a granite cliff that was directly in front of us. So, as another intermediate landmark, we set out for a large boulder at the top of a cliff. We climbed around the rocky cliff up a forested mountainside. We pulled ourselves from one tree to the next until we reached the top. The steep climb consumed valuable time. We had to make frequent rest stops. The incline was so steep we had to hug trees to keep from falling while we rested.

It took thirty minutes to climb to the clifftop. From there, however, the peak looked deceptively close. One more obstacle stood between us and the base of the peak. It was a tall, gently sloped and forested mountain.

So, the top of the mountain became our next intermediate landmark. Along the way, we found dozens of deer antlers scattered randomly on the ground. I made my long-sleeve shirt into a sling so that I could take some souvenir antlers home with me. Since they were so abundant, I kept only the best shiny white antlers. It was an awkward bundle to carry, but I was so proud of my collection that I didn't mind carrying the cumbersome extra weight.

Even though we set a fast pace up the intermediate mountainside, time was fleeting. The peak was an elusive objective. It mysteriously seemed to slip further into the distance, and we had to make it back to the cabin by three o'clock. We didn't want to get the grownups mad by being late.

From the top of the forested mountain, the base of the peak was only a mile across a flat, open meadow. We quickly trekked across the meadow to the base of the peak.

There, at the base, we saw our first snow bank. We ate snow to conserve our canteen water. Small shrubs, flowers, rocks and a few scattered pine trees covered the ground near the base of the peak. We were too tired and hungry to continue without taking a lunch break. So, we sat upon a "comfortable" rock and ate our lunches. Even though we were near a snow bank it was warm enough to be comfortable without shirts, so I shed mine to soak up some extra sunshine.

Despite my earlier regrets of having David tag along, I enjoyed his company. He carried his weight better than I thought he would. Surprisingly, he kept up with my pace very well. He compensated for shorter strides by making quicker steps, and he didn't nag or complain at all.

After a light lunch, we spent some personal time relaxing in the sunshine. David aimlessly wandered around the area occasionally tossing a stone. He amused himself by looking at the array of rocks and pebbles that covered the ground. I lay on the ground relaxing with my eyes closed.

A few minutes later David said, "Hey, TJ, look at this!

I jumped to my feet to see what he had discovered. He held his hand out displaying his find. It was an Indian arrowhead! A real artifact. I recognized it because my dad and I frequently searched for arrowheads in the wheat fields of Colorado's Great Plains. It was in perfect condition. It was an amazing find. The ground was covered with small rocks and pebbles, but he just happened to look down at the right moment as he walked across it. Encouraged by his discovery, we eagerly searched the area for other Indian artifacts. We didn't find any, but David had an adventure memento to keep forever. And for me, I still had my deer antlers for mementos.

By the time we finished piddling around and resting, it was noon. We were only at the base of the peak. The summit was another 2,000 feet higher. And we had to be back at the cabin by 3:00 P.M. Besides being short on time, we were exhausted. My legs were sore, I was dehydrating, and our progress was paltry. We both wanted to make the final trek to the top, but we didn't have the time or energy. The reality of the situation was disappointing. We had to abort the climb and start the long journey back to the cabin. I underestimated the time that it would take to climb the peak; it was farther away than it appeared to be.

It would take us at least three hours to get back to the cabin, if we traveled fast. We had hiked about five miles of diverse mountainous terrain, but the route that we came was not the quickest way back. From our high perspective we saw an easier route back to the cabin. Down in the valley we recognized the road that passed to the west of the cabin. We could eliminate a considerable amount of ups and downs by heading straight west to the road, then following it back to the cabin. That was our new plan.

Discouraged by our failure, we regretfully gathered our gear and souvenirs for the journey home. Slightly recharged by the rest, we began our descent. The return trip was pure work; the excitement was gone. We failed to make our objective, and there was nothing to look forward to on the way back. It was a matter of getting back to the cabin in time to get in the car to go back home to the flatland. The return trip gave us plenty of time to vent our frustrations.

The afternoon sun baked us, drained our energy levels and dehydrated us. I put my shirt back on to protect my skin from the intense ultraviolet rays; I had already exposed myself to more sun than I should have.

As we descended, we kept our thoughts to ourselves. I thought about how wonderful it was to wander freely about the mountains exploring new territory and overcoming challenging obstacles. No parents dictating our actions, or telling us what to do or which way to go. I freely made my own decisions. The mountains seemed like an illimitable wilderness full of fascinating obstacles, animals, plants and natural wonders. Hiking in the mountains made me feel wonderful about myself, and about being alive. The mountains were the one place that I felt truly free to be myself. I didn't have to obey any rules. I didn't have to worry about doing something that might be considered socially unacceptable behavior. And I felt free to listen to my instincts. To explore the mountains was to experience true freedom.

We trekked through the same type of terrain as on the ascent, sparsely scattered pine trees, waist-high brush, gullies and scattered rock outcroppings. An hour and a half into the return trip we stumbled across a grisly sight. We came across a tree with a fresh chunk of deer meat dangling from a branch on a string. From the way that it was set up it looked like coyote or bear bait. Dangling raw meat could certainly attract any carnivorous creatures. I had no desire to meet anything that might be drawn to the bait. While in the vicinity of that meat we were also bait for anything that might be attracted to it. Encountering a bear was my most dreaded fear. If we were in a bear's territory, we could already be in grave danger. What if a bear had already smelled the bait, or us?

It was enough to get my imagination stirred up into a frenzy of fear. We were so scared that we ran from the area in a near panic. We intermittently looked back as we ran, to see if anything was after us. My imagination went on a rampage. The worst possible scenario ran through my mind: Two grizzly bears chasing us across the brush-covered terrain with only one tree in sight. It was a horrifying vision from a previous nightmare.

I forced myself to think of something else. I convinced myself that we weren't in any danger. After all, bears wouldn't be out in the daylight. And bears are supposed to be afraid of people. We finally put enough distance between ourselves and the bear bait to subside our fears, and we didn't see or hear anything pursuing us. After settling back into a steady pace, we pulled our thoughts back under control.

The remainder of the return trip was uneventful. After reaching the valley, we had to hike two miles without water, but it was just a matter of pure perseverance.

Amazingly, we dragged our weary bodies back to the cabin fifteen minutes before three o'clock. Even though we told the adults where we were going, I thought that we would still get scolded for being gone so long. Surprisingly, they were understanding. They questioned us about our day of adventure without the formal interrogation that I expected.

Before leaving, I looked at the big peak wondering if I would ever stand upon its summit. I wondered if I would ever return to that part of the Rocky Mountains. As always, I dreaded leaving the mountains. But I left the mountains that day with vivid memories of another satisfying high country experience. Even though I failed to reach the summit, my spirit had been enriched by the climbing experience.

Δ

We hiked about ten miles that day, and in our minds it truly was just a day's adventure in the mountains. We didn't have any conception of the risks that we took that day nor a concern in the world. I didn't consider the possibilities of becoming lost, encountering wild animals or getting hurt. Climbing to the top of the big peak on the horizon was my only concern. At that age my naïveté precluded me from worrying about potential hazards. However, my first big hike was a turning point. It was the beginning of a new period of life for me, teenage life. At thirteen, my carefree outlook on life started giving way to a more realistic understanding of life. I began looking beyond the beauty of the mountains. I sought to learn more about the science of the mountains: the geology, ecology and climate.

But naïveté, innocence and a carefree existence made my early years a very special period of discovery and exploration. During my early years, I spent my mountain time enjoying carefree fun. I pretended to be explorers, mountainmen, soldiers, prospectors, cowboys and other adult characters that fit into mountain settings. The more I explored, the more I learned about the wilderness, and the farther I ventured alone, the greater my confidence grew.

During 1978 I continued to broaden my early mountaineering experience with several firsts. I visited the majestic Indian Peaks Wilderness Area for the first time. The abundance of quality hiking trails makes it a hiking paradise. When I first saw the trails, I wanted to hike them all to their ends. My first trek into the area was a one-mile family hike to Mitchell Lake. The picturesque beauty and serenity of the forest, streams, peaks and lakes consumed me. The area quickly became my favorite Rocky Mountain recreation area.

In July 1978, I climbed my first 12,000-foot-plus peak. A cousin and I scraped the bottom of 13,000 feet when we climbed Pawnee Peak's 12,943-foot summit.

During the fall of 1978, I went on my first backpacking trip. I went with my junior high Outdoor Recreation class on a two-mile backpacking trip to Diamond Lake. It was a super experience! I enjoyed depending on the wilderness and feeling close to nature and have thoroughly enjoyed backpacking since that first trip. Living with and experiencing nature through backpacking is an enlightening experience.

After that trip in the fall of 1978, I had a long adventureless wait for my next trip to the mountains. It was a dreadful dry spell. I was at the mercy of my parents for transportation to the mountains. I lobbied for a trip to the mountains at every opportunity. I pleaded, begged and occasionally threw teenage temper tantrums. I wanted to get back into the high country, to breathe the clean fresh mountain air, hear the sound of the wind blowing across the tree tops, smell the piney aroma of the forest, see the massive snow-capped peaks and feel the natural rush of standing upon a mountain top. I had a terrible case of high-country withdrawal symptoms.

Finally, after an unbearably long time in the flatlands, I made it to the mountains in a big way. I broke the 13,000-foot contour by climbing Mount Audubon. Standing atop Mt. Audubon was a momentous occasion. It was the beginning of my loyalty to the high peaks. The beginning of my quest for mountaineering excellence.

Mount Audubon

ON A WARM July day in 1979, I broke into the over 13,000 foot club after successfully climbing Mt. Audubon (13,223 feet). Mount Audubon is a massive peak in the Indian Peaks Wilderness Area of Colorado's Rockies. It is the 459th highest peak in Colorado. Colorado is one of only nine states with peaks above 13,000 feet, and there are 741 peaks over 13,000 feet high scattered across the Colorado Rockies. Wyoming has at least fifty named peaks over 13,000 feet high. Compared to the world's highest peaks, thirteeners are only minor in magnitude, although many thirteeners are just as awe-inspiring as the fourteeners. In fact, many thirteeners offer more challenging climbs than higher peaks, and for a beginning mountaineer, thirteeners offer a formidable challenge. Thirteeners are just as potentially deadly as the world's highest mountains if approached without adequate knowledge, training and preparation.

As many avid climbers will attest, it isn't the size that makes a peak difficult to climb, it is its character. The Rocky Mountains contain a wide variety of mountain types to meet every mountaineer's expectations. There are peaks for sightseers, photographers, recreational climbers, technical climbers, backpackers and seasoned climbing veterans. Some are easy to access and can be climbed in a day; some are remote and require two or three days to climb.

Atop a thirteener the air is thin, cool and clear; vegetation is sparse and dwarfed, trees are nonexistent; and the weather is highly variable. If you're not accustomed to high elevations, you can get altitude sickness atop a thirteener (and at lower elevations as well). Thirteeners offer the climber a wide range of technical and nontechnical challenges. Some climbs are easy, half-day hikes with only 2,000 feet of elevation gain; some thirteeners require lengthy backpacks (over twenty miles) and climbs of 5,000 to 6,000 feet elevation gain. One unnamed peak (13,762 feet) in San Isabel National Forest requires a twenty-four-mile hike and elevation gain of 5,000 feet. Some thirteeners cannot be climbed without some technical climbing and rope work. Some thirteeners, such as Ice Mountain (13,951 feet), should only be attempted by experienced climbers.

Now that I have significantly hyped up thirteeners, let me tell you about my first "thirteener."

It was a midsummer morning when my mom, dad, sister, and I drove west in the family car. Our destination was Brainard Lake, located in the Indian Peaks Wilderness Area—a gateway to high adventure. We planned to go fishing and have a barbecue dinner, and, as usual, I was ecstatic about going to the mountains.

The lake was a two-hour drive from our home. The two-lane mountain highways are sinuous; they wind back and forth with the natural bends of the valleys they follow. Throughout most of the drive I had my face halfway out the window to absorb as much of the mountain surroundings as possible. The swift forty-five m.p.h. breeze washed my face with pure mountain air and filled my nose with a piney aroma. I fully attuned my senses to the sights, sounds and smells of the Rocky Mountains. As we whizzed steadily up Boulder Canyon, I scanned the passing scenery. I saw old, abandoned gold mines, mountainsides forested with pine trees, waterfalls and Boulder Creek paralleling the highway. My ears were stimulated by the sounds of the rushing and tumbling white water of Boulder Creek and the humming of the car as it whizzed by the guardrails along the highway.

The drive through Boulder Canyon was a scenic drive through the present and a memory-stimulating drive through the past. Seeing the places unlocked memories: old family picnic sites, mountains that Dad and I had climbed and streams that we had fished. We passed the road that we got stuck on during a late May snowstorm, we passed the first mountain I climbed and we passed many roadside picnic and fishing areas that we frequently visited. Many of my best childhood memories are of weekend family outings in Boulder Canyon and surrounding areas.

By midmorning we arrived at Brainard Lake—the gateway to the alpine paradise of the Indian Peaks. The skies were clear blue, the temperature was forty-five degrees Fahrenheit and warming. From the east end of the lake the view was panoramic. The western horizon was a jagged ridge of picturesque peaks along the Continental Divide. From south to north the chain of peaks include: Niwot Ridge (12,284 feet), Navajo Peak (13,409), Apache Peak (13,441), Pawnee Peak (12,943), Mount Toll (12,979), Paiute Peak (13,058), and Mt. Audubon (13,223). Even in midsummer the rugged granite mountainsides were speckled with snowfields and scattered patches of snow. In the foreground of the Indian Peaks, the lower mountainsides were blanketed by a rich, pine-tree forest. Lower in the valley, mountain creeks link turquoise tarns and finger lakes that stretch down the U-shaped glacial valleys. The creeks flow with stinging-cold, clear, fresh water from the melting snowfields high on the mountainsides. Deer, squirrels, chipmunks, birds and trout were frequent sights from the lakeshore of Brainard Lake.

Continuing a tradition that I started several years ago, immediately after Dad parked the car, I bolted out into the forest! My goal was to disappear without a trace as quickly as possible. I dashed into the cover of the alpine trees and ran until I heard Mom's familiar yell, "TJ! Get back here! Don't just take off like that. You stay close to the car so you don't get lost." As usual, I rebelliously dragged my feet back to the car to receive a dose of parental guidance. And as usual, their guidance entered my left ear, passed through my brain without triggering any responses and exited my right ear. They gave me the normal spiel of advice, "Don't wander off too far. We're going to eat lunch in a while. Don't take any unnecessary chances. Someone is always getting lost in the mountains. We don't want you to get lost."

I said, "I'll be fine. Don't worry about me. I'm just going to fish for a while." Until I get bored, I echoed to myself. Which will be in ten minutes if I don't catch a fish.

I grabbed my fishing pole from the trunk, and walked down to the lake to fish with Ma, Pa and Sis. I stuck a worm on the hook and cast it into the ripple-surfaced lake. Then, I perched myself on a big rock on the shoreline next to my blonde-haired, younger sister. At that time in my life, she was an undesirable annoyance and hindrance that I normally avoided.

A few minutes after we sat down, Dad reeled in a silvery rainbow trout. Encouraged by Dad's big catch, I fished for another thirty minutes. After that, the lure of the wilderness drew me away from the lake. I couldn't bear another minute of staring at the lake hoping for a passing fish to feast on my worm. It was especially difficult to sit passively fishing when I could be exploring the surrounding wilderness. Drawn by the call of the wilderness, I reeled my line in and packed the fishing pole back into the car trunk. I wanted to explore new territory, test my backcountry skills and boldly go where no boy had gone before. My sister seldom went hiking with me because she was a crybaby and she couldn't keep up with me.

At my first chance, I aimlessly dashed into the woods. I just wanted to get away from the cars and people around the lake. I carried some snacks, a light jacket and a canteen of water in a knapsack. I hiked deep into the forest, not really caring where I was going. After a while I came to a grass-covered clearing. From there, my destination unveiled itself to me. Above the treetops, I saw a massive granite mountain towering high in the sky. It had to be

Mount Audubon. It was a very tempting objective, but I knew it was further away than it looked. I sat down by a boulder and contemplated my situation.

Audubon looked awesome! Its base spread out over miles, patches of snow and snowfields spotted the upper portions of the mostly gray peak, and its lower elevations were wrapped in an evergreen blanket. Its rounded summit rose well above the timberline, extending high enough to touch the clouds. More massive than the surrounding peaks, Audubon prominently stood as the king of the Indian Peaks. On its east side a long gentle-sloping ridge extended up to the summit, like a giant ramp.

Thinking grandiosely, I imagined myself effortlessly climbing up Audubon's east ridge. I had no idea how long it would take to make the ascent and descent. I didn't even know how far I would have to travel. Audubon's impressive appearance was too much to resist; it magnetically pulled me toward. My desire to stand atop its summit took control of my actions. Empowered by the mountain, it didn't matter whether I had time and adequate provisions to make the climb. Audubon became a quest. I would have to find potable water somewhere on the mountain. As for time, I would have to climb quickly. I guessed that I had until dinner to make it back to the lake. After that, Mom and Dad would have the forest rangers searching for me.

I charted a straight course to the summit, through the forest that surrounded its base, up through timberline and then into the tundra above. After leaving the clearing, I lost sight of Audubon in the thick of the forest. However, I kept on course by watching the angle of my shadow and following the upward sloping terrain. The forest obstructions slowed me down: I had to highstep and climb over fallen timber, climb across or go around large boulders, wade across marshes and bushwhack (without a machete) through thickets. I dreaded crossing marshes because they were typically teaming with swarms of mosquitoes. Mosquitoes loved the taste of my blood. Sometimes the other obstacles were enjoyable, rather than a nuisance; they added a dash of spice to lonely treks through forests. I enjoyed balancing myself while walking across logs. I also liked scrambling over boulders. Sometimes I actually sought appealing obstacles that weren't too far from my travel route.

Near the base of Audubon, I stumbled into a low-lying marsh. Just as I feared, the mosquitoes greeted me. Several of them drove their needles through my shirt and into my skin. Few of the attackers escaped to enjoy their bloodthirsty dinner. Nevertheless, they still delivered many painful bites before meeting their deaths.

Sloshing through the marsh and swatting mosquitoes diverted me off course. While resting on a partially dry mound in the marsh, I reoriented myself. Using the angle of my shadow, I determined the general direction in which I had to continue. I confirmed my orientation with tree moss which primarily grew on the north sides.

Finally, I made it through the dense forest to the acclivity of Audubon's base. The trees continued up Mt. Audubon, but it wasn't as dense as the lower forest. After the trek through the forest, I reached the base, the starting point of the climb, and my pulse quickened as I started up the steep slope. The footing was slippery because of the steepness and a layer of pine needles that covered the ground. On steep inclines I preferred to climb on rock.

By chance, I came across a talus formation (rocky slope). It was much easier to climb up the rocks, than tangle with the inherent obstacles of a wooded mountainside. The talus provided an unobstructed, but potentially dangerous, climbing path. Many of the rocks teetered precariously upon one another, threatening to slide when stepped upon. Stepping onto the wrong rock could trigger an avalanche.

The slope wasn't dangerously steep, and the talus seemed fairly stable. A few rocks teetered when I crossed them. One dislodged after I stepped on it, but it quickly stopped against a larger rock below. There were just enough loose rocks to keep me alert.

The combination of the vigorous exercise and intense sunshine caused me to sweat, and often I wiped the sweat from my forehead to keep it from getting in my eyes. Despite my growing thirst, I had to ration my canteen water. I didn't know how far I would have to travel before finding drinkable water. I drank just enough to wet my mouth and throat.

Above the talus slope, I re-entered forested terrain; however, the trees were smaller and sparser—the first sign of the changing alpine environment. My heart and lungs worked much harder than normal to fulfill my body's oxygen demand.

The summer mountainside burgeoned with beauty. I was climbing through the transition zone between the forest and the higher alpine environment. Short grass, pink and violet flowers and short brush flourished in abundance between scattered boulders and dwarfed pines. Furry rodents, like squirrels, pikas and marmots were the most prevalent creatures. I passed several of them during the day. As I approached two pikas, they chattered, squeaked, scurried about the rocks and curiously carried on. They watched me from a safe distance. While resting, I saw a golden eagle proudly perched high on a dead tree limb, scanning the mountainside for prey. I envied its grace and ability to soar over the mountains and through the valleys; I wished I could fly to the top of Audubon like it could.

After a short rest, I continued the increasingly difficult ascent. Higher on the mountainside, I saw a puzzling man-made line of rocks across the mountainside. It looked like a trail, which would certainly decrease the difficulty of my climb. I eagerly climbed up to the rocks, and sure enough, it was a trail: a rocky, narrow footpath that angled up the mountainside. Even though I wasn't sure that the trail led to the summit, I decided to follow it. Since I was on a spontaneous excursion, I hadn't studied any maps of the area to learn about any possible trails. Normally, I avoided trails because they always seemed to follow the longest route up a mountain, and I liked following more direct routes. Sometimes I avoided trails just to make the climb more challenging. However, as I later learned, direct routes were seldom the quickest or the easiest ways to the peaks.

For the time being, I buried my inhibitions about trails and followed it. About a half-mile up the trail, just above timberline, the first snowbanks appeared. Where there was melting snow, there had to be streams flowing with pure water. The thought of sipping water from a cold spring was very enticing. My canteen was almost empty, and I became thirstier by the minute. The thought of having a dry canteen made me even thirstier. I hated to travel or camp without an adequate supply of water, and when camping, I always kept a full canteen of water within reach; otherwise, I couldn't sleep comfortably.

Relief came at timberline. A cold stream of sparkling water crossed the trail. It was fed by a melting snowbank. With the stream's source in view, I felt confident that the water was safe. I knelt at the water's edge and drank the crystal-clear water like a camel at an oasis. It tasted as pure as it looked. I drank a few handfuls, then filled my canteen. It was pure Rocky Mountain spring water, compliments of nature. I wished that our well at home was filled with it.

Above timberline, the landscape transformed. A shorter growing season, harsher environment, thinner air and rockier terrain produced a treeless, sparsely vegetated landscape. I entered the tundra zone, between timberline and the barren, rock-laden landscape of higher elevations. The tundra vegetation consisted of dwarfed evergreens (Krumholz), short grass and a colorful assortment of flowers. The topography was rocky and rugged. Without trees, there was little protection against the high winds that frequently occur at higher elevations. The wind-swept surface and short growing season made it extremely difficult for vegetation to grow.

The above-timberline elevation also posed a greater danger to hikers and climbers. Natural shelter from high winds and stormy weather was virtually nonexistent. Boulders and rock overhangs provided limited shelter, if they were found. Afternoon thunderstorms were a regular occurrence. A clear blue sky commonly transformed into a dark, stormy sky in less than thirty minutes. Likewise, temperatures can plummet fifteen to thirty degrees just as quickly. Mountaineers and other high-country explorers that are often caught off guard by rapidly moving storms which frequently bombarded the peaks with lightning and wind-driven rain and hail. Thunderstorms have also blind-sided high-country visitors by approaching from behind objective mountains. In addition to thunderstorms, snow was always a possibility. The Rocky Mountains have received several inches of snow in June, July and August. However, most summer snows were light and quickly melted.

After climbing well above the last stand of trees, a few cumulus clouds began forming around the peaks. In my impromptu preparations, I packed a long-sleeve shirt and light jacket, but no rain gear. However, I wasn't worried; I expected to be back into the shelter of timberline before the first bolt of lightning flashed. I hadn't been caught in a thunderstorm before, but this was to be my first climb above 13,000 feet. I was adventuring into new realms. Heeding the early warning, I accelerated my climbing pace.

The trail followed a circuitously lengthy route. It was time to pursue a shortcut. So, I abandoned the trail to follow my original route—straight up the long, gentle-sloped ridge to the summit.

At first, the shortcut worked to my advantage. The gentle slope of the east ridge made the climbing easy. Unfortunately, the gentle, easy-going slope turned into a steep, rugged slope. My shortcut backfired. By then, the trail was out of reasonable reach.

Above 12,000 feet, I entered the upper alpine zone, commonly referred to as a rock ocean. The high landscape was dominated by small to large rocks, a harsh environment whose only inhabitants included spiders, insects, pikas and marmots. Lichen was the closest thing to plant life. It was a gargantuan mound of gray granite.

Climbing was treacherous, and my feet took a beating from scrambling over boulder after boulder. I frequently lunged across wide gaps and crevices between boulders. Most of the boulders had jagged, sharp edges capable of gashing and bruising legs, extremely hazardous for ankles. A broken or sprained ankle could be fatal, especially when climbing alone and far from the trail.

Step by step, I steadily climbed up the rocky mount. What started as a leisurely hike through the woods transformed into a grueling climb to the top of a prominent Colorado thirteener. I pushed my young body to its limits, and at times I had to rest every ten steps. The high elevation, intense sun and fatigue were taking a toll on my body.

As I pushed myself, I realized the important relation between mind and body. An internal battle erupted; my mind wanted to continue, but my body wanted to stop. My body's self-defense mechanisms engaged to avoid bodily injury. My body grew tired and sent warning signals of pain to my mind. That was when I first discovered that the mind could overrule the body. "Mind over matter." The meaning of that oft-quoted phrase became evident. My body wanted to quit, but my mind forced my sore muscles up the mountain. I wondered if I would reach my limit. How much pain could I endure? Someday, I would reach my limit, but it would take a much greater mountain than Audubon.

I persevered and continued climbing the rocky ridge. The summit, or so I thought, was in sight and lifted my spirits. I took fewer breaks, forcing my lungs to work harder and my legs to work faster.

At the top, I was disheartened to discover that it was only a false summit (a rocky knoll, screening the actual summit). I rested a few minutes and convinced myself to continue. The summit, or perhaps another false summit, was another 100 feet higher. Once again, I charged for the summit.

It was another false summit! Once again my hopes were crushed. How many more false summits were there? After recovering from the summit assault, I recharged my spirits and pushed for the next high point.

After topping another false summit, I wondered if there was a real summit. Maybe it was just a chain of false summits leading to the heavens. It was extremely frustrating. From below, the ridge appeared to be a smooth incline to the summit. But in reality, the ridge had numerous false summits that stepped upward. Each one lured me another 100 feet up the mountain. Finally, I quit expecting to reach the top. I prepared myself for more false summits.

It was my first experience with false summits. From my earlier climbing days in the lower elevations, I remember climbing to the top of one mountain to find another higher one behind it. It was a pattern that endlessly repeated itself, but it was different on Audubon. This was an isolated mountain with a definite summit which eventually I would reach.

Finally! About mid-afternoon, I reached the summit of summits.

The pinnacle was reality. I climbed onto the highest rock on Mt. Audubon. I felt a rush of adrenalin and a wave of euphoria wash over my body. What an accomplishment! I stood 13,223 feet above sea level. Only a few hours earlier I stood at the bottom looking up with admiration at the awesome peak. The vista from the summit was astounding. The pain and hardships of the climb immediately began to dissipate.

Over fifty miles away and 8,000 feet below I saw Denver, nestled against the base of the Rockies. Straight east were the fertile plains and rolling hills of eastern Colorado, the rich farmland that received water (a life source) from the peaks that surrounded me. Towering into the clouds a few miles to the north was the dominant king of the northern Front Range, Longs Peak, (forty-fifth highest peak in North America, fifteenth highest in Colorado). To the south, a sea of mountains stretched over a hundred miles to New Mexico. To the west, mountains also stretched to the horizon. Miles and miles of snow-capped peaks, forest, canyons, white water rivers and rugged wilderness filled the panorama. It was truly a view to behold. The view, the feeling of accomplishment and the beautiful environment made every ounce of lost sweat worthwhile.

Looking north, I gazed at Longs Peak. Although its summit rose another 1,032 feet above Audubon, it wasn't as domineering as it looked from home (in the plains), where it distinctly towered above surrounding peaks. The next closest fourteener was Mount Bierstadt, forty miles south. From Denver, north to Ft. Collins, and east to Ft. Morgan, Longs Peak was a focal point. It was the northernmost fourteener.

Many times I stood in the yard at home looking at the high peaks wondering what the view would be like from the top of one. Finally, I knew the feeling, the realization of a childhood dream.

Unfortunately, I couldn't afford to savor the summit sensations too long, for I had to return to Brainard Lake before my parents reported me as missing. Fortunately the weather wasn't a factor. The puffy cumulus clouds never developed into thunderclouds, and, after bathing in the august beauty of the surrounding scenery and resting my stressed muscles, I started the descent. To save energy, I followed the trail for the four-and-a-half-mile trip back to the lake.

Fatigue crept into my tired muscles and bones as I ambled down the trail. I switched my energy conservation switch on, letting my body's downward momentum do most of the work. I just placed one foot in front of the other and avoided tripping over rocks. The best aspects of the trail were its gentle grade and lack of boulders. I wasn't feeling very adventurous on the return trek; the climb stole my enthusiasm for challenge, and I didn't have enough energy to boulder hop and take on the challenges of offtrail descending. The remainder of the descent was uneventful.

Just in time for a barbecue dinner, I innocently emerged from the treeline to join my family around the barbecue grill. When I enthusiastically told them about my day's adventure, Mom lectured with the usual, "You shouldn't have gone off by yourself like that." Other than a few words of advice, my parents weren't mad at me; they were getting accustomed to my high-country antics. They showed me a stringer full of rainbow trout, which had them in good spirits, so it was a good day for everyone.

Audubon looked different than it did before I climbed it. It seemed like a friend, rather than a distant stranger. It wasn't just another foreign peak in a sea of many. I discovered Mt. Audubon's character. I saw it from different perspectives, high and low. I noticed features that weren't apparent before. Thousands of people saw Audubon from a distance; only a few have stood on its massive summit. The rigors of the climb made me respect the awesome character of Audubon, and my perspective of it was forever changed. I had gained a new mountain friend.

The successful climb of Mt. Audubon was an important milestone in my mountaineering career for several reasons. I broke into the thirteener club. I loved the feeling of accomplishment that I got from making the climb. I discovered that I really enjoyed mountaineering. It was also the beginning of a deep feeling of respect and an almost spiritual relationship with the mountains. Prior to climbing Mt. Audubon, my feelings toward the mountains weren't as profound. I began viewing the mountains as an integral part of the environment, rather than just places for recreational pleasure. I began to see that the mountains were important to our existence. Their recreational value is important, but their environmental significance is paramount.

Mt. Audubon marked the beginning of my quest for high adventure. It was my first "big" mountain. The memory of that climb will always be especially meaningful. Mt. Audubon is the cornerstone of my Rocky Mountain Adventure Collection and my mountaineering career.

Someday, when I am standing upon my highest summit, I will reflect upon the mountain that persuaded me to continue striving for higher goals. Only then will I appreciate fully my mountaineering origins. I share the same dreams as many mountaineers: to stand upon the highest peak on every continent and to climb the classic peaks. But for now, until I can afford to become a full-time mountaineer, I am content with high adventure in the Rocky Mountains. Climbing every thirteener and fourteener in Colorado is an interesting challenge. Maybe. Someday.

If you're interested in climbing Mt. Audubon, just follow the directions that I will give at the end of the next subchapter. It is a three-and-a-half-mile climb up the trail from the Mitchell Lake Parking Area in the Indian Peaks Wilderness Area. It is an easy half-day climb.

Kiowa

KIOWA PEAK reaches 13,276 feet into the Colorado skyline. It can be seen from 100 miles away, from the eastern plains of Colorado. It is one of the many prominent and challenging thirteeners that are scattered throughout Colorado. It is Colorado's 421st highest peak. It is located in the Indian Peaks Wilderness

Area of the Front Range, and, relative to the other Indian Peaks, it is about average in height and climbing difficulty. From the Indian Peaks Campground it is a long hike to the base of the massive peak, and there isn't a trail to follow. It is a physically demanding climb following a lengthy trek. Kiowa, like the rest of the Indian Peaks, demands that climbers be in top cardiovascular condition. When I climbed it, I could run a mile in under six minutes; it still proved to be an exhausting climb.

From the east side of Brainard Lake, just the tip of Kiowa's summit is visible. It is hidden behind Niwot Ridge and across a secluded alpine valley. At first glance, it could be mistaken for a pile of rocks on Niwot Ridge. Because most of the mountain is hidden, Kiowa has an air of mystery about it. I wanted to see the rest of the hidden mountain. My curiosity was galvanized. It lured Craig and me toward it by exposing just enough to tempt us.

The Kiowa climb was an especially important one. It was the beginning of Craig's and my mountaineering partnership. Craig was fifteen and I was sixteen when we climbed Kiowa Peak. We had been friends for three years, but hadn't had much of a chance to get up to the mountains on our own because we lacked a means of transportation to the mountains. Finally, I received a driver's license and the keys to Dad's black, 1963 Buick Le Sabre. We broke the strings that tied us down at home, and now had a way to get to the mountains of adventure.

Craig and I met during wrestling practice in eighth grade. He moved to Colorado from Oklahoma. We both had strong interests in athletics, especially football, a sport we both loved. Our friendship grew stronger as a result of our common interests and outlooks on life. Physically, we were about the same size and had about the same strength. He had light brown hair that covered his ears, stood six feet tall, weighed 145 pounds and had a medium frame build. To enhance our football playing skills we started religiously lifting weights in ninth grade. Initially, I put on more weight and increased my strength faster, but we maintained a fairly equal balance. When we weren't in the mountains we spent our free time playing catch and weight lifting. After our first mountain climbing adventure, we found a deep mutual interest in the mountains, which strengthened our friendship and gave us a healthy alternative to the weekend high school party scene. For the most part, we alienated ourselves from our classmates, and strove to achieve intellectual and physical freedom in the fostering mountain environment.

The Indian Peaks Wilderness Area became our favorite high-country playground. It was only a two-hour drive from our homes (even in a 1963 Buick). We escaped to the Indian Peaks to enjoy the wilderness, discuss our problems, discuss political issues, enjoy life, relieve the stresses of teenage life and occasionally pursue women. One day, we read a comedy play from a mountainside in Boulder Canyon.

Craig and I climbed the mysterious peak in August, 1980, on a spectacularly pleasant summer day. The following is how the adventure unfolded.

From the east side of Brainard Lake, we watched the final slice of the dark orange sun dip behind the Continental Divide. We stood silent and still, hypnotized by the colorful sunset. Streaks and wisps of pink and orange colors radiated outward from the center of the setting sun against a darkening sky. It was a spectacular sight! It was one of the most beautiful sunsets that I had watched.

Shortly after sunset, Kiowa drew our attention to the tip of its barely visible peak. Niwot Ridge rose against the skyline like a long, gently sloped ramp for a giant earth-launched space rocket. In the middle of the rising ramp, Kiowa Peak poked up like a pile of rocks on Niwot's smooth ramp. It obviously wasn't part of Niwot Ridge; it was behind the ridge.

Spontaneously, we decided to climb Kiowa Peak. Its hidden nature was intriguing, and it posed a challenge that we had to take. We could see its pyramid-shaped summit, but we wanted to see the rest of it. We knew of no trails going to the peak, so we had to find our own route. Niwot Ridge would be our first obstacle. We discussed our possible routes. Kiowa appeared to be about ten miles away, as a goat would travel, over at least one 12,000-foot ridge, and across at least one valley. Without a map, we would be trekking blindly into unknown terrain, not knowing what obstacles we would encounter or whether to carry climbing equipment. With the exception of 1,000 vertical feet of forested mountainside, the remainder of the climb up Niwot would be across the tundra above timberline, with a few patches of snow remaining in shaded, mountainside niches. The ridge was blanketed with short, tundra grass and resembled the beautiful, green, alpine pastures of the Swiss Alps.

We chose to follow a straight course between Brainard Lake and the peak. It would take a full day to complete the roundtrip trek. Of course, a full day could be until sunset or later. With the next day's agenda set, we went back to camp to cook dinner and hit the pine needles.

Our adventure began on a cool August morning in 1980. As was usual during our climbing trips, I awoke before Craig, at dawn. I hiked through a peaceful stretch of forest, downhill to the river. Along the way, I came face to face with a deer. I stopped dead-still in my tracks, and it froze with its ears pointed upward. For a few seconds, we both stood motionless, staring at each other. I knew that it would dash off as soon as I moved, and it did. I took a step forward. It bolted away, sprinting gracefully between the trees. At the river, I dunked my head in the cold water, washed my face and brushed my teeth. Few sensations are more invigoratively stimulating than dunking your head into a stream of cold creek water!

On the way back to camp, I gathered some firewood to fuel a breakfast campfire. After building the fire, I rousted Craig from the tent and announced, "We're burning daylight!"

After breakfast we packed daypacks with lunch, water, a compass, spare clothing and some other little items (sunscreen, insect repellent, aspirin, etc.). We both started the hike wearing sweatshirts, pants and tennis shoes. We didn't have enough money to afford professional mountaineering attire, so we improvised. The sky was clear, the temperature cool and a gentle breeze rustled the treetops as we embarked on our quest.

Kiowa disappeared behind the forefront of Niwot Ridge as we

approached our first climb. We noted Kiowa's last position on the top of Niwot Ridge and made that an intermediate objective. We spotted several prominent landmarks to help us dot-to-dot our way up the ridge. The first reference point was a cliff with talus at its base, surrounded by forest. Climbing the cliff and talus would be easier than fighting through tangled vegetation, trees, and fallen timber.

We stopped at the foot of the talus to choose a route and assess the advantages and disadvantages of climbing the cliff. The talus slope looked stable; the cliff would take some concentration, but it would still be faster than going around up the densely forested mountainside.

Carefully taking our steps, we climbed up the talus toward the cliff. Near the top of the talus at the base of the cliff, the rocks were smaller and less stable. Our footing was poor and the slope steep. If we fell, we would land in a rocky grave. Utilizing firmly rooted plants and a few embedded rocks, we pulled ourselves up the talus into a fissure in the cliff face.

Without looking down or thinking about the risks, I started up the rock face. Craig followed behind at a safe distance. It would be a challenging free climb up the granite cliff. We should have belayed each other with ropes, but we didn't have any with us. Our lives depended upon finding firm footholds and handholds, because a fall would probably be fatal. I was scared, but I kept it to myself and maintained my concentration, gritted my teeth, and carefully climbed from one hold to the next. After perspiring a quart of sweat each, we safely topped the cliff.

Above the cliff we climbed back into the forest. From there, we had a steady climb through the forest to the openness of the tundra. We wouldn't be able to see Kiowa again until we got above the trees and atop the ridge. In the thick of the trees we couldn't see our intermediate landmarks, so we just kept climbing.

We saw a few of the typical, and more sociable, mountain critters on our trek up the mountainside: woodchucks, pikas, rabbits and squirrels. There were probably coyotes, black bears, bobcats and mountain lions prowling about in the forest, but they normally remained hidden.

Huffing and puffing, we broke out of the woods into the open tundra, and for the first time since the cliff, we stopped for a water-and-rest break. We rationed our canteen water, because we didn't know where we would find drinkable water.

We trekked quickly across the open tundra of Niwot Ridge. Searching for our bearings, we traveled toward an unnamed sub-peak on the ridge's spine. It was too close to Niwot Ridge's summit to be considered a separate summit. As we climbed, Kiowa gradually unveiled itself to us, like a lady slowly lowering her towel. Atop the 11,679 feet subpeak, we saw Kiowa's north face for the first time. All of its magnificent features were visible.

Kiowa's east face was too steep for our climbing desires. To the southeast a long, three-mile spur connected Kiowa with the rest of the mountains. The north side facing us was steep but climbable. Due west of Kiowa, Arikaree Peak (13,300 feet) appeared. The two peaks were bridged by a ridge that dipped down to form a pass between the two mountains. That ridge looked like the best route to follow up Kiowa.

The most disappointing feature that we saw was the mile wide, 1,000-foot-deep valley that cut between us and Kiowa's base. It was a beautiful, isolated valley pocketed with tarns and finger lakes, but we would have to lose our hard-earned altitude just to reach Kiowa's base.

We grumbled about the situation for a few minutes, then shook our frustrations off. The sparkling alpine lakes were very appealing, because our canteens were getting low and our throats dry. Unwilling to let the valley keep us from Kiowa's impressive summit, we descended into the valley.

We ran downhill most of the way to the Green Lakes of the valley floor. North Boulder Creek, in the valley's trough, split the sides of the valley and the bases of Niwot and Kiowa. At the highest lake (closest to Kiowa's west base), we took a long, refreshing break. We saturated ourselves with pure Rocky Mountain stream water and drank directly from the lake-fed creek. We probably shouldn't have done that, but the water was to us as the apple was to Eve.

The fresh water, rest, sunshine and a couple of snacks replenished our energy. But it wasn't energy levels, bad weather, snowfields, cliffs or exhaustion that could keep us from reaching the summit. Our minds would determine whether or not we would make it.

Then we began our ascent of the mysterious peak. We simply scrambled up the first pitch of the rocky mountainside. It was demanding, but relatively easy, climbing up and over boulder after boulder. The mountain slowly wore us down, and halfway up the mountainside I grew so exhausted I almost had to lift my weary legs with my arms. My body wanted to quit; my muscles were sore, fatigued and on the verge of collapse; my lungs were tired from working twice as hard as normal. The long hike to the base, the steepness of the mountain, our quick pace and the intense sunlight drained my energy. I thought about telling Craig to press on without me. I wanted to reach the summit, but my body wasn't cooperating. An internal war erupted between my mind and body. Will power would be the key factor that would spur me to the pinnacle of Kiowa. I had to overcome the physical pain that tried to break me. That climb became the hardest physical exercise of my life.

After every ten steps upward, I rested a minute. Intermittent resting combined with focusing my psyche on reaching the summit was the winning prescription. Trailing several paces behind Craig, I gutted it out and maintained the distance between us.

Fighting off fatigue, we forced ourselves upward. It didn't seem that we had hiked far enough, but the summit appeared to be just ahead of Craig. I hustled to close the gap between us; I wanted to be with Craig when he topped the peak.

I shouted ahead, "Is that the summit?"

"It looks like it," said Craig. "I certainly hope so."

Before I could catch up, he climbed up onto the apparent summit. "What does it look like" I asked. He was out of sight and didn't answer.

Climbing over the edge, I saw it was just a false summit, a familiar feature encountered on Mt. Audubon. It was just a knoll blocking our view of the actual summit. The false summit was a setback. But, the summit, or another false one, was just another eighty feet higher.

Together, we climbed toward the summit, pulling and propelling our weary bodies over the granite boulders. After reaching the top, we discovered another false summit! And, as before, there appeared to be another summit about fifty feet higher. A pattern of false summits began. It reminded me dearly of Mt. Audubon.

How many more deceptive summits would we cross? More importantly, how much farther could I push my body? I was almost to my mind-over-matter limit.

At that second false summit Craig got a pounding, painful head-ache. It was the first symptom of minor altitude sickness. Neither of us was adequately acclimated for the high altitude. I also felt slightly dizzy and light headed. Craig's splitting headache, my fatigued body and the repetitive false summits forced us seriously to consider quitting. But we were so close. We had to be very near the summit. Besides, we never bowed to defeat; we weren't quitters, not in the mountains, not in sports and not in life. So, we mustered our remaining strength and again pushed for the summit.

We proceeded up the mountain with the attitude that the next apparent summit was just another false summit. That way, we wouldn't get our hopes up. And sure enough, we crossed more false summits.

Finally, after climbing over several false summits, we made it! In a final burst of energy, we charged to the highest rock on Kiowa Peak. It was fifty-three feet higher than Mount Audubon. Kiowa Peak became my new high. It felt wonderful finally to be at the top! It was like standing on the top of the world (or at least the top of Colorado). Even after all of the pain and fatigue, it was well worth the effort. It was an accomplishment that gave me a distinct feeling of self-satisfaction.

After a few minutes, the summit experience washed away the agony of the past hour, and the invigorating fresh air carried the pain away. Additionally, the spectacular view drew our attention from our sore muscles.

From the summit cairn, the view was spectacular. To the east, the mountains gave way to the plains which stretched to the horizon toward Kansas. To the north, south and west a sea of mountains stretched to the horizons. Denver, the mile-high city, was far below and many miles to the southeast. It looked like it would from the seat of an airplane.

After enjoying the first wave of euphoria, we noticed another summit cairn, possibly higher than the one on whch we were standing, twenty paces east. After some debate, Craig hustled over to claim first rights atop the man-made rock mound. Like the chief of Kiowa Peak, he stood proudly atop the cairn. If it was the highest point, I also had to stand upon it in a token effort. After Craig stepped down from the throne I stepped up to assume it for awhile. One of the two cairns was certainly the summit.

The skies were still fair, but we couldn't chance staying too long. It was getting late in the afternoon, and we had a long descent back to camp. Gathering cumulus clouds forecasted that the tell-tale thunderstorms were not far away. The thought of climbing back up and over Niwot Ridge made me weak, and I wished that we could spend the night on the peak and start back fresh in the morning. Reality told us that it was time to leave the summit, because waiting would only exacerbate our sore muscles.

Once again we ignored our pains, and we fought against fatigue all the way back. Despite a few blossoming thunderclouds, weather conditions remained favorable for the return trek. It was a grueling descent back into the valley, a battle against fatigue up Niwot Ridge; and only our momentum carried us back to our camp east of Brainard Lake.

On the verge of collapse, standing in the shadow of the Indian Peaks at a vantage point near the lake, we looked back. There it stood, just as the night before. It was tinted orange by the glow from the setting sun. It looked the same, yet different. It wasn't a mysterious, hidden mountain anymore; we had discovered Kiowa's secret character. It was like the face of a friend peeking over the ridge.

The climb changed us and our perspectives of Kiowa Peak (and the mountains in general). We enjoyed it so much that we vowed to make mountain climbing a regular recreational activity. On the long list of sports that we enjoyed, mountain climbing was second only to football.

As darkness encroached upon the remaining light, we returned to camp, built a campfire, ate dinner, then recapped the highlights of our climb. We talked about our adventure while watching the flickering campfire flames cut through the darkness.

Δ

The Kiowa climb affected us in two major ways. It strengthened our friendship, and it strengthened our respect and understanding of the mountains. It established another mutual interest that continued to bring Craig and me together for many mountain adventures. A bond was formed by the mutual memories of that spectacular summer adventure. Even though we are now hundreds of miles apart and leading completely different lives than we did then, we will always share the memories of that adventure. It is a bond of friendship and a bond to the Rocky Mountains. Even while writing this, I still see the orange glow of Kiowa in the light of the setting sun.

The Kiowa adventure was also another step up the trail of mountaineering experience. We learned more about the mountains, nature and mountaineering itself. Mountaineering extends beyond the physical challenges and risks. It is a mindset, a way of experiencing life. Anyone who blindly climbs without absorbing the wonderful sensations of the mountains is not a mountaineer. Mountaineering is a holistic experience which encompasses physical, emotional, intellectual and spiritual aspects. A mountaineer is free to wander about the mountain wilderness and between the various states of existence. A mountaineer understands human relationships with nature, our impact on nature and our role in the global ecosystem. A mountaineer is truly a part of the alpine environment, a free spirit who wanders high and low.

As you embark on your own adventures, I encourage you to

listen to nature's message. While enjoying yourself, take time to think about the environment and your role in the environment. Are you an integral part of nature, or are you (and humankind) separate from nature? Should you live in harmony with nature, or in conflict with nature?

Now, if you're interested in climbing Kiowa, let me tell you how to get there. As previously mentioned, Kiowa is located in the Indian Peaks Wilderness Area of Colorado. To get there, from Nederland, Colorado (west of Boulder), follow highway 72 north to the north side of Ward, Colorado. Turn west at the sign marking the paved road to the Indian Peaks Wilderness Area. From there it is about a ten-minute drive to Brainard Lake campground. Kiowa is to the southwest, mostly hidden behind Niwot Ridge. Since most of the wilderness between Brainard Lake and Kiowa is off limits for camping, you'll probably have to stay at the campground or just park at the west end of Brainard Lake. Unlike many of the other peaks, there isn't a trail to Kiowa from Brainard Lake. It is a grueling climb, and depending on your physical condition and experience, you may or may not be able to make this climb in one day. The Kiowa climb is for mountaineers with climbing and backcountry experience. If you're a beginner, I suggest that you follow a trail to the top of one of the other Indian Peaks. And no matter which peak you set out for, start early and pack rain gear, water, food, sunscreen, a jacket and a camera, as a minimum.

Longs Peak

LONGS PEAK, towering dominantly above its neighbors, stands apart from Colorado's other "fourteeners." Its location, physical characteristics, history and prominence puts it in a class by itself. It is the northernmost fourteener in Colorado and is over forty miles north of the next closest Front Range fourteener. As the Rockies dip into northern Colorado and southern Wyoming, Longs Peak thrusts upward to 14,225 feet. It is the forty-fifth highest peak in North America. Longs Peak is visible from several major cities, including Fort Collins, Greeley, Boulder and Denver. Because of its high visibility, it is well known to many Colorado residents. It is easy to point out, because it is clearly the tallest mountain in the northern Front Range.

It typically remains spotted with snowfields throughout the summer. During the winter months (including late fall and early spring) it is predominantly snow-covered, except for the steep vertical faces. Longs Peak's 1,675-foot east face is a Rocky Mountain hallmark. Furthermore, its east face is magnificently highlighted by the 1,000-foot sheer-walled Diamond Face. It was climbed for the first time in 1960, after the National Park Service lifted climbing restrictions of it. The east face attracts technical climbers from around the world.

But its popularity isn't limited to technical climbers. Longs Peak offers challenges and rewards for every class of mountaineer from youngster through senior and from beginner to professional. It is a spectacular peak with many interesting facets. The alpine scenery along the trail to the summit treats climbers to a broad spectrum of topography, flora and fauna.

Aside from its physical nature and spectacular characteristics, Longs Peak has a sentimental meaning to me. During my childhood days, in the eastern plains of Colorado, Longs Peak was always my focal point on the western horizon. Every time I gazed west, Longs Peak captured my attention. I first noticed it when I still depended on Dad to carry me up mountains and Mom to change my diapers. It was a distant point that seemed beyond reach; it was a dream place.

I was twelve years old when I learned its name. Even though it wasn't the highest peak in Colorado it meant more to me than Mt. Elbert did. At that time in my life, Mt. Elbert was so far away that I couldn't even imagine what it looked like. Other popular mountains, such as Pikes Peak, weren't as important either. Pikes Peak is much farther away, and it has a road to the top. Although I had been to the top of Pikes Peak with my parents at a very young age, I pictured a congested freeway winding to the top (even though it is just a simple two-lane road). The thought of driving to the top of any mountain upset me. It was appalling. Mountains are meant to be climbed by human power.

During my early teenage years, I gathered more knowledge of the mountains and formed impressions about mountain climbing. For the first time Longs Peak became a place that I could visit, rather than just a far away point on the horizon, and I realized that it could be climbed, and that I would one day stand on its summit.

After thoroughly studying Longs Peak, I learned that it can only be climbed without equipment during July, August and September. The popular, recreational route (the Keyhole route) traverses the steep west side. The west side is icy and snow covered throughout most of the year. The Narrows ledges and the Homestretch are extremely treacherous when they are snow covered and moderately dangerous when they aren't. In fact, those two areas require an ice axe, crampons, belays and some experience if they are to be climbed safely with snow on them. And they may have snow on them in July.

Over twenty fatalities have occurred on Longs Peak. However, over 100,000 have climbed it. Most of the fatalities resulted from falls, lightning, and exposure.

I learned enough about Longs Peak to give it my full respect. It is not a mountain to be taken lightly. Hence, I opted to prepare myself adequately before scaling its lofty heights and chancing its portending pitfalls.

Thoughts of climbing Longs Peak remained in the back of my mind as I set out to train my way up to its heights. I concentrated on climbing several 12,000- and 13,000-foot peaks to get the experience that was necessary for a fourteener. For two years I climbed and climbed with the goal of climbing Longs Peak in mind. An intuitive force instructed me to prepare gradually for Longs Peak, and that is exactly what I did. After all, I was preparing to reach a new milestone in my mountaineering achievements.

Finally, by the summer of 1981 I felt confident about climbing Longs. Craig and I planned an early August climb to take advantage of Colorado's best summer weather. We climbed up the east side, actually spiraling completely around the cone of the peak before reaching the summit. The climb to the top is seven and a half miles and rises 4,725 feet from an elevation of 9,530 feet.

Inclement weather forced us to abort our 7 August attempt for the summit. Overcast skies and rain blanketed the entire area, covering most of Rocky Mountain National Forest. Fortunately, we planned an extra day into our schedule for some unforeseen delay. We probably could have made it to the summit on the 7th, but we opted to wait another day hoping for better weather. Our decision was beneficial. Here is how our Rocky Mountain adventure unfolded.

In the predawn dark on 8 August 1981, we awoke from a comfortable night's rest on the hard ground floor of the pup tent. The inside of the tent was wet with dew that felt like ice. I rousted Craig awake as I crawled out of the tent. It was too early to determine if the weather had improved. Some typical morning fog filled the valley blocking visibility of the sky, but at least it wasn't raining.

After a hot campfire breakfast, we broke camp and drove to the trailhead on Longs Peak's east side. In rain, sleet or snow, we were determined to climb Longs Peak. Fortunately, the morning sun burned the fog away, revealing a blue sky. The signal of good weather elevated our spirits to a jovial mood. The world looked fantastic! I felt like I could leap to the summit in a single bound!

We packed our backpacks lightly with lunch, water, spare clothing, a camera and some other small survival-type items. We started the climb from the Longs Peak Ranger Station at an elevation of 9,530 feet. The first stretch of the climb took us through a serene fantasyland forest. As we climbed up through the quietude of the forest we transcended into a dream-like world.

A mysterious feeling of peaceful, quiet tranquility washed over my body as we hiked through the first stretch of forest. It was a very romantic setting for both fantasy and reality. Natural, wholesome sounds and sights transported me into another mind-set, away from the everyday worries of the urban setting. Distant sounds of Alpine Brook reverberated through the trees creating a soothing, hypnotic background sonance. Closer to us, the mixed intermittent sounds of birds and squirrels enlivened the forest.

We welcomed the warm rays of sunshine that filtered through the trees onto our backs. The air was still cool, chilled by the cold granite of the mountain and the snowfields of higher elevations. Still in the prime of our early adulthood, we set a vigorous Olympic-style climbing pace.

Longs Peak was our Mt. Everest, and we could pretend to be anything that we wanted to be. I chose to be a professional climber training for a future Everest expedition. Relaxing and enjoying life were two reasons that make mountain climbing and backpacking fulfilling experiences. While the body exercised, the mind was free to wander. It was a great time to rejuvenate the mind.

At the first fork in the trail a few aspen trees appeared in the changing mountainscape. The light green aspen leaves contrasted beautifully against the dark green of the pines. Had it been October the aspen leaves would have been gold and fluttering in the breeze like butterflies. The trail to the right led up to the Eugenia Mine, and to the left it led on upward toward the summit. The pine forest thinned slightly as the rocky ruggedness of the terrain increased.

Beyond the fork, farther up the trail, the sound of rushing water gradually grew louder as we neared Alpine Brook. The presence of more moisture thickened the vegetation. Soft-needled subalpine fir and sharp-needled Engelmann spruce trees thrived in the cool, moist environment along the brook.

The next stretch of trail paralleled Alpine Brook leading us into Goblins Forest. Goblins Forest was mysteriously different from its neighboring forest. Trees were denser, and the forest was darker and extremely calm. Its name suited it well, and the environment stimulated my imagination with images of the mythical Middle Earth.

To avoid being captured by the elusive goblins we trekked

through Goblins Forest without any rest breaks. After crossing a feeder stream, we continued to parallel Alpine Brook until finally crossing it via a convenient bridge provided by the National Park Service. Across the creek, the heavily forested terrain changed into a higher alpine environment, the evergreens were shorter and sparser because of a shorter growing season and harsher conditions. The colors gradually turned from grassy green to rocky gray. The high peaks that we longed to stand upon came into view in the openness of the alpine terrain. As we climbed, a chilling breeze swept across us bringing cold from the snowfields above. The intense alpine sunshine drove the chill from our bodies.

The rockier terrain made climbing harder as we entered a section of broken-down rock that was especially hazardous to the ankles. Hiking boots provided good ankle protection against the abrasions and twists that often resulted from slipping and tripping on the rocks.

Telltale signs of the wind's powerful influence on the alpine landscape appeared as we neared timberline. The trees were shorter and the branches were concentrated on the leeward side of the trees. Trees and boulders received the full force of the strong winter winds, which played a major role in sculpting the high country landscape. The winter drastically differed from the relative calm of the alpine summer.

Higher on Longs Peak's mountainside, we entered another zone with different vegetation. The shrub-like trees were well adapted to extremely harsh conditions. They grew low to the ground and clustered in wind-sheltered groves. Krummholz (crooked wood) type trees were most common. Their trunks were often twisted and their bark was thick. Even the young trees looked like veterans of their harsh climate.

"Bear brush!" I said as we approached a grove of Krummholz.

"Bear!" Craig jocularly responded.

Short, shrub-like evergreens were what Craig and I commonly called "bear brush." Somewhere, probably from a public television-sponsored nature program, I learned that bears like hiding in this type of brush. Although we never had any bear encounters in the bear brush, we jokingly continue to refer to them as such. Every time we cross the characteristic brush, one of us says, "bear brush," and the other responds with "bear." It was a saying that instantaneously rolled off our tongues several summers ago. Then it became a traditional saying. Hopefully, we'll never have a real bear encounter in the bear brush.

Beyond the tough, stubby bear brush, I took a moment to reflect upon the tundra that covers the alpine mountainside. Several years ago I didn't even think about the damage that I did while hiking across the fragile tundra. I was oblivious to the damage that I caused. Just above timberline everything that plants need to survive was scarce. The growing season was short, and there was very little soil for the plants to root. Plant life itself was limited to only a few types. Short tundra grass and flowering plants were the most prevalent types of alpine flora.

Still climbing at a strong pace, we arrived at the second trail intersection before 9:00 A.M. The left trail led to Chasm Lake and the august glacial valley of the Roaring Fork. We went right, continuing toward the summit. Just past the intersection, we crossed back over the Alpine Brook. At that elevation, the brook was just a narrow mountain stream and we simply rock-hopped across it. It was just a baby compared to its size farther down the mountainside. Fed by numerous other streams, it grew eventually into a raging white water creek.

At Jims Grove we passed through the last stand of natural shelter. A grove of spruce and fir formed timberline. Above Jims Grove, the landscape transformed into an ocean of rock, with vegetation limited to tundra grass and similar stunted plants. The landscape was barren, but not devoid of beauty.

The beauty of the landscape was in the eye of the beholder. To me, the high country was beauty in its purest state. Beauty was in the natural wholesomeness of the alpine landscape, giving the illusion that it was beyond humankind's destructive reach. But, unfortunately, it wasn't.

Craig and I continued our ascent like two mountaineers racing to claim a virgin peak. We conversed sparingly and pointed out distinctive natural features as we passed them. It wasn't that we didn't have much to talk about; we chose to conserve our air intake for breathing.

The familiar, high-pitched chirp of a pika occasionally cut through the silence. Pikas were among the few, ever-present rodents that inhabited the rocky alpine landscape. They were brown rat-like creatures that incessantly release high-pitched chirps. They border between being a novelty and an annoyance. Aside from the pikas, the other predominant animals were the marmots and ptarmigans.

Marmots were my furry favorites. They were big, brown, furry woodchucks well adapted to the alpine environment. They calmly moved about from one lounging place to the other. I envied their carefree life styles and their beautiful alpine homes.

The slow-moving, grouse-like ptarmigans were undoubtedly around, although we hadn't seen any on this climb. Because of their excellent camouflage, they were the least likely to be seen. They had gray and black feathers that almost matched the color of the granite mountainside.

Other types of wildlife, such as Rocky Mountain sheep, mountain goats, mountain lions, deer and elk were also abundant; however, they were rarely witnessed during the summer daytime hours. They were especially rare along the more popular hiking trails.

Continuing to push our bodies harder, we climbed toward Granite Pass, across increasingly rugged terrain. The beauty of the lower alpine meadows faded behind us. Longs Peak began revealing another of its many characteristics: steeper and more arduous trails.

Climbing in the rugged natural surroundings of the mountains triggered thoughts about my primitive ancestors. Even though humankind evolved from a very primitive, natural world, I felt somewhat displaced in the backcountry. Had it been that long since humans ran wild and naked about earth? It seemed as if I had been artificially conditioned by the easier existence of modern times. I wondered how long I could survive if I were stripped of my clothes and left in the wilderness. I would certainly have to seek lower ground and migrate south for the winter. I felt alienated from nature in some ways, but in other ways I felt that I belonged to nature. Of course, I knew that I was a direct result of natural processes as we all were. While we depend on the earth for survival, we are an integral part of nature. And it's possible that humankind's modern evolution was also part of nature's master plan. Survival was nature's game, and if we are to survive throughout eternity, we will have to continue to adapt and evolve with the rest of the universe. If that is the case, some day in the distant future humankind will have to set sail for a new planet with a younger sun. Or we will somehow evolve so that we no longer need an earth-like planet for survival. But until we advance beyond our earthly ties, if we ever do, we will have to live as a part of nature, not as conquerors of nature. In that way, I feel very much like a part of the natural alpine environment.

More and more I viewed earth's natural environment as home. The wilderness is not a place to destroy; like a home, it is a place to cherish and preserve. Polluting the wilderness is like throwing trash in our backyards. Throughout my backcountry adventures my sensitivity for the environment continued to increase, and I developed a deep sense of respect for nature.

Next, we crossed Granite Pass, another landmark. The weather remained good, the sky crystal blue. When the air was calm, we stayed comfortably warm, but the slightest breeze quickly carried the warmth away; wind chill seriously influenced our relative warmth.

The terrain between Granite Pass and Boulderfield was rock-laden, but not too steep. And, as the name implies, Boulderfield was a field of boulders. It was in a valley north of the summit. At Boulderfield's elevation the soil and plant life was almost nonexistent, and the environment was much harsher; consequently, it didn't require the same cautious respect as the wilderness at the lower elevations. In fact, if you try to abuse the boulders you'll damage yourself far more than the environment. It was an excellent place for bouldering. You could spend the entire day climbing from one boulder to the next. For the more passive—sun worshipers and meditators—there were thousands of boulders that were perfect for lazing upon. Unless you have a companion who can carry you down five miles of mountainside in the event of an emergency, sun bathing is the recommended activity. Boulderfield was abundant with ankle-twisting and leg-breaking booby traps. If we weren't blazing for the summit, we would have stopped for some bouldering. We never seemed to have enough time to fully enjoy the mountains we climbed.

At Boulderfield we entered an extremely dangerous area. From here on thunderstorms were deathly dangerous. They can transform a jovial climb to the summit into a terrifying fight for survival (I know from experience). Even though we were only two hours from the summit, bad weather conditions could force us to abort the climb.

Beyond Boulderfield, our next milestone was the Keyhole, a notch through a jagged ridge demarking the east side of Longs Peak from the west, a more demanding climb with steeper terrain and thinner air. As our muscles worked harder to carry us up the slope, our lungs vigorously worked harder to supply our bloodstreams with oxygen. At 13,000 feet I began feeling the effects of high altitude. My pulse increased; I had to take rapid short breaths and I felt slightly dizzy. Despite being well acclimatized from a summer of climbing, Craig and I still felt mild cases of altitude sickness. As long as the symptoms didn't get worse, it wasn't harmful. To the contrary, it felt relaxing, slightly euphoric. We were getting a Rocky Mountain High.

Between Boulderfield and the Keyhole, we passed dozens of other climbers who desperately gasped for air as they crept up the mountainside. They were dropping to the sides of the trail like flies in a cloud of insecticide. Farther up the trail, on the east side of the Keyhole, we climbed into a mass of recouping climbers. About sixty hopeful Longs Peak climbers were strewn about the steep-sided ridge. It looked like a rocky coast strewn with seals basking in the sunshine.

At first glance the crowd confused me. I thought the park service was charging a toll to pass through the Keyhole. As we got closer, I thought for sure that we would find a hotdog stand selling snacks to hungry climbers. I never saw so many people congregated that high on a mountainside. Some were having second thoughts about finishing the climb. Out of group pressure we felt compelled to stop and chat with the mass of mostly tourists. But out of sheer determination (and the fact that we weren't tired) we trekked onward to the Keyhole pass.

After weaving through the crowd, we approached the Keyhole. It looked like I thought it would. It was a convenient notch that allows climbers to avoid the dangers of climbing over the jagged ridge. We hiked through the Keyhole and passed from the sunny side to the shaded side of Longs Peak. As we emerged from the Keyhole, the terrain changed drastically. The west side of Longs Peak was still in the morning shade. The massive chunks of granite were still cold. The temperature dropped at least twenty degrees, and the rocks were barely above freezing. My hands became cold from occasionally touching the rocks to keep my balance. Scattered ice formations and ice on the trail were common. The previously easy-going trail transformed into a precarious stretch along the Narrows Ledges. In many places the trail was a mere ledge traversing the steep west side of Longs Peak.

It became apparent why the Keyhole area was a gathering point; beyond it, the climbing terrain became considerably more dangerous. It was a good place to make final preparations for the treacherous journey ahead. It was the last safe haven to put on an extra shirt, eat a snack, and mentally prepare for treacherous trail ahead. If that were my first mountain climbing trip I would also be a little shaken by the ominous Narrows. When we climbed up through the scattered group of resters, I remembered some ghostly white faces. They had obviously experienced or started to experience the Narrows.

We were young, strong and full of gusto; we thrived on rugged and dangerous terrain. Facing life and death danger charged our systems better than a cup of double-strength coffee. In fact, I liked the "hairy" terrain better than easygoing, happy-go-lucky terrain. Steep, narrow and icy trails with loose rock were good catalysts for turning brown hair gray (not that I wanted gray hair). The challenges of mountaineering were embedded in my spirit, and I enjoyed the personal satisfaction of overcoming the challenges.

Putting the cold aside, the vistas from the west face were spectacular! Snowcapped mountains stretched to the eye's limits. Far below, we saw a beautiful, secluded valley blanketed in green, split by a river and spotted with lakes. From our high perspective, it looked like a backpacker's paradise. Someday, I would like to backpack into that secluded valley and spend several days exploring it. Someday, I would like to visit every mountain, every mountain valley, and every alpine wilderness area. I hoped that "someday" would become reality.

Despite the harder climbing conditions, we continued upward at a staggering pace. The weather remained spectacular. Only hints of changing weather appeared in the form of cotton-ball cumulus clouds. But, as all Colorado mountaineers know, fluffy cumulus clouds frequently foretell afternoon thunderstorms. I've seen harmless looking cumulus clouds evolve into towering thunderstorm-bearing cumulonimbus in less than thirty minutes. That doesn't give climbers much time to get off of exposed summits, especially if belays are necessary.

As we spiraled around the dome of the peak the trail crossed a couloir, the beginning of the homestretch. Actually, the trail ran into a steep rock face in front of us. Standing a few steps back from the steep pitch, we searched for the best route. We gladly welcomed the challenge. I was starving for some good recreational rock climbing, so for us, it was pure fun. But for tourists and less-seasoned climbers the craggy couloir face presented a formidable obstacle. However, with concentration and a sprinkle of tenacity even frightened first-timers can make it to the top.

Then, just as Craig and I found our first handholds, we heard the cracking sound of tumbling rocks. It sounded like a small avalanche! I didn't have to look up to know what was headed toward us. Instinctively, Craig lunged to the left and I lunged to the right, covering our heads and hugging the mountain. Golf ball to volleyball sized rocks bounced over me and to the sides. After about five seconds, it was over. I peeled myself from the rock face. Sometime after the first rocks struck our area, we heard a belated warning from above, "Rocks! Watch out below!"

Thankfully, neither of us was hit. A few small rocks brushed harmlessly across our backpacks. The culprit was another climber about fifty feet above, who continued to carelessly kick rocks loose; we quickly scrambled out of his drop path.

The unbelayed free climb was a good break from the monotony of the trail. The rocks were cold, slippery and booby trapped with loose patches. It was just enough of a challenge to put a smile on my face.

We scrambled up the craggy couloir face without trouble. I climbed carefully above Craig, trying not to kick any rocks loose. We slipped a few times and harmlessly jarred a few rocks loose; otherwise, we climbed the spur without incident. Upon topping the couloir, we emerged back into the sunshine that wrapped around the south face. After thirty minutes in the cool shade, the sunshine felt great. From there, the summit was only a rock-hop, skip and jump away. We began the final leg of the home-stretch.

Years of anticipation and excitement were rising to a climax. For most of my childhood, Longs Peak was a distant place at the limits of my imagination. I knew that it was the highest point on the western horizon. I knew that I wanted to climb it someday, but other than that I knew little about Colorado's northernmost four-teener. However, as I grew into adolescence, my interest in Longs Peak (and the mountains in general) intensified. After I discovered a gold mine of knowledge in the school library, my ignorance of the outer (beyond home) world dissipated. Reading books opened doors to the rest of the world and enabled me to visit vicariously exciting places around the world. I read any book that appealed to my mood at the time, and believe it or not, on a few occasions, I actually skipped class so that I could go to the library to read about subjects that interested me. Eventually, as destiny carried out its course, I picked up a book about the Rocky Mountains. That was when I first learned about Longs Peak's history and physical char-acteristics. The more I read, the more it intrigued me. Finally, after years of building anticipation, I was about to stand upon the distant peak on the horizon.

At 10:50 A.M. we topped Longs Peak's broad flat summit. One hundred thirteen years after the first recorded climb of its summit by John Wesley Powell, we too had climbed its 14,255-foot summit. The success of our climb probably placed us at around the 100,500th and 100,501th persons to reach the summit. Our only chance at any claim to fame (and it was a weak chance at that) was for the speed of our ascent. We made the seven and a half mile climb to the summit in three hours and thirty minutes at a normal, unforced pace. We didn't set out to break any records, and probably didn't, but I'm sure that we were in the top five percent of fastest ascents. Out of at least 100,000 climbers, that would put us in the company of 5,000 others. Since few climbers keep such records, it was difficult to guess at our ranking. Records aside, the self-satisfaction of climbing Longs Peak was more rewarding than having my name in a history book.

One thing that I'm sure John Powell didn't encounter, that we did, was a crowd on the summit. It was like a summer summit festival. It took some of the sense of accomplishment out of the climb after we saw nearly one hundred others scattered atop the expansive summit. I shouldn't describe the crowd's composition. If I mentioned the toddlers, the glory of our climb would be in serious jeopardy (just joking, we didn't see any toddlers). We had to get in line and wait our turn to stand upon the highest rock. So, we joined over a hundred people to climb successfully Longs Peak on 8 August 1981. The numbers sound much better when compared to earth's total population. Out of a possible five billion persons we were two of a hundred or so to climb Longs Peak on 8 August 1981. After recording the pinnacle of our adventure on film, we stepped aside so that others could bask in the glory of standing upon the forty-fifth highest point in North America. Someday, we will share our adventure photos and stories with our children and grandchildren.

Absorbed in the elation of a successful climb, we relaxed upon the summit for thirty minutes. We inhaled the surrounding panorama and privately celebrated our accomplishment. It felt wonderful to achieve such a long-sought goal. Too bad we couldn't stay longer, but omnipotent thunderclouds formed overhead. Staying on the summit too long would increase our risk of getting pelted by a thunderstorm during the descent.

Before leaving the summit, I gazed across the eastern plains searching for a landmark that would pinpoint home. Somewhere down there was the place that I looked from when I gazed west at Longs Peak—the king of the northern Front Range. Standing atop Longs Peak was the realization of a childhood dream. If I never return to Longs Peak's lofty summit, I am happy to have the memory of making it at least once.

We started our descent at 11:20 A.M. and followed the same route as on our ascent, arriving safely back at the Longs Peak Ranger Station at 2:05 P.M., officially ending our descent.

The memory of our Longs Peak adventure will be remembered as one of my most rewarding climbs. It is special because of its physical prominence, its place in my past and because it was my first fourteener.

If you're interested in climbing Longs Peak it is easy to find. I recommend the Keyhole route for beginners and recreational climbers. To get to the trailhead, follow Colorado 7 ten miles south from Estes Park, and turn west for a one-mile drive to the Longs Peak Campground and Ranger Station. From the ranger station it is a seven and a half mile climb up 4,855 vertical feet to the summit. For technical climbers, there are numerous challenging routes to take, such as the 1,000-foot vertical Diamond Face. To avoid encountering snow on the Narrows ledges, August is about (no guarantee) the best time to make your ascent. If there isn't snow on the Narrows you can make the climb without climbing equipment. However, if the Narrows and other areas are snow covered you will need an ice axe, crampons, belay rope and some experience to make a safe ascent. Camping on Longs Peak is restricted to certain areas, and you must have a backpacking permit to stay overnight. If you get an early start (a wise thing to do), you can probably make the climb in a day. Beginners and less expe-rienced climbers should start before 5:00 A.M.

My next attempt at climbing a fourteener came six years later when two friends and I fell short of Mt. Princeton's summit. A late start, inadequate training, and threatening thunderstorms forced us to abort the climb only 500 feet below the summit. Our foolish descent down Princeton's Chalk Cliffs almost cost us our lives (see my story titled "Death Defying Descent"). Seven years after Longs Peak, I once again stood above 14,000 feet. Sean and I climbed Colorado's highest, Mount Elbert, during the summer of 1988. The Mount Elbert adventure is the most appropriate story to end this mountain climbing chapter.

Mount Elbert

On 10 July 1988, Sean and I climbed Colorado's highest peak, Mt. Elbert (14,433 feet), the loftiest Rocky Mountain and the second highest peak in the contiguous United States, surpassed only by California's Mt. Whitney, sixty-two feet higher. Mt. Elbert is the eighteenth highest peak in the United States and the twenty-ninth highest in North America. From the Black Cloud Creek trailhead to the summit it is a six-mile climb up 4,730 vertical feet. Despite being Colorado's highest, it is a relatively easy climb in terms of vertical steepness, and there are numerous nontechnical routes to the top. The most difficult aspects of climbing Elbert are dealing with the rapidly changing weather conditions and the physiological effects of the high altitude.

We originally planned to climb Mt. Antero's prominent pyramidal peak on 10 July. Antero is Colorado's tenth highest peak. Aesthetically speaking, Mt. Antero is a grander peak than Elbert and has more topographic character. It is steep, rugged and more challenging than Elbert. Mt. Antero captured our attention during our attempt at Mt. Princeton. From Princeton's southern slope Mt. Antero is a very impressive looking mountain, and as we ascended and descended Princeton, I couldn't keep my eyes off Antero. It was like trying to avoid looking at a scantily clad attractive woman. During our Princeton climb we agreed to return the following summer to climb Antero.

Three weeks before the scheduled climb, we switched objectives. Although Antero is very impressive, the temptation of climbing "the highest" made us rescind our previous decision. After moving to Georgia in 1987, I had become highly selective in my mountain climbing objectives. I do not have the luxury of being a full-time mountaineer. Climbing Colorado's highest justified the 1,208-mile flight to Denver.

Mt. Elbert is almost at the dead center of Colorado and is one of fifteen fourteeners in the Sawatch Mountain Range, surrounded by august Rocky Mountain beauty. The picturesque Elk Range is to the west and the Mosquito Range is to the east. Elbert's rivaling neighbors are Mt. Massive to the north, and La Plata Peak (the Silver Peak) to the south. Within a fifty-mile radius of Elbert there are at least seventeen ski areas, numerous lakes, several rivers, and thousands of acres of mountain wilderness. Some of Colorado's richest precious metal mining communities are in the surrounding area. Leadville, Climax, Fairplay, Alma and Silverthorne are all within fifty miles of Elbert.

Prior to Elbert, our last climbing expedition was when the Chalk Cliffs of Mt. Princeton nearly claimed our lives. Since that climb neither of us had logged much high-country time. Sean spent some time backpacking and climbing in the Canadian Rockies, and I did some low-altitude climbing in the Smoky Mountains and North Georgia's Blue Ridge Mountains. I hiked to the top of Tennessee's and Georgia's highest mountains, Clingmans Dome (6,643 feet) and Brasstown Bald (4,784 feet), respectively. Even though I am accustomed to climbing at much greater heights than the Appalachian Mountains, you won't catch me laughing at them. Climbing Clingmans Dome proved to be my most physically exhausting climb. A climb that Craig and I grossly underestimated. We started the climb like we were going on a Saturday afternoon picnic. We each packed light daypacks with the bare minimum of provisions, and the forest ranger laughed at us when we told him that we were going on an afternoon hike to Clingmans Dome. We started the climb at the Deep Creek Campground, twelve miles from Clingmans Dome according to the trail guide (it felt farther). On the first afternoon, we barely made four miles before dusk. We purposely didn't pack a tent and slept on the ground under the stars. Then, around midnight, I was frightfully awakened by a snorting bear. It was very close to us, but we couldn't see anything in the extreme darkness of the forest's canopy. We managed to scare it away by talking loudly, but I didn't sleep the rest of the night. At the crack of dawn, we started the grueling climb to Clingmans Dome. After a painfully long climb, we made it to the top. It was then that we also discovered a road leading to a parking lot within one mile of the summit. We were discouraged to see others comfortably riding almost to the top in their cars. On the fifteen-mile descent, by way of the Noland Divide Trail, I hiked in excruciating agony. During the last five miles my feet felt raw with pain. I remember looking down at my feet expecting to see my tennis shoes red with blood. Somehow, we managed to make it back to the car at Deep Creek Campground. That was my first Appalachian climbing adventure.

That agonizing climb of Clingmans Dome was my only training for climbing Mt. Elbert. Although I was in good cardiovascular condition, I wasn't ready for the thin air of Elbert's lofty heights.

From my window on the jet, I eagerly gazed west after the pilot announced that he was starting his descent into Stapleton International Airport in Denver, Colorado. After six months away from the Colorado Rockies I got my first refreshing view of them as the plane sped toward Denver. Pikes Peak was the first peak that I pinpointed, and the sight of the majestic Rocky Mountains, my home, nearly brought tears to my eyes. Being away from them for so long really made me appreciate them, for I was long overdue for some revitalizing mountain air purification.

At daybreak on 9 July 1988 my dad, Sean and I piled into the pickup and camper for the three-hour drive to Twin Lakes Reservoir, near the base of Mt. Elbert. Dad planned to fish while Sean and I climbed Elbert. He magnanimously volunteered to take us up into the Sawatch Range. Dad's camper cooking is the best in the west, and I wouldn't trade America's best hotel and restaurant for his camper bed and breakfast.

Craig, Brent and Sean each were invited to join the Mt. Elbert adventure, but Sean was the only one who could make it. Craig was stranded in Puerto Rico, and Brent couldn't get away from work.

Our tight climbing schedule didn't give us any time to train for the climb, and it only allowed one day of altitude acclimatization.

We spent Saturday acclimatizing ourselves to the high country air and enjoying the mountain environment. We went on an afternoon exploring trek up the eastern slope of Parry Peak (12,682 feet). We climbed up Gordon Gulch and visited some of the local ghost mines. We didn't push ourselves too hard, but our little climbing excursion was enough to get our hearts pumping fast and our lungs working vigorously. After only three hours, I felt the symptoms of mild altitude sickness, light-headedness with a slight headache. At least we received some high-altitude exposure before making our ascent. It was more than enough exercise for the day before our climb.

The weather forecast for the climb was favorable, but not ideal. Thunderclouds formed in the late morning on Saturday, and the weather pattern would probably be the same for Sunday. We also heard reports of mid-summer snowfall in other parts of the mountains. However, summer snowfall and thunderstorms were typical and nothing to worry about. Both of us have backcountry experience during adverse weather conditions. We knew always to prepare for the worst.

We camped at the Twin Peaks Campground in the peaceful valley between Mt. Elbert and La Plata Peak. After one of Dad's delicious camper dinners, I took some aspirin to relieve a throbbing headache that was spurred by the altitude. After a refreshing night's rest in the plush comfort of the camper, we awoke at the break of dawn. Dad served a delicious sausage and egg breakfast with hot coffee to wash it down. After breakfast, we packed the essential provisions in daypacks and made our final preparations for the climb.

There are four popular routes to Elbert's summit. There is the Main Range Trail, the Mt. Elbert Trail, the Echo Canyon Trail and the Echo Canyon Trail from Black Cloud Creek. We chose the latter route. From the trailhead at Black Cloud Creek to the summit is about five miles.

Shortly after sunrise we started our ascent. The air was dry and cold for a July morning. It felt especially cold to my Georgia tempered body. I started the climb wearing wool pants, tennis shoes, a head band and a sweatshirt with daypack on my back. It was cold enough that I had to keep my hands in my pockets for the first half-hour of the climb. The sun was still too low to reach us.

The wonderful feeling of the mountain morning made me realize how deeply I missed the mountains and disliked city life. The mountain morning vitalized me with energy-giving, invigorating stimuli, while city mornings drained my body's energy with stress-inducing nuisances. Determined to rejuvenate my mind and body, I concentrated on absorbing as much of the wholesome natural environment as I could. Throughout the climb, I galvanized my body, mind and spirit with the invigorating sensations of the alpine environment. I cherished every moment, every sensation and every facet of our Mt. Elbert adventure.

After the first twenty minutes on the trail, we settled into a fast, comfortable climbing pace. During the first two hours of the ascent, the steep terrain forced us to rest about every ten minutes. The beautiful mountain vistas also encouraged us to stop at regular intervals to enjoy the scenery. Every rest stop revealed a spectacular vista; La Plata Peak was an especially inspiring sight to behold. At every stop, I spun in a complete circle to see the changing views of the valley, the mountainsides and the snow-spotted peaks.

After an hour on the trail, the sunshine spilled over the mountains breaking the shadows in which we had hiked, immediately warming our skin, chasing the morning chill from our bodies. Shortly after the first rays of sunshine struck our faces we hiked into a grassy meadow, low on Elbert's southern slope.

To our satisfaction the meadow was heavily concentrated with an abundance of lovely blue and white petaled columbine scattered about on both sides of the trail. That was the largest concentration of columbines that I had seen. Hence, I named the columbine patch the Columbine Meadow. As we crossed the meadow I wandered off the trail to get a closer look and to smell the aroma of the columbine. I recalled the quote, "One should take time to smell the roses in life." Well, for me, it was time to smell the columbines.

Back on the trail, we left the beautiful Columbine Meadow behind and pressed steadily toward the beckoning summit. From our vantage point, Elbert was tucked elusively behind its 14,143-foot subsidiary peak, South Elbert, which looked like an independent peak. It is one mile south of Elbert, but because of the shallow elevation drop of the connecting saddle, it isn't officially recognized as an independent fourteener.

Just below timberline, on South Elbert's southern slope, at the site of a ghost mining camp, we stopped for a rest. A cabin and some caved-in mines were the only remnants of the mining site. The two-room cabin was still in relatively good condition considering the harshness of the environment. The heavy weight of the winter snows had collapsed half of the roof.

It was a little mining operation looking much like hundreds of other such sites that were scattered about in the Rocky Mountains, remnants of Colorado's Gold Rush days. The cabin stood at an elevation of 11,800 feet. Two hundred feet to the east, a mine cut into the mountainside, and farther up, there were other mines scattered about on each side of the gulch. Digging for gold was a strenuous, back-breaking chore. Blasting, picking and shoveling through solid granite was a painstakingly slow process, measured in feet per day. If they found gold, a good vein would yield five or six ounces of gold or more per ton of ore. Life was a continuous uphill battle against stormy weather, rugged terrain, brutal winters and long work days. Miners were driven by the glow of gold fever in their eyes. The dream of finding the mother lode fueled their furious search for the elusive, yellow metal.

After locating our position on the topographic map (topo), we found that we missed the Black Cloud Creek trail turnoff. It was a half-mile back down the mountain. We decided to blaze our own route up the south side of Elbert, rather than backtracking. Our new route went up a grass-covered ravine, straight up South Elbert.

Continuing toward the summit, we started up the ravine. It took us above timberline, where we were more susceptible to the thunderstorms and wind chill. Shelter was limited to hard-to-find rock overhangs and crevices.

Step by step, we climbed up the side of the steep ravine. Up, up and up we went on a quest that seemed endless. We paralleled a stream that flowed in the bottom of the ravine. At its source, pure Rocky Mountain spring water emerged from the mountainside. We wisely filled our canteens, and quenched our thirsts; it might be our last source of water.

Just above the spring we cut across the ravine and angled up South Elbert's south ridge. To conserve energy, we trekked up the green mountainside at a very comfortable pace, but the climbing was still hard work. I've never been on a really comfortable mountain climb. You have to be partially masochistic to really enjoy putting your body through so much pain. I must have some masochistic tendencies because I really love pushing my body to its physical limits, one of the reasons that I enlisted in the Marine Corps right after high school.

My pulse checked in at 160. It stayed there for the next hour or longer. We were pushing above 12,000 feet. I began feeling effects of the altitude, a light head and throbbing temples. Considering that I hadn't climbed a high mountain in over a year, I was lucky that I just had symptoms of minor altitude sickness.

On South Elbert's southern spur, we stopped to pinpoint our position on the map and take a much-needed break. Slightly disoriented (sort of lost), we couldn't determine where to look for Mt. Elbert. Looming on the other side of a dismal looking valley was a peak that would be impossible to reach in the time that we had. If it was Elbert, the success of our climb was in serious jeopardy. Then we looked up at South Elbert thinking that it might be Elbert. After ten minutes of comparing the surrounding topography with the map, we resorted to using a compass. Surprisingly, the compass worked like a charm! I knew that there was a good reason for always packing a compass.

We determined that the peak across the deep glacial valley (cirque) was Bull Hill and convinced ourselves that we were on the spur of South Elbert, rather than Elbert itself. Satisfied that Elbert was still hidden behind its massive subsidiary peak we stretched out to relax.

After five minutes, the portending signs of a thunderstorm incited us to get moving again. Just like the day before, scattered clouds darkened the late morning sky. We were at least an hour from the summit, with rain gear our only source of protection. We were far above the safe havens of the forest.

We still had to skirt around South Elbert's southwest face, cross the saddle to Elbert and then make our final assault up Elbert's south ridge. It looked simple enough on the topo. Then I stared up at the steep, rocky mountain slope in front of us. We still had 1,400 vertical feet of rugged climbing ahead of us.

Pacing up the ridge, we rested one minute for every twenty steps upward. The one minute rests weren't much, but they kept my lungs from bursting. Unfortunately, our pace wasn't fast enough to beat the rapidly forming thunderstorms. A darkening sky loomed overhead, and the higher we climbed the more vulnerable we became. A bad thunderstorm would force us to abort the climb and retreat down a dangerously slippery mountainside.

Then, three-fourths of the way up South Elbert's ridge, it began to hail! The hail pebbles were light, but that didn't mean they couldn't grow. "Why didn't we start earlier?" I thought, as it looked more and more like we would have to abort the climb. We should have been on our way back down, rather than pushing for the summit. Fortunately, the hail storm passed quickly; it was just enough to spot the rocks. It gave the mountain a white, snow-like coating. The hail storm blew over, but thunderclouds kept rolling across us. The clouds looked like they could throw anything at us at any time. Rain, mist, hail, sleet, snow and lightning were all valid possibilities.

After enduring a light pelting from the hail storm, we topped the rocky ridge, only sixty feet below South Elbert's summit. The wind picked up as we exposed ourselves to the top of the Rockies. The temptation to climb to the nearby summit of South Elbert was strong. I hated to pass so close to another summit without climbing to its pinnacle. But with the deteriorating weather conditions, and our inner drives to reach the highest point in Colorado, we skirted around South Elbert's tempting summit.

Finally, at the crest of the saddle that bridged Elbert with South Elbert, Elbert came into sight! It looked incredibly massive. From our position the connecting saddle dipped, then linked with Elbert's south ridge. The south ridge gradually sloped upward to Elbert's summit, and to our tired bodies it appeared incredibly distant. It was a mile away. For a few moments we stood in the wind gazing at the massive mountain of granite. If necessary, we would continue in rain, sleet or snow; we weren't going to turn back before reaching its summit. Without uttering a word, we stepped off toward our objective. From that instant, we committed ourselves to reaching Elbert's summit.

Next, it rained. It was just a light, passing shower, but just enough moisture to aggravate climbing conditions. It made the rocks slippery, forcing us to climb more cautiously. On both sides of the saddle the sides dropped off into cirques, over a thousand feet below. Across the saddle we stood at 14,000 feet, at the base of Elbert's south ridge.

From there, Elbert rose prominently to its height of 14,433 feet. It was more mountain than I expected from my study of it. From my readings, I had the impression that it would be a cake walk to the top. That impression was from reading a story about someone driving a jeep to the summit. I wish that I could have seen that feat! That must have been one nerve-racking trip. I don't doubt that it happened. Rocky Mountain jeepers are crazy! When it comes to mountain climbing, I would rather rely on my feet.

The south ridge was our homestretch to the summit. It would be like climbing from the back of a brontosaurus, up its long neck, to its head. Our pre-summit adrenalin pumped our bodies up enough to get us up the ridge. Like swimmers preparing to take a dive, we took a deep breath of air and started the final push for the summit. First, we crossed a snowfield, then pushed ourselves up the rock-bound ridge.

Shortly after noon, climbing abreast, Sean and I stepped onto the highest point in Colorado! The twenty-ninth highest peak in North America. Simultaneously, we topped the 14,433-foot summit of Mt. Elbert. It was the climax of my mountain climbing career! We stood upon the highest point within hundreds of miles. I was exalted about being atop Elbert, but even as I stood there, lost in personal glory, I thought about higher places.

A Canadian or Alaskan climbing adventure brewed in the back of my mind. And further back in my mind, thoughts of even higher objectives were tapped.

After the euphoria dissipated, we signed the Colorado Mountain Club's climber's log, snapped some photographs (to preserve our historical moment), ate lunch and absorbed the spectacular pano-rama. We sat in a picture-perfect alpine setting. Mountain valleys and high peaks surrounded us. To the north, Mt. Massive, Colora-do's second highest peak rose into the clouds. To the south, La Plata Peak, Colorado's fifth-highest peak, stood proudly above its neighbors. As we turned a full circle, to the northeast we saw what appeared to be a freak summer snowstorm hitting one isolated peak. Amid a sea of blue-gray mountains the freshly coated white mountain stood apart. A ring of fluffy, white clouds hovered above it.

Trying to stock up on the alpine sensations, I concentrated on every facet of the summit experience: the cool air, the light wind, the fresh smell of the air, the enduring hardness of the summit itself, the surrounding sea of beauty and the squeaking sounds of pikas. I had to return to Georgia with a large enough supply of alpine sensations to last until my next Rocky Mountain adventure. I wanted to stay and savor the sensations for the rest of the afternoon, but my instincts and experience warned against staying any longer.

The sky was filled with turbulent dark clouds swirling and

dancing about. A couple of mountains away a bolt of lightning split the air, and thunder rumbled across the mountaintops. We were already in danger. It was nature's command to descend as quickly as possible. We decided to descend by way of the Bull Hill—Mt. Elbert saddle. It was a different route, but it was the shortest way to get safely to lower ground.

Regretfully, we said goodbye to Elbert and began our descent back down the south ridge. We quickly scrambled for lower ground. Then, just as we started across the saddle toward Bull Hill, light, feathery snowflakes landed on us and quickly melted. It didn't last long.

Glissading down every snowfield that we crossed, and zigzagging down the mountainside, we dropped several hundred feet in minutes. Although the summer heat melted most of the snowfields, there was still enough left to make the descent exhilarating. I loved the free feeling of whisping down snowfields! It felt great to jump spontaneously onto a snowfield and slide down it without relying on any special equipment. I enjoyed the rush of adrenalin and feeling of freedom that accompanied the glissading.

We glissaded down the last snowfield into the bowl of a cirque. While hiking across the bowl, a heavy rain accompanied by lightning and thunder erupted. The elements struck again! We donned our rain gear, then continued our descent. The moisture made the grass and rock-covered mountainside precariously slippery. It rained steadily for fifteen minutes, just long enough to soak everything thoroughly.

We angled across the mountainside, back toward the abandoned mining cabin that we passed during our ascent. At the cabin, we intersected with the trail, and followed it back across the same terrain that we crossed on the ascent. Except for a second visit to the Columbine Meadow, the remainder of the descent was uneventful. On time, nine and a half hours after we started the climb, we met my dad at the rendezvous point.

In the dimming light of the advancing evening we drove away from Mt. Elbert. I left the mountains feeling enriched with the sensations of another spectacular Rocky Mountain adventure. The day's adventure passed into history as another subchapter in my adventure collection and another page in the book of my life.

Climbing Mt. Elbert didn't make me a world-class mountain climber, but it did give me a strong feeling of accomplishment. It wasn't a spectacularly dangerous feat like climbing the Eiger; however, it was another milestone in my mountaineering career. It was another step toward bigger, more challenging objectives. Had I waited a few more years to write this chapter, it might have ended with a story about Mt. Logan or Mt. McKinley. And then again, had I waited, I might not have ever finished the book.

Climbing Mt. Elbert won't make you a world-class mountain climber either, but if you want to experience a precious day of climbing in the Rockies you'll need to know how to get there. If you make it to Elbert's high summit, you'll also be able to claim rightfully that you have stood upon the highest mountain in the Colorado Rockies. Once you get near Mt. Elbert there are numerous routes to its summit. To get there following the route that we took, take Highway 24 south from Leadville to Highway 82. Follow Highway 82 west toward Aspen. After you pass through Twin Lakes watch for the Twin Peaks Campground. The trailhead is an eighth of a mile past the campground on the right side of the road. If you follow the trail, you will parallel Black Cloud Creek and then intersect with the Echo Canyon to Bull Hill Trail. Take the necessary provisions, start early, and don't be afraid to turn back if the weather gets bad. There are many routes from which to choose. A good topographic map will help you select the most appealing route, and a compass will help you keep oriented. And please, if you drive a jeep to the trailhead, park it and use human power to climb Mt. Elbert.

Through the adventures and experiences in this chapter my mountaineering career emerged and matured. It was born when I was just a knee-high tyke climbing at my dad's side. It matured through my teenage years as I ventured out into the Rocky Mountain wilderness. And the beginning stage of my mountaineering career culminated with the successful climb of Colorado's highest. From there, I entered an intermediate stage in my mountaineering career. I am going forward to broaden my climbing experience, to increase my climbing skills and to prepare for the difficult challenges that await.

Although this chapter ends with my Mt. Elbert adventure, my mountaineering career is ongoing. In the summer of 1989, Brent and I successfully climbed Mt. Lincoln and Mt. Cameron. It was our first climbing adventure together. Likewise, my wife and I climbed our first peak together when we climbed Wyoming's Medicine Bow Peak on 21 June 1990. Those adventures and subsequent adventures will have to be included in my next collection of Rocky Mountain adventures.

3. Skiing

To ski is to experience the stimulating sensations of the alpine winter wonderland: the quietude of isolated trails, the adrenalin rush of speeding down a mountainside and the invigorating feeling of cold air rushing by.

OES SKIING DOWN a mountainside at 100 m.p.h. seem incredible? How about 120 m.p.h.? In 1988, C.J. Mueller flew down a ski slope at 136.3 m.p.h.! He was the first recorded skier to exceed 130 mph. Skiing can be a fast-paced, dangerous sport for amateurs and professionals.

Every year there are numerous skiing accidents and fatalities. However, relative to the large number of skiers that flock to the slopes every winter, the fatalities are very low. You're more likely to get killed in a car accident than you are skiing down a ski slope. Of course, if you try skiing off of the east face of Longs Peak your odds of surviving will be dramatically lower.

Wintertime in the high country is very cold. You have to dress appropriately to enjoy skiing or any other winter recreational activity. The wind chill on a person skiing at 40 m.p.h., on a calm day, at a temperature of ten degrees Fahrenheit, is minus thirty-six degrees Fahrenheit. As I know from experience, properly dressing for the weather conditions is the difference between enjoyment and misery. Nature taught me a lesson that I'll never forget.

One winter morning Craig and I arrived at a ski area early enough to be among the first to ski fresh powder. At the base of the mountain the air was calm, the sky clear and the temperature was twenty-five degrees Fahrenheit. It felt warm. I foolishly left my gloves and stocking cap in the car. We ascended over 2,000 vertical feet from the base of the mountain to the top of the highest ski slope. Before getting off of the chair lift I knew that I was in trouble. At the top of the mountain the wind was blowing and the temperature was much lower than at the base. We went to the top of the longest ski slope at the ski area. It was over two miles back down to the ski lodge. As we neared the top of the lift I was very concerned about making it back without getting frostbite. I decided that my best course of action was to make a beeline for the bottom of the mountain. It would be a race against time. As I skied away from the lift, I passed through a chilling whirlwind of snow swirling across the barren, wind-swept mountaintop. It was dreadfully cold. My head and hands felt the cold immediately. Exercising my only alternative, I bolted down the mountainside, a race against the clock. Midway down the slope my hands began to numb, my ears stung and I could barely hold onto my ski poles. At that point, I knew that I was in serious jeopardy of getting frostbitten fingers. The pain increased, and by the time I neared the final stretch to the car, the ski poles hung on my wrists, I lost most of the feeling in my fingers. My finger tips were white with frostbite. Fortunately, the car had a good heater. After thirty minutes with my fingers over heated air, the color returned to my fingers.

Guess what? Since then, I've never underdressed. I'll carry a backpack full of extra clothing if I have to. My philosophy is, "It's better to carry too much clothing, rather than too little." You may go for hours without needing the extra clothing, but when you do need it it is worth its weight in platinum.

The following skiing adventure stories are accounts of my most emotional skiing experiences. The downhill skiing subchapter includes experiences of my first skiing trip and my worst wipe-out.

The second subchapter on cross country skiing is about my winter adventure in the Indian Peaks Wilderness Area.

Cross country skiing is a slower-paced, endurance sport compared to downhill skiing. That is partly due to the fact that you don't have a chair lift to carry you to the mountaintops. You have to supply all of the energy for cross county skiing, like the wintertime equivalent of backpacking. It allows you to get close to nature and to experience the wintertime wilderness environment as a quiet, unobtrusive visitor. As you silently glide into the depths of a forest, you begin to feel like a part of the environment. The wintertime Rocky Mountain wilderness is a very peaceful place to visit. Cross country skiing and snowshoeing are the best ways to access the wintertime wilderness without disrupting the harmony of the natural environment.

Without further ado, please turn the page and glide with me into the winter wonderland of the Rocky Mountains.

Downhill Skiing

AT THE TOP of the highest ski slope we stood poised and ready to zip down the slope. It was early in the morning, and Craig and I were the first two skiers to make tracks in the fresh powder. The night before it snowed three inches, coating the slopes with a blanket of fluffy white powder. Without saying a word, we looked at each other, nodded our heads and pushed off down the slope. Hell-bent for leather, like bats out of hell, we took off! We knew that the first run of the day was always the best run. We wanted to go for the gusto before the ski slopes filled with multitudes of skiers. The wind chill on our faces was about minus twenty degrees Fahrenheit. The cold numbed my cheeks. The skiing was fantastic! The fresh powder provided me excellent skiing control. I swished back and forth down the mountainside with precision. My adrenalin pumped wildly. I felt alert, and in total control of my destiny. Craig was slightly ahead of me into the first turn. I cut sharply to take the inside of the turn. Without a warning, we came out of the turn onto an advanced (black diamond) slope. It was very steep and riddled with deep moguls. It surprised both of us. I shot over the edge, catching air and not wanting to land. I landed hard and fast, immediately accelerating down the mogul-laden slope. My legs acted like shock absorbers as I bounced across the moguls, struggling to stay up. Gaining some control, I finally made it into the groove of the moguls, where I zigzagged back and forth with some resemblance of control. I fought with complete concentration to stay up on my skis; my leg muscles ached from the constant shock-absorber-like battering. If the moguls didn't get me, the fatigue in my legs would surely drop me, but somehow I stayed up. Fortunately, relief was in sight at the bottom of the advanced mogul run; the slope leveled and turned sharply to the right. The outside edge of the turn had a guard fence around it, because it looked like the mountainside dropped off over the outside edge of the turn. I had no inclination for testing the strength of the safety fence. Craig was out of sight somewhere behind me. Despite desperate efforts to gain control before reaching the turn, I sped faster and faster down the slope. Just before going into the turn I caught enough snow with the edge of my skis to make the turn. It was a hairpin turn that opened up into a smooth straight slope. The straight stretch was just long enough to let me catch my breath. While trying to rest I continued accelerating downward toward another sharp turn, and if I missed that turn I would fly off into a patch of pine trees. I slowed myself by making two sharp zigzags. With the most control since pushing off at the top of the mountain, I spared myself multiple broken bones by making the turn. Out of the turn, I skied onto a large flat area toward the start of another black diamond slope. From my approach, all that I could see was blue sky beyond the edge of the flat area. Slightly out of control, I approached the edge too quickly, and attempting to stop, I turned sideways and slid across the surface of the snow, right over the edge onto the steepest slope that I ever saw. Before I could do anything I was sliding sideways and accelerating toward a wicked mogul field. The previous mogul field looked like an intermediate slope compared to this one. At the mercy of the slope, I accelerated into the moguls. At that point, I felt like a rag doll. I just went with the flow, doing everything that I could to stay up. In an attempt to get into the groove, I pointed my skis down the slope. Instead of getting into the groove, I rammed head-on into a large mogul. I caught air off of that mogul and landed on the downward side of another mogul. Gaining even more speed, I hit hard in the dip between two moguls. My momentum carried me up the next mogul and again into the air. By then, I lost all control. That time I cleared an intermediate mogul and landed full force into the face of another mogul. My legs finally collapsed under the impact of the landing. My downward momentum caused me to skid up and over three downslope moguls before coming to rest in a rut. One ski came loose as I skidded over the moguls. Other than being a little shaken, I escaped without injury. Using a ski pole, I pulled myself to my feet, brushed the snow off of my body and retrieved my other ski.

Still no sign of Craig. I decided to wait for him at the bottom of the slope, if I could make it to the bottom myself. After a rest, I continued my descent of the ski slope. The fall trimmed my gung-ho vigor and stole some of my gusto; I just wanted to get down in one piece.

The fall installed enough fear to make me slow down. I made it safely back to the start of the lift line at the bottom of the mountain. Ten minutes later, Craig skied up to me. He didn't even have to tell me that he had wrecked. He was covered with a light coat of white powder. His ordeal was similar to mine. We talked about the "first run of the day" while riding the ski lift up the mountain for the second run.

Contrary to my original thoughts, skiing was not as easy as it looked. Other skiers (experienced skiers) made it look easy. I'll learn how to ski just as easy as any other sport, I thought. I was a well-trained, healthy athlete. Well, I finally got a chance to see just how easy it was.

Riding up the lift for the first time, I thought that it would be simple; I would just stand up and swish down the mountain. Shortly after that thought crossed my mind, Craig and I lay in a tangled mess at the top of the lift. It wasn't the glorious start that I had envisioned. I stood up from the lift chair and slid straight forward without any idea how to stop or turn.

Like most beginners, I spent most of my first day snow plowing down the beginner's slopes (slopes symbolized with a green circle). The beginner's slopes are supposed to be easy, but when you are skiing for your first time nothing is easy. It was hard enough just skiing on flat terrain. The slightest incline was a major challenge. After a long repeating cycle of falling and getting back up, I started to get better. Better at falling, that was. Falling is the first thing that you have to get good at. By midday I mastered falling, and decided to move on to the dreaded intermediate slope (symbolized by a blue square). It was easy, until I got off the chair lift at the top of the mountain. I spent the next stretch of time standing at the edge of, what seemed to be, an impossibly steep slope. After thoroughly psyching myself out, I inched my ski tips over the edge and accelerated down the slope. Out of control, and erratically bouncing across moguls I fought to stay upright. Instinctively, I tried to initiate a snow plow to slow myself. My skis crossed, I slammed into the snow, and slid down the slope on my stomach. My skis and poles were strewn about the slope. Seeking to amend my fall, I brushed the snow off and strapped my skis on for another go at it. Unnerved, but in one piece, I made it back to the base of the mountain. I retreated to the sanctity of the bunny slopes to polish up on the basics.

Even though I ate a lot of snow on my first ski trip, I left the mountains feeling satisfied with my progress. Skiing added a winter dimension to my Rocky Mountain adventures. Skiing lured me into the wintertime beauty of the Rockies. It ignited my curiosity for winter adventure. By the end of my second ski trip I was hooked. Visions of becoming a ski bum tempted me to stray from higher career aspirations in engineering. However, I chose to become an engineer in hopes of later being able to afford to become a ski bum or full-time mountaineer.

As my skiing ability matured, I skied faster and faster. Skiing faster became an obsessive challenge. It almost grew into a fatal addiction. Whisping full speed down snow-covered mountainsides gave me a feeling of elation. It was a type of wintertime Rocky Mountain High. I began competing against Craig and my own times. As I mastered the intermediate slopes, I naturally progressed toward the advanced slopes. On several successive ski trips I spent my days skiing almost constantly, sometimes without breaking for lunch. Once downhill skiing was in my system, I became dependent upon speed. After my skiing ability reached advanced intermediate, I lost all sense of fear and went over the edge. I lost the instinctive fear that kept me balanced upon the ridge between life and death. Eventually, I had to regain my instinctive fear or prematurely meet the Grim Reaper.

Finally, the inevitable happened. One afternoon, after a morning of head-to-head racing, I regained my fear. Craig and I found a great downhill racing slope. We stuck to skiing on it most of the day. Like a couple of Olympic hopefuls, we tenaciously worked at improving our times. We milked the slope for every ounce of speed that we could get. Unlike training Olympians, we had to share the slope with other skiers. The owners of the ski area didn't close the slopes on our behalf. So we had the additional challenge of avoiding numerous unpredictable moving obstacles.

The race started the instant we got off the chair lift. Like racers out of the starting gates, we sped down the mountainside. We raced at speeds in excess of 50 m.p.h. Side by side with Craig at the fastest turn on the slope, a cluster of skiers forced me to go wide into Craig or slam into a mass of unsuspecting bystanders at full speed. My skis slid over the top of his, taking us both to the snow. Tangled in each other's skis, we hit the snow in a cloud of white powder. Our momentum and force of impact scattered us, our skis and our poles across the ski slope. I helplessly slid down the mountainside toward a bright orange warning barrier at the edge of a cliff. I desperately scratched at the snow and tried to sink my heels into the icy crust. Inches from the cliff's edge, I slid to a halt. Craig lay a few paces upslope, also near the cliff's edge. We slowly picked ourselves up and brushed the snow off. Amazingly, we both walked away unscathed. Fortunately, we completely avoided hitting any bystanders. A couple of concerned onlookers asked us if we were all right.

Afterward, we skied away with born-again fear. Our little accident reinstilled the instinctive fear that I had lost. It also pounded some better judgment into my head. Crowded ski slopes are not the place to practice downhill speed skiing. Since that day, I quit skiing like a speed-starved maniac. I have finally accepted that I am not going to pursue Olympic downhill skiing, although I would if I had another life to live.

Δ

Rocky Mountain downhill skiing is the ultimate sport for winter recreation and adventure. Despite the picture portrayed through my adventure accounts, skiing is a safe, enjoyable sport if you ski sensibly and smartly. You don't have to ski "on the edge" to have a good time. One of the greatest pleasures of skiing is the serenity of gliding silently through the forest, a good way to get attuned to nature's winter splendor. You can even experience this serenity at the most popular Rocky Mountain ski areas; it is only a turn away. Just turn down a less traveled trail away from the main slopes, and glide into the forest.

Since there are well over thirty ski areas in Colorado alone, I will not list them or attempt to describe how to find them. There are many ski areas scattered throughout the Rocky Mountain states. Most of them are widely publicized and easy to find.

If downhill skiing doesn't appeal to you, maybe cross country skiing is better suited for you. If you like the thought of gliding peacefully through the wilderness, then you'll probably enjoy reading about one of my cross country adventures.

Cross Country Skiing

ISOLATED IN THE labyrinth of the vast Rocky Mountain wilderness, we glided quietly across the winter landscape. The peaks were covered with a deep layer of snow that glistened in the morning sun. The mountainsides were predominantly white, except for a few patches of forest. The air was still and quiet; the swishing of our skis and the panting of our lungs were the only sounds breaking the silence.

We were skiing in a winter wonderland, moving slowly up the U-shaped valley toward a towering wall of jagged-edged peaks. The ridge line of the peaks before us was the Continental Divide. The three of us skied single-file through the forest. Time seemed to stop; all my worldly worries faded away as I distanced myself from civilization. It felt gratifying to escape the hustle and bustle of the synthetic world to enjoy the simple pleasures of the natural environment. We spent the rest of the day skiing harmoniously through the placid wilderness.

Cross country skiing is another unique way of perceiving and enjoying the natural environment. Cross country skiing allows you to escape the large crowds at the ski areas. You don't have to negotiate with the ski slope traffic, and you don't have to wait in lift lines. Of course, you don't have the conveniences of the ski area either. There are no chair lifts to carry you uphill, there are no heated lodges to warm up in and there are no hamburger stands. Cross country skiing is an excellent means of observing and enjoying the winter wilderness.

Although it may sound like a passive sport, there are inherent or objective dangers associated with cross country skiing. Some of those dangers are hypothermia, exposure, frostbite, avalanches, getting lost and blizzards. With smart preparation and education the risks can be minimized. Common sense, experience, education and intuition are the best safeguards against potential trouble.

Extra caution must be taken when skiing in avalanche-prone areas; avalanches can strike like lightning. Every year avalanches claim the lives of some cross country skiers and other winter backcountry explorers. Fast-moving winter storms can also be perilous to the unprepared cross country adventurer. Getting lost is another cross country skiing pitfall; in the winter, the trails are harder to follow, and the problem of staying on the trail is intensified by deep blowing snow. Many of the common landmarks are buried with snow, a light wind can bury your tracks, and a blinding wind can disorient you.

With adequate preparation, cross country skiing is a rewarding backcountry escape, an ideal sport for discovering the hidden beauty of the wintertime Rocky Mountains. I've tried tapping the winter beauty of the Rockies by other methods, but nothing equals cross country skiing. Snowshoeing is equally good for getting in touch with nature, but it is more physically demanding. Hiking is also a good way to get close to nature, but wading through waist-deep snow is extremely exhausting. Snowmobiling is great entertainment, but it is a motorized activity that destroys the quiet of the wilderness experience. Cars, jeeps and trucks are all right on the roads, but they don't go far in waist-deep snow. My wife could tell you about horseback riding in deep snow, but I haven't tried that yet.

My first cross country skiing adventure was in the Indian Peaks Wilderness Area on 31 December 1986. I went with Sean and Craig. We were three greenhorns. After three weeks of studying and taking final exams we were primed for an adventure into the Rockies. We longed for the type of relief that only the high country offers. We needed to free our minds from the confines of the classroom in the solitude of the mountains. Sean was between semesters in graduate school at the University of North Dakota. Craig was between semesters as a senior at the University of Oklahoma. And I had just graduated from the University of Wyoming.

Sean and I met while he was an undergraduate at the University of Wyoming. He is a genuine friend with an appetite for adventure like mine. We have skied, backpacked, climbed, caved, explored and rappelled together in the Rockies. Sean is very high spirited and confident. He has strong qualities that make him an invaluable asset to any adventure party. He is backcountry wise and keeps his composure in difficult situations.

Friendship, camaraderie and teamwork have made my Rocky Mountain adventures especially meaningful. Many of my friends and I are bound together by the spirit of adventure. My friendships are strengthened by the experiences that my friends and I share. It is always reassuring to have a trusted friend belaying you down a mountainside or helping you up a difficult pitch. The complimentary nature of our backgrounds is a vital component in the success of our adventures. One person's weakness is another's strength. That is one aspect of teamwork; and friendship that is invaluable, especially when things don't go as planned.

Drawn together by the magnetism of the Rocky Mountains, we gathered for our first cross country ski adventure. We rented our skiing equipment at a ski shop at the foot of the Rocky Mountains, in Boulder, Colorado. From Boulder, we drove an hour up into the Rockies. The joke for most of the road trip was Craig's and my 1985 snowshoeing adventure. It was a joke because of the fact that our snowshoes didn't work very well. On that particular day we experienced two types of snow: deep and shallow. In the shallow snow we didn't need snowshoes; in the deep snow we still sank up to our knees, despite wearing snowshoes. So we joked about our snowshoeing adventure while enroute to our high country destination.

We arrived at the Indian Peaks Wilderness Area trailhead early in the morning on 31 December 1986. The air was crisp, cold and refreshing. The forested mountains were blanketed with a thick coat of snow. In the distance, towering up from beyond the trees, the majestic Indian Peaks glistened in the soft morning sunlight. They sparkled as if they were covered with diamonds. Under a clear sky, a light westerly wind stirred the air just enough to drop the wind chill a few degrees.

We parked the car in a turnout near the snowdrift that closed the remainder of the road. We packed daypacks with the usual

essentials: lunch, water, matches, some extra clothing and a mis-
cellany of other small necessities. Unsure of our destination, we
strode off in a westerly direction. We hoped to make it to Long
Lake, but the numerous unknowns made it impossible to know
how far we could make it. We didn't know how fast we could
travel. We didn't know what the skiing conditions would be like.
And we didn't know how long the good weather would last.
Between the three of us, we could end up anywhere from Long
Lake at 10,600 feet, to the Continental Divide at 12,000 feet.
When we were together, the sky was the limit. When we felt less
energetic, we pushed until our instincts told us to quit.

From the outset of our adventure it was evident that cross
country skiing was work. Our first stretch of skiing was uphill; the
surrounding terrain was forested and mountainous. For the first few
miles we simply followed the snow-covered road to Brainard Lake,
struggling up the gentle inclines and gliding down the declines.
There were a few small groups of other skiers and adventure seekers
along the way. As we skied down a long flat stretch of trail I saw
two hard-core adventuring souls trekking toward us on snowshoes.

Those two rustic guys looked like mountaineers from a page of
early Colorado history. They were dressed in leather pants, wore
fur coats, carried heavy overnight packs and towed sleds packed
with provisions. They had a miscellany of climbing items protruding from their packs—ice axes, crampons and coils of rope. I
looked at them in awe as they rigorously trotted past us on their
way toward lower ground. I wondered what adventures they had
delved. From their appearance they could have done a number of
alpine feats. They could have been training for a major expedition,
like Everest or McKinley. Professional mountaineers frequently
train in the Colorado Peaks. Whatever their purposes were, we all
shared the commonality of enjoying the mountains.

They reminded me of the previous winter when Craig and I
snowshoed into the high country. It was apparent that they had
more experience than Craig and I; they made it look easier than it
was for us. As we continued to ski, the best method of getting
across snow-covered terrain was still an enigma to me. From my

experiences I wasn't sure what was the easiest means of winter mountain travel: snowshoes, skis or, for that matter, trudging through the snow in hiking boots. It became easier as we went, and by the end of the first hour, we started developing some resemblances of technique; it seemed there was an advantage to wearing skis. We took our first break on the frozen, wind-swept surface of Brainard Lake.

The view from Brainard Lake was incredible. The granite towers of the Indian Peaks stood as mammoth monuments of nature, forming a jagged wall across the western horizon. We hypnotically stared at the beautiful alpine backdrop. No matter what happened the rest of the day, that view made the trip worthwhile. It was especially meaningful to me, like looking at good friends and recalling fond memories; I felt like I personally knew the peaks. I had climbed every peak in sight, I had seen all four of their seasonal faces from the same view and I had experienced both the calm and violent sides of nature while afoot on the mountains.

After a rest, we continued our trek through the forest and into the U-shaped valley between two spurs of the high peaks. We pushed for Long Lake, the next finger lake up the glacial trough. We were confident that we could make it at least that far; beyond Long Lake the terrain was steeper and more difficult.

After a lengthy trek through thick forest, we broke out into a clearing at the west end of Long Lake. A gusting wind struck us, sweeping across the frozen lake and down the valley; the wind chill temperature had to be well below zero. That arctic wind discouraged all thoughts of continuing farther up the valley.

We stopped to rest, eat lunch and take some pictures. Making the most of a cold, potentially miserable situation, I lit a can of Sterno and boiled some water for hot tea. After sipping a cup of hot tea with lunch, I set the camera up for an automatic photograph of the three of us. After the shutter clicked, our images were frozen in time in the snowy wilderness setting.

Afterward, fighting images of being in warm places, we decided to continue up the Long Lake trail. The trail cut through the forest around the lake, providing a welcome wind break, yet the frigid, wind-driven air sliced through our clothing. We were getting uncomfortably cold, and the trail conditions were deteriorating: snow became powdery, deep and difficult to ski upon. We struggled up the difficult trail for a while longer before deciding to turn back. We needed our remaining energy to get back to the car. As we started back, I felt uneasy about how far we had traveled and how far it was back to the car. I convinced Craig and Sean to follow me across a shortcut. I was familiar with the surrounding wilderness and therefore knew of many shortcuts. So, we abandoned the firmly packed trail for the loosely stacked snow of the forest.

We made great progress for the first few minutes, until we hit waist-deep powder while descending a heavily forested mountainside. It was our first opportunity to downhill ski on cross country skis. It became a fiasco. Fortunately, none of us stayed upright long enough to gain much speed. Speed was the enemy, especially when you are frequently colliding with trees. Dodging trees and digging out of deep snow consumed any time savings that we might have gained by taking the shortcut. I spent as much time buried in snow as I did skiing, and Craig and Sean had similar problems. We skied and fell, skied and fell, and skied and fell throughout most of the shortcut. On the positive side, Murphy's Law failed to apply itself. We could have become lost, but we didn't. Eventually, we made it back to the firmly packed trail.

After some difficulty, we emerged from the untamed forest back onto the main trail at Brainard Lake. We were exhausted from our labors in the woods. From there, we still had three miles of enduring skiing before us. My shortcut made a great conversation topic to help pass the time. Craig and Sean teased me all the way back to the car about my long shortcut.

Δ

Cross country skiing is vastly different from downhill skiing; nevertheless, both types of recreational sports have their own merits and associated risks. Downhill skiing is more for the hyperactive speed demon, and cross country skiing is more for the mellower nature lover. Although we avoided avalanche-prone areas during our adventure, avalanches are the primary danger of cross country skiing. You should take extreme caution when skiing upon or at the base of steep, treeless, snow-covered slopes.

Since you've been introduced to my shortcuts, I will elaborate for you. Oftentimes, while venturing about in the mountains, I am compelled to take shortcuts. As you know, sometimes my shortcuts turn into long-cuts. On two other occasions my shortcuts nearly had fatal consequences. If you look ahead, to the chapter on Miscellaneous Adventures, you'll notice two stories, "Dripping Water Rock" and "Death Defying Descent." Both of the harrowing experiences in those adventures are results of my shortcuts. In spite of my shoddy record of shortcuts, I'll probably continue utilizing them in future adventures. I often enjoy the increased challenge of offtrail adventures, and I like to explore new territory.

If you're interested in making your own cross country skiing adventures in the Indian Peaks Wilderness Area, just follow the same directions given in a previous chapter. You won't be able to get to Brainard Lake in your car during the winter. The road to Brainard Lake is typically closed from October to June due to deep snow. Just drive until you reach a wall of snow, then park the car, strap your skis on and enjoy the wintertime beauty of the Rockies.

4. Running

Alpine running is the breathtaking activity of rapidly navigating down a mountainside that is strewn with ankle-breaking obstacles.

F ROM ATOP A rocky pinnacle, high in the Colorado Rockies, I stood in awe as I stared down upon the tiny cars parked along the raging river in the bottom of the valley. The river cut through the surrounding green of the forest like a bubbling white streak, the mountainsides sloped steeply down to the river's edge. Although they looked only like colored specks, I saw some people fishing and picnicking along the banks of the roaring white water.

I climbed for an hour to reach my vantage point. After reaching the top of a rock outcrop, high on a mountainside, I perched myself upon a rock like a resting eagle. The view was beautiful! It felt very satisfying to absorb calmly the sights and sounds of the mountains.

After filling my senses with the rejuvenating sensations of the high country, I felt a burst of energy. I had a hankering to spring to my feet and skip down the mountainside like a mountain goat fleeing from a predator, so that was exactly what I did.

After swinging down from my rocky crest, I landed on the mountainside running. I skipped, slid and zigzagged. Gravity gave me all of the downward acceleration that I could handle. The mountainside was forested, rock strewn and scattered with logs, stumps, plants and occasional streams. To keep my momentum, I had to plan my steps instantaneously. My eyes continuously scanned the terrain in my immediate foreground. While avoiding the ankle-breaking obstacles I also had to avoid large obstacles that would force me to stop (namely trees and boulders). I had a couple near falls, but managed to keep my balance on both instances. My concentration was very intense; I had to keep focused on the rapidly approaching mountainside before me. My mind and body worked in harmony toward getting me safely to the bottom. A few breathtaking minutes after leaving my perch on the rock crest, my momentum nearly carried me into the torrent of the river in the valley bottom. I had to latch onto a tree to stop myself from lunging into the cold water.

That description of one of my numerous downhill runs is what I call alpine running. It is the activity of getting down a summer mountainside as fast as possible. The level of control is the key aspect that distinguishes alpine running from falling. Alpine running is a controlled activity; falling is an uncontrolled activity. Sometimes alpine running and falling go hand in hand; however, a good alpine runner keeps the falling to a bare minimum. Falling, of course, is very dangerous. On a steep mountainside or a rocky mountainside falling can result in serious injuries or death; it all depends on how extreme you want to get.

An extreme skier is someone who skis down slopes so steep that if they fall they die. The same definition can be applied to an extreme alpine runner. I am not an extreme alpine runner or skier. There are very few extreme alpinists anywhere; most of them have very short lifespans. One extreme alpinist once quoted an old Chinese saying: It is better to live one day as a lion than a month as a sheep. I believe in a Chinese philosophy that promotes moderation in everything. I would rather live two weeks as a wolf. The extremist lives for the rush of participating in life-threatening activities. I live for the euphoric feeling that I get simply by being in the mountains.

Three types of mountain running are alpine, trail and forest. They each involve moving at seven miles per hour or faster: the minimum speed that is considered to be running. They each have unique characteristics, and I find enjoyment and challenge in all three types.

Trail running is probably the safest of the three; it gives you the opportunity to focus more on the environment and less on staying afoot. It is the mountaineer's equivalent to a city dweller's sidewalk running. It gives you a chance to experience the highcountry sensations, to concentrate on something else or to let your mind freely wander. Running a couple of miles on a peaceful mountain trail, just after dawn, is a vitalizing experience. It is just you and the wilderness; while your body follows the trail, your mind is free to drift.

Forest running is a step more dangerous and less harmonious than trail running. Running through the wild forest requires more agility and alertness. You have to navigate through the obstacles of the forest as you rapidly travel. Your level of awareness has to be higher because you have to dodge trees, leap logs, skip between rocks, forge streams and navigate.

Which type of mountain running do I like the best? It depends on my mood. I like all three. When I am in a calm, relaxed mood or just trying to get some healthy exercise, I normally choose to run on a trail. If I am in an energetic, semi-wild mood, I like to run through the forest. If I am feeling physically indominable and wild, I like to take the extra challenge of the downhill alpine run. With all types of alpine activities you have to balance your mood against the inherent risks. Even when I'm at my wildest I am not willing to take the risks of going to the extremes.

The two running adventures that follow are both about alpine running experiences. Please forgive me for focusing only on alpine running. "Summit Run" and "Race for Shelter" seemed most appropriate for this adventure collection. "Summit Run" was an alpine running adventure that I was compelled to do in a burst of spontaneous energy. "Race for Shelter" is an alpine running adventure about Craig's and my plight from an approaching thunderstorm.

Summit Run

RUNNING IN CIRCLES around an oval track is not exciting enough for me any more. During junior high school, I used to run my heart out trying to improve my running speed. Five minutes and forty seconds was my best one mile run time. That is an average speed of ten and six-tenths of a mile per hour. Once I broke the six-minute barrier, it became pure work trying to run a faster mile. Sports are supposed to be fun, so in high school I traded my track shoes for football cleats. I enjoyed running toward the goal line with a football in my arms, more than running around a track.

Later, during Marine Corps recruit training in San Diego, California, I traded my football cleats for combat boots. Running took on a whole new meaning. I ran every day whether I wanted to or not. I ran with a rifle, pack, canteens and a steel helmet; I ran up and down hills, across sandy terrain and beneath the baking hot sun of southern California. At the end of the longest summer of my life, I ran the fastest three miles that I'll probably ever run. During the final physical fitness test I scored the top score on the three mile run by finishing in exactly eighteen minutes (average speed of ten m.p.h.). I fell one pull-up short of getting a perfect score on the complete physical fitness test.

Running has always been a part of my life. In elementary school I ran just to burn off excess energy, in junior high and high school I ran for sport, in basic training I ran to stay in shape and for a living, and now I run to stay in shape and for fun. Recreational running in the mountains is my favorite type of running. High country running is very invigorating.

I started running in the mountains shortly after I started walking in the mountains. I started out by running through the forest, on trails and down small stretches of mountainsides. Later in life, I sought greater challenges accompanied by greater risks. Alpine running became a favorite pastime. Alpine running is the recreational activity of running up and down steep mountainsides. The degree of risk and challenge is proportional to the ground cover and the steepness of the mountainside. It is closely related to screeing and glissading. Sometimes all three activities come into play. Screeing is the activity of running and sliding down scree, loose rock debris commonly found at the base of cliffs. Glissading is the activity of sliding down snowfields on your feet or rear. During my summit run, I ran, screed and glissaded. "Summit Run" is a recount of my most harrowing alpine run to date.

On a warm summer day in August of 1983, I got a wild idea. Craig and I were frolicking in the serene beauty of the Indian Peaks Wilderness Area. On that August day I ran up and down an 11,500-foot peak in twenty-four minutes. I started my alpine running feat from the west end of Long Lake at an elevation of 10,800 feet. It took me seventeen minutes to scramble to the top of the summit, and seven minutes to return to my starting point. On the descent, I dropped an average of 100 vertical feet per minute (1.67 feet per second).

Craig and I were on one of our annual retreats to the Indian Peaks Wilderness Area when I decided to "go for it!"

It was the day after our futile attempt for Crater Lake. The day before it was cloudy and rained heavily most of the day. Craig and I had planned to go on a backpacking trip to Crater Lake, an eight-mile trek across the Continental Divide. We waited all day for the clouds to dissipate, but they never did. Just before dark the rain lightened and we decided to hike as far as we could before nightfall. That decision was a stroke of stupidity. We didn't get far, and we had a miserable night.

Mother Nature taught us both a lesson. I felt like a child that had been left out in the rain for doing something wrong. My body felt like it was soaked to the bone.

The following day, we went on a short hike to Long Lake in search of a good place to lie in the sun to dry out. At the east end of Long Lake, we found a large boulder in an open meadow. Like two wet rats, we lay on the boulder to let the sun drive the deeply embedded coldness out of our bodies.

It didn't take very long for the sun to drive the cold misery from my body. But it didn't do anything for my emotions from the night before. I learned a valuable lesson, but I still felt that I had to avenge myself. I had to do something to help regain my confidence.

When my eyes opened, I saw a challenge. It was an 11,500-foot peak that rose up from a forested valley on the northeast side of Long Lake. The lower half of the mountain was tree covered, and the upper half was rugged and rocky. The summit was partially ringed with a cliff. It looked like a crown. My selfmade challenge was to make it to the top of that mountain and back to the boulder as fast as possible.

I told Craig about the feat that I was about to attempt, and because he knew my nature, my proposal didn't surprise him. It didn't prompt him to join me either; he opted to stay put. In fact, he didn't budge from that boulder.

I analyzed the mountain for a few minutes to find the best route. I mentally pictured the climb, the obstacles and the objective dangers. After setting my mind on a route, I set the timer on my wrist watch and "went for it!"

I leaped to my feet and sprinted across the glen toward the base of the mountain. Before entering the thick forest around the base, I made a final glance at my ascent route. I dashed across a foot bridge, then the hiking trail, and disappeared into the forest. I ran through the forest dodging pine trees, leaping over logs, busting through brush, and barreling over large boulders and rock outcrops.

Two minutes into the run, I reached the base. The terrain sloped steeply upward, forcing me into a rapid climb. I aggressively climbed upward, sometimes using the pine trees to pull myself upward. Fallen timber on a mountainside is a menace. It is often loose; and of course it tends to roll downward.

In alpine running, the primary challenge is overcoming gravity. Gravity constantly tried to pull me over backward, knock me off balance and steal my footing.

After breaking above timberline, the summit came into view, and the terrain became rugged and rocky. Slightly above, a three-story-high granite cliff crowned the summit. I thought about circumnavigating the cliff, but that would add too much distance to my climb. Instead, I decided to climb straight up a narrow avalanche chute in the crag. The base of the crag was covered with loose talus that I had to climb across carefully. I still lost my footing on a couple of precariously balanced rocks and kicked them loose down the mountainside.

Standing next to the wall of granite, I took a few seconds to catch my breath and examine the characteristics of the rocky face. It had plenty of hand and footholds. Nonetheless, it would still be a near vertical free climb without belay. It was a class-5 climb.

Without looking down, I vigorously assaulted the crag, hugging the rock wall and climbing hand over hand. A fall would be fatal; each hand and foothold had to be firm. I focused all of my attention on finding solid holds. Balancing speed and safety, I climbed up the crag. The rim of the granite crown came into view. I pulled myself over the top onto the grass covered summit.

At the highest point I rested for a brief moment. My heart was pounding wildly, and I was breathing frantically. The afternoon sun beat down upon my face. The cool, dry air, moved by a slight breeze, absorbed most of the sweat that formed on my face.

Downclimbing down the cliff would be tediously time consuming; therefore, I chose to go around the cliff and down a snowfield. Without further delay, I ran down the summit toward the top of the snowfield. The snowfield looked steeper from above. It bridged the summit mound with the mountainside. As I ran toward it, I made a discouraging observation: the bottom of the snowfield was rocky. It was a snow slide that was abruptly terminated by large rocks. As I approached the top of the snowfield, I seriously considered climbing down the snowfield, rather than sliding down it. In a moment's hesitation, I tried to slow my downward momentum. I was running down the mountainside so fast that I would have to fall onto my seat to stop before reaching the snowfield. Instead, in a flash of lunacy, I leaped out onto the snowfield and "went for the gusto!" As I foresaw, I rapidly accelerated down the slippery snowfield. The instant my feet hit the snow I started thinking about how I was going to stop myself from hitting the rocks. I only had seconds to spare. Instinctively, I dropped to my seat. As the rocky terminus approached, I dragged my hands and sank my heels into the snow. While frantically trying to slow my descent, I mentally rehearsed my rocky collision.

An instant later it happened. Sliding on my rear, feet first, I slammed into the rocks. Surprisingly, my momentum popped me back up onto my feet. Flowing with my momentum, I haphazardly skipped across the talus below the snowfield. Amazingly, I was unscathed by the impact and managed to stay afoot. God was definitely watching over me. Taking advantage of my fortune, I shook my awe-struck amazement from my head and skipped on down the mountainside.

I ran wild and out of control for about ten seconds afterward, somehow keeping my balance, wrestling to control my downward momentum by zigzagging. Just before reaching timberline I regained a slight resemblance of control. Then, I raced right into the trees for the greater part of the entire run.

Alpine running down a forested mountainside was my forte. It made me feel at home in the mountains like a deer gracefully bounding through the forest. Not to imply that I was as graceful as a deer. To the contrary, I made a lot of noise as I ran down the mountainside. I whisped by the trees, hurtled logs and leaped over streams as I finished out the lower part of the mountain.

At the bottom, it was a forest run and a sprint back to the boulder from where I had started. I reached the boulder in twenty-four minutes, from the time that I had left it.

Craig hadn't budged. He was still lying on the boulder, basking in the sun. I was panting so hard that I couldn't talk. It felt great! After walking myself back to normal vital signs, I sat down on the boulder and stared up at the mountain that I had just climbed. I mentally retraced my footsteps and imagined my feat from a distance.

Summit Run was my greatest alpine running feat. I'm sure that many extremists have taken greater risks. That doesn't bother me. I'm not out to get my name in any record books, or prematurely on a tombstone. I like to practice balance and moderation in about everything that I do. Although my adventures sometimes take me to the edge of disaster, I always try to balance pleasure, challenge and safety. My aim is to have a lifetime of enjoyable mountain adventure, rather than having a short-lived career consisting of a few spectacular feats.

If you are interested in alpine running all that you need is the mountains. Any mountains will work: the Rockies, the Sierra Nevada, Appalachians, the Ozarks, the Andes, the Swiss Alps and so on. I suggest that you start with trail running and gradually work up to alpine running. Alpine running is a very demanding and dangerous activity. It is full of pitfalls: one misplaced step can result in a broken ankle or leg, a fall can be fatal, and a host of other injuries can result from trips, falls and stumbles. Before you embark on any alpine running adventures, I suggest that you balance the risks that you are willing to take with a reasonable factor of safety. Be wary of wild-haired decisions that pop into your mind while you are under the influence of a Rocky Mountain High.

Race For Shelter

THIS IS A short story about an afternoon high-country trek for Craig and I. We were up enjoying a beautiful, clear, sunny day in the Rockies. We were just out for a relaxing hike around the Long Lake trail. We had no intentions of climbing above timberline. But, as often happens with us, a simple pleasure hike escalates into a greater experience. We are highly susceptible to getting side-tracked from our original intentions.

The allure of the majestic peaks takes control of our actions. Once our eyes gaze upon the beckoning peaks we can't resist their appeal. It is almost as if the peaks hypnotize us. It can happen any time that we are within sight of the mountains, but it frequently happens on beautiful summer days. When it happens, we just start climbing for the highest point around. Sometimes we don't say anything, we just follow the lure of the peaks.

The mysterious attraction of the peaks is the only way that I can explain how we got atop Niwot Ridge on that summer afternoon. We weren't dressed to be frolicking around above timberline. We certainly weren't prepared for the rattling that we received.

It was mid-afternoon when Craig and I reached the top of Niwot Ridge (12,000 feet). We hadn't brought jackets because we didn't plan on climbing above timberline. We started on a relaxing stroll around the Long Lake trail, but the magnetism between us and the peaks drew us high up the green slopes of Niwot Ridge. So, there we sat in the lush grass of the alpine pasture, in the comfortably cool air. We just sat upon the mountainside savoring the serenity of the alpine environment. From our vantage point the view was astonishing. We overlooked the glacial valley of South St. Vrain Creek. The valley starts just east of the Continental Divide at the cirque that was once the bed for Isabelle Glacier. From there, the valley runs eastward and contains the three alpine lakes of Lake Isabelle, Long Lake and Brainard Lake. Totally absorbed in the serene surroundings, we ignored the storm that was brewing overhead.

Then, a loud crackling of thunder snapped us from our tranquil state! A wicked thunderstorm crept into the skies, engulfing the peaks with dark, heavy clouds. The sky darkened, lightning flashed and crackling thunder enlivened the sleepy landscape. It moved so swiftly that we were caught totally off guard. Sheets of rain poured down on the peaks just west of us. Lightning was flashing dangerously close, and the thunder continued sounding its ominous booms.

Karoom! An earsplitting crackle of thunder brought us smartly to our feet. The peaceful, quiet atmosphere of a few minutes past disintegrated; we were about to get drenched. We were high above the shelter of timberline, and the alp-like scenery reminded me of some of the settings in the musical, *The Sound of Music*. It compelled me to sing, "The hills are alive, with the sound of thunder!"

"Let's get out of here!" I said, while starting down the mountainside.

The temperature dropped a few degrees. The sound of thunder echoed between the peaks. And it started to pour. Within seconds the mountainside became precariously slippery. We didn't have any choices. We had to get down to a safer elevation.

The mood switched from serenity to survival. Our leisurely hike became a slippery alpine run for timberline. Zigzagging down the mountainside, we raced for the shelter of the trees surrounding Long Lake. It would have been challenging if the mountains were dry; with the rain, we had to contend with slippery rocks, mud and grass on a steep mountainside. We ran as fast as we dared, slipping and sliding downward.

Craig was first to lose his footing on the slippery slope, and I followed shortly after. I heard an "ouch" from Craig, and the crashing of tumbling rocks. Trying to stop, I lost my footing, and fell smartly onto my rear. I slid a few feet before coming to rest against a rock. A few feet up the slope, behind me, Craig was getting up. We were uninjured. Shaken by the falls, we momentarily slowed our pace. Nearby, another bolt of lightning struck with a loud crack of thunder. Images of my remains and smoldering tennis shoes incited me to pick up the pace again. My fear of falling was subdued by my fear of being vaporized by lightning. I broke into a full alpine run down the precarious mountainside.

My blue jeans and sweatshirt were soaked through to my shivering cold skin. The rain continued to pour down on us with no signs of letting up. As the ground became saturated, a thin sheet of flowing water covered the mountainside. It was extremely difficult to find firm footing.

Then the inevitable happened again. I stepped onto a rock that was loosened by the rain; it gave way, and I fell. I slid down the steep slope, dislodging more rocks in my path and starting a mini rock slide. I tried to arrest my slide by grabbing larger rocks as I slid by them. Sliding down a rock-laden mountainside wasn't as thrilling as glissading down a snowfield; my rear end took a beating. Finally, I grappled a firm rock and stopped myself. Craig barreled past me as I recovered from the fall. I didn't hear him fall again, but his shirt told the story; it was streaked with mud.

We slipped and slid the rest of the distance to timberline. We kept running until we were safely below timberline in the partial shelter of the forest. As soon as we entered the forest, the rain lightened into a drizzle.

A simple jog through the forest would have been too easy. So, we happened into a mucky swamp in the valley at the bottom of Niwot Ridge. There was no easy way around it, so we had to go through it. We couldn't jog because our feet sank into the mud. In places, we sank up to our shins in muck. Eventually, after struggling through the mire, we stumbled across the familiar Long Lake trail. We received some strange looks from passing hikers. We looked like we had been wallowing in the mud.

By the time we got back to camp we were just wet. The continuing rain washed most of the mud off.

Δ

"Race for Shelter" was a forced alpine run, for we ran to escape the dangers of the thunderstorm. At that altitude, we were extremely vulnerable to lightning and hypothermia.

When you distance yourself from the comforts of civilization you put yourself in the hands of nature, and you never know what is going to happen. You have to prepare for and adjust to the ever-changing conditions in the backcountry. The dynamic nature of the alpine environment is what makes mountaineering extremely challenging.

Alpine running is an adventure sport; it takes dexterity, agility, balance, quick thinking, excellent conditioning and absolute concentration. If you're interested in alpine running, you should gradually work up to the difficult slopes. I started by jogging down hillsides. And, as always, balance the risks with safety. If you elect to enter the domain of Rocky Mountain Wilderness, you are voluntarily exposing yourself to objective dangers of the mountains. If you elect to run down a steep mountainside, you are risking your life. Every adventure sport and alpine activity has a degree of risk associated with it, and everyone should be aware of those risks before engaging in those activities. Minimize the risks by increasing your experience or decreasing the difficulty level of the activity.

If you want to enjoy the pleasures of mountain running, without the great risks, I recommend trail and forest running. If you are a thrill-seeker who has to have high risk for high pleasure, I'm sure that alpine running can satisfy your needs.

5. Backpacking

*Backpacking is the ultimate way to experience life
in the Rocky Mountain Wilderness.*

O UR OBJECTIVE WAS Mt. Lincoln (14,286 feet), Colorado's eighth highest peak. In the mid-afternoon of 26 June
1989, Brent and I strapped our hefty backpacks to our backs and
started our trek for base camp. We started our trek at the west end
of Montgomery Reservoir (10,800 feet). We crossed the Middle
Fork of the South Platte River just below the abandoned Magnolia
Mining Mill. From there it was a grueling backpack trek up the
lower eastern base of Mt. Lincoln. The mountainside was steep,
heavily forested, rocky in places and wet in other places. There
wasn't a trail to follow, so we had to do our own navigating.

We had a base camp location selected and marked on our
topographic map. We just had to get there in the few remaining
hours of daylight that we had. It looked like a fairly simple task on
the map, but the terrain was quite challenging due mainly to the
extra weight of the packs.

We fought our way through an entanglement of pine trees,
shrubs and other forest vegetation. After one section of heavy
forest, we climbed up a rocky section of boulder talus at the base of
a cliff. We weren't even midway to our base campsite when I really

started feeling the weight of my backpack. Knowing that we were on a short one-night backpacking trek, we heaped more than we needed into our packs (including a couple cans of beer).

Midway to the base campsite, we encountered a difficult obstacle. We were blocked off by a swampy area and a sheer rock wall. We either had to get wet or free climb up the cliff. Since we didn't want to get wet, and we liked rock climbing, our choice was easy. We carefully worked our way up the cliff with our packs hung loosely about our shoulders. During the most difficult pitch, we had to pass our packs up the cliff in relays.

Shortly before sunset, we found a super campsite just below timberline, about 100 yards from Putnam Gulch. We were relieved to get the backpacks off of our backs. We set camp in a small clearing at about 11,800 feet. Afterward, we climbed up to a rocky ridge overlooking the Lincoln Amphitheater. From our high vantage point, we saw the tip of Mt. Lincoln's snowcapped summit.

"Tomorrow we will stand upon its lofty summit," I said.

We sat in awe as the sun sank behind the backdrop of a ridge of rocky peaks.

The following day we climbed Mt. Lincoln from the advantage of our base camp. We packed only the essential provisions and left the rest at our base camp.

That was just a brief introduction to one of numerous backpacking treks in which I have participated. On our Mt. Lincoln climb, backpacking was an important part of our journey. By backpacking to a base camp, the final stretch to the summit wasn't as far; it made the climb more enjoyable. We had plenty of time to make it to the summit before the inevitable thunderstorms moved in.

Backpacking is a useful and enjoyable way of getting into many backcountry locations. Backpacking is the only self-reliant way of getting your provisions into remote wilderness areas. Backpacking is used for many different backcountry activities including climbing, fishing, camping, prospecting, wilderness photography, seeking solitude and even caving.

Backpacking

During backpacking treks, you are dependent upon the wilderness and the few things that you can pack with you. It is a superior way to experience the wilderness. I feel comfortable in the wilderness; at peace with the universe. Some people get a little uneasy over the thought of camping ten or twenty miles deep in the wilderness. That is where I am in harmony with the environment. I enjoy distancing myself from the noise, pollution, convenience and chaos of the civilized world. However, backpacking is not a carefree activity without risk. It has all of the natural dangers of the wilderness: fickle weather, wild animals and dangerous obstacles. The deeper into the wilderness you go, the more susceptible you become to the dangers. The risk associated with injury becomes especially high. Depending on how far from help you are and who you are with, some injuries can be fatal. But, I always justify the risks by the fact that I feel safer in the backcountry than I do in a city or in a car. That is just my nature. I feel more in control of my destiny when I am in the wilderness versus in a highly populated urban area. When I backpack into the mountains I have to seek out death to find it. In the city, death can come from many directions.

I went on my first backpacking trip at age fourteen. My outdoor recreation teacher took a group of students and me on a three-day backpacking trip to Diamond Lake. That first backcountry experience in the fall of 1978 was the spark that ignited my interests in backpacking. It was only a two-mile trek. But that was far enough for my first backpacking trip. I wasn't very well equipped for the trip. I had to carry a heavy canvas pup tent with railroad spikes for tent stakes. After the first mile I wished that my backpack was lighter.

I have a list of reasons why I enjoy backpacking. First of all, I enjoy staying at the hotel Pine Tree. I would rather be meditating next to a stream than vegetating in front of a television set. I enjoy sitting on a rock or with my back against a log. I love sitting by a crackling fire and gazing into its hypnotic flames. I would rather wake to the sounds of the wilderness than to the sound of a buzzing alarm or a screaming siren. Most of all, I enjoy feeling like a part of the natural environment rather than like a consumer of it.

Since 1978 I have been on several memorable backpacking trips. I have selected two of them to share with you. The first one, "Over Pawnee Pass" is a challenging summer backpacking trek across the Continental Divide and through deep snow. The second adventure, "Five Days in the Backcountry," is about my greatest backpacking experience. It was a sixty-mile trek that took us across the Continental Divide twice and over some very high mountain peaks. As you read the following two adventures, remember that Craig and I are not story-book backpackers. Aside from my first backpacking trip, all of my other treks have been "wild," without an experienced guide. We don't do everything in an orthodox manner. We don't recommend following our approach to back-packing; we made some mistakes and broke a few rules during our backpacking adventures. Remember that I became a mountaineer through experience, not by reading a book or going to a special school.

Over Pawnee Pass

WE CONJURED UP the objective of our adventure during a hot, dry summer day at my home on the plains of eastern Colorado. As we sat at the kitchen table with a topographic map in front of us, the objective seemed simple. Our objective was to climb over Pawnee Pass (12,540 feet), and set camp at Crater Lake on the other side of the Continental Divide. We planned to make the twelve-mile roundtrip trek in two days, on 6-7 July 1983.

After making our plans, we stepped outside to gaze at the section of the Rocky Mountains that we would be crossing. Because of our familiarity with the Indian Peaks, it was easy for Craig and me to pinpoint the individual peaks even though they were about fifty miles west of us. The large, rounded summit of Mt. Audubon was the easiest to pick out; once we located it, the others were easy to isolate. Snow. Lots of snow. That was the most striking feature that we could see from our distant vantage point.

It had been a heavy winter. The mountains were whiter than usual for July. Above 10,000 feet the snow was just starting to melt. The snowcapped high peaks glistened in the summer sunshine.

We planned to start our trek from the Long Lake trailhead in the Indian Peaks Wilderness Area. From there, we would hike past Long Lake, past Isabelle Lake, over Pawnee Pass, down past Pawnee Lake and up the valley to Crater Lake. Our greatest fear was getting caught by inclement weather before getting camp set. Even though we saw that the mountains were snowcapped, we didn't foresee the vast amounts of snow that we would have to cross. We knew that the Pawnee Pass would be snow-covered, but at the lower elevations we only expected to cross occasional patches of snow.

Even after we had driven to the Indian Peaks Wilderness Area, there didn't seem to be any more snow than usual for July. Not expecting abnormal amounts of snow, we hadn't packed snow-shoes, ice axes, rope, skis or snow boots. In fact, Craig made the journey wearing badly-worn tennis shoes; I at least had waterproof hiking boots. We packed plenty of extra clothing and enough provisions to last three days.

This would be Craig's first climb of Pawnee Pass, and my second. Neither of us had ever descended into the valley on the other side. It was a clear, sunny Rocky Mountain summer morning when we started our ascent toward Pawnee Pass.

Determined to trek across the snow-covered Continental Divide, Craig and I started our ascent early in the morning. We carried everything that we expected to need in our backpacks. Pawnee Pass was a four-mile climb from the Long Lake trailhead. From Pawnee Pass it was two miles down into the valley to Crater Lake. We had a long day's trek before us.

We had fantastic expectations of what the valley across the divide would be like; the only information that we had about it was what we could determine from the topo map. Its remoteness was its most appealing feature. The valley, Cascade Valley, was isolated by several miles of forest and rugged mountain wilderness. We envisioned a peaceful valley of endless natural beauty. We were sure that the trek to get there would be worth the effort.

The trail to Long Lake was in good condition, although a little wet and muddy in places from the early summer runoff. The air was fresh, with a hint of pine aroma in it. We passed several day-hikers who were hiking around Long Lake and up to Isabelle Lake. Few, if any, were out to cross the divide.

We felt high spirited! This was our first backpacking trip of a new summer. Since the previous year, we had longed to return to the august beauty of the Indian Peaks. We greeted everyone that we passed with a hearty, "Good day," or "Hello." Most of them returned our greetings, but a few were too snobby.

Commenting on passing hikers was a favorite hiking pastime of ours. We joked about anything that struck us as unusual, such as habits, gestures, facial expressions, clothing, equipment and even eyewear. Some of our famous comments were: "He looks like he just crawled out of a cave. That guy looked like he spent three days inside his tent. Those two guys have enough gear to last them a summer. They look like flower children from the sixties." I'm sure that we received some similar remarks from passers-by.

I especially enjoyed seeing the stereotypical serious backpacker. He carries a stuffed backpack, so full that he has to tie pots and pans on the outside. He has an ice axe sticking out the top of the pack and a coil of rope strapped to the back. His hair is a tangled mess, and he has a few days worth of stubble on his face. I have fit that description on a few occasions.

During our many hours of high country trekking, we noticed an unusually high percentage of hikers wearing round glasses. We interpreted round glasses as a symbol of peace or passivity. They seemed to be vogue for the high country hiker. They conveyed a simple, passive, earthly lifestyle. I vowed to wear round glasses, if I ever needed them.

Like most young adult males, women occupied a large part of our conscious thoughts. To pass the trail time, we often told each other about our fantasies about women. We often fantasized meeting two gorgeous women who were out hiking to the same place that we were. They were usually nymphomaniacs, and crazy about us. We would set camp somewhere in the wilderness and stay there for days. But they were just fantasies. Reality never produced the fruits of fantasy. Whenever we met single women they were returning from a trip when we were starting, or they were breaking camp when we were setting camp. It was ludicrous to expect to meet fantasy women at the places we hiked to. Cavewomen would have had problems making it to some of the places to which we hiked.

The invigorating high country air filled our minds with various thoughts. It stimulated our thoughts and invoked conversations on various topics ranging from the simple to the abstract. Sometimes we talked about our philosophies, global peace, politics, astronomy or our destinies. Discussing profound and controversial issues helped pass the trail time.

At the west end of Long Lake the trail got wetter, steeper and rockier. The trail conditions were still good, but we passed more snow drifts the higher we climbed. We crossed several snow drifts before reaching Isabelle Lake (10,868 feet). That was an uncomforting warning of the higher terrain. The trees grew thinner and the mountainscape more barren as we neared the alpine lake.

We reached Isabelle Lake just before noon. It still looked like winter. The trail disappeared beneath the snow; we would have to make our own trail the rest of the way to the pass. I didn't expect to encounter that much snow. It ranged from two to ten feet deep. We were in for a challenging afternoon. It was already noon, and we weren't even to the divide. Craig's tennis shoes could hardly pass for sandals. I tried to convince him to buy a pair of hiking boots from a second-hand store, but he wouldn't do it. I wondered if my waterproof hiking boots would keep my feet warm. It was Craig's nature to underprepare grossly for our adventures. I'm not sure why he did it. It was either stubbornness or masochism.

For the moment, the weather looked great. Unfortunately, that didn't mean much. The weather in the Rocky Mountains is extremely fickle, and we had no way of telling what the weather was like on the other side of the divide. The towering Indian Peaks completely blocked our view of any storm that might be approaching. We still had 1,500 vertical feet to climb, and several miles of snow-covered terrain to cross before dusk.

There were a number of other day hikers at Lake Isabelle, but they didn't have plans of hiking any further. They were picnicking, playing in the snow, relaxing and photographing the alpine landscape. They would probably be spending the night back in the comfort of their homes.

Our overnight packs drew the attention of one passer-by. "Do you think you'll make it?" he asked with disbelief.

"We'll be on the other side of the Continental Divide by nightfall," I said.

Filled with the gusto of adventure, we left the frozen shores of Lake Isabelle. We tried to stay atop the crust of the snow, but occasionally we sank waist deep. For some insane reason, we continued to tredge on up the mountainside.

Surprisingly, the climbing became easier as we ascended to the wind-swept terrain above timberline. The snow was packed harder from the colder temperatures and wind, and some small stretches were windswept to the ground. We trekked across alpine meadows and knolls. Where possible, we climbed across dry ground; although there wasn't much of that in sight.

Our feet were cold and wet; Craig's feet were already getting uncomfortably cold. Fortunately, the sun still shone brightly overhead, giving us a psychological advantage over the cold. The air was warm enough to keep the rest of our bodies warm. My greatest fear was getting caught by a thunderstorm. The higher we climbed, the more vulnerable we became. A shower of cold rain would put us at a high risk of getting hypothermia. Any such occurrence would jeopardize our adventure.

Our greatest challenge loomed before us. At midafternoon we reached the base of a massive, steep snowfield. It was the side of the north-south ridge that formed part of the Continental Divide and Pawnee Pass. This steep, snow-covered face was one of the faces we had seen from home, fifty miles away.

Fighting against the fleeting daylight, we vigorously assaulted the snowfield. Beneath the snow the ridge was a boulder-strewn slope. In places, the jagged-edged rocks stuck up through the snow or were barely covered by the snow. There were also cavities beneath the snow about which we had to be cautious. At the bottom of the snowfield there were intermittent patches of exposed boulder fields; if we fell and slid to the bottom, those rocks would be our nasty greeting party. The slope was steep enough to make it difficult to break a fall, especially since we had no ice axes. If we fell, we could easily slide to the bottom of the slope.

The crust was hard from surface melting during the day and refreezing at night. It was difficult to get good footing. Since Craig couldn't possibly carve footsteps into the snow with his shredded tennis shoes, I blazed the path up the snowfield. We zigzagged back and forth in a diagonal pattern up the large snowfield. We frequently had to punch our hands into the snow to get additional traction. Occasionally, a foothold would give way; and the backup handhold saved a fall. Isolated on the vast snowfield, there was no relief from the cold snow.

Craig followed a few paces behind. He was having problems getting adequate traction with his ragged tennis shoes. His feet were painfully cold. He had a couple slips and near falls. They were close enough to give him some fear. We were nearing a section of the slope that would put us in a direct line above the exposed boulders at the bottom. It was the most dangerous section of the Pawnee Peak snowfield. Craig knew the rocks were down there. His voice trembled slightly. I could tell that he was nervous, but there wasn't much I could do to calm him.

I carved the steps as deeply as I could to provide the best possible footing. That was the first time I ever had to encourage Craig to keep climbing. Psychologically, the mountain had him beat. Once that happens, fear becomes one's greatest threat. Fear leads to panic; panic causes thoughtless mistakes; and mistakes can be disastrous, especially in precarious situations.

Then, midway up the slope, Craig slipped! He was about ten paces behind me when it happened. He yelled and hit the snow with a thud. By the time I turned my head he was sliding down the snowfield, accelerating rapidly. I couldn't do anything to help. We should have been roped together and carrying ice axes, but we weren't.

"Dig in! Dig your hands and feet into the snow!" I yelled frantically.

He tried to dig in, but his efforts were in vain. He slid helplessly out of control at the mercy of the mountain. I anxiously watched my climbing partner slide down the mountainside toward the rocky bottom. The slope leveled some before the rocks, but I wondered if it would be enough to slow him.

It was over in less than ten seconds. Miraculously, he stopped himself before smashing into the rocks. Two hundred feet below my position, he lay motionless on the surface of the snow. His backpack was about twenty feet from him, and some of its contents were strewn across the snowfield.

Just as I started to descend, Craig moved. He gave me an okay signal with his arms. It took him a few minutes to shake off the fall. I dug into the snowfield and waited for him to climb back up to my position. The delay cost us about thirty minutes, but it could have been much worse. As I waited, I thought about the descent into the valley on the other side. I wondered when and where we would be able to set camp. By dusk, we would desperately need a place to warm up and dry out.

After Craig climbed back up to my position, I saw his physical and psychological wounds. He had minor scrapes on his hands from the abrasive surface of the snow. He would recover from the abrasions. The psychological wounds, however, cut far deeper. He was really rattled. We had been through many risky situations together during our years of high adventure. But this particular fall affected him more than any other incident. The fear went deep, and it followed him the rest of the trek. Some veteran climbers would say that he lost his "edge," that is, he lost his ability to subdue fear and focus on the task at hand. That can be extremely dangerous.

We finished the snowfield in the same manner as before, except at a more cautious pace. Late in the afternoon we topped the pass. We stopped at a sign that marked the Continental Divide. We were at 12,540 feet. We took a short break, then crossed the pass to see what was ahead of us in the valley on the other side.

The other side was steeper and rockier than the side we had ascended. At the bottom of the steep portion, it leveled out into a serene glacial valley. Pawnee Lake, a small alpine lake, occupied the cirque. It was all snow covered. Below Pawnee Lake the valley became forested. Somewhere, down in the valley, we would set camp. It was obvious that we wouldn't make it all the way to Crater Lake.

Our new objective was to find a dry patch of ground for a campsite before nightfall. We quickly descended into the valley by glissading down the snowfields. Footskiing with backpacks is very challenging. It is difficult to compensate for the extra unbalanced weight of the pack. I fell several times before reaching the valley floor.

It was early evening when we started trudging through the waist-deep snow in the forest. The shadows darkened the landscape as the sun sank behind the mountain ridges. There were a few scattered patches of clouds in the sky, but most of the sky was azure. We were wet, cold and wondering if we would find a dry place to set camp.

Traveling through the deep snow was grueling. The snow was soft from the day's melting. We sank up to our thighs with every step. I felt the first signs of fatigue creeping into my sore muscles. As we continued descending into the valley, I thought about the warmth of the campfire beside which that we would soon be sitting. Eventually, the snow cover would have to start dissipating.

The wintry, summer forest was quiet. The lull gave me a strong sense of our isolation. The nearest road was across eight miles of wilderness to the west; and the nearest road to the east was across seven miles of wilderness and the Continental Divide. We found the isolated wilderness for which we set out. But I hadn't expected so much snow.

Then the silence was broken by the sound of flowing water. It was Cascade Creek. For the first time, the creek emerged from the snowy landscape. Our spirits were lifted by the sight of the flowing water. Flowing water was assurance that we would have drinking water; and that the landscape was thawing out. We followed the creek, continuing our search for a campsite.

Finally, we saw bare ground. We found a clearing next to Cascade Creek in the narrow valley floor. It was surrounded by snow and forest. The valley walls climbed steeply on both sides. To the north there was a vertical granite wall, divided by a cascading waterfall. The water tumbled down the cliff, and disappeared into a heap of talus at the bottom.

It was a dry little haven amongst a snow-covered landscape. It was the Pine Tree Inn, and it had vacancies. We didn't think twice about setting camp there. In fact, without saying a word, we automatically unslung our packs and proceeded to set camp. Craig went into the woods to gather firewood, while I pitched the tent.

Shortly after sunset, we had a small campfire flickering against the encroaching darkness. We laid our socks next to the fire to dry and cooked dinner. At last, we could relax.

After dinner, we crouched close to the fire and began to appreciate the beauty of our mountain haven. The Indian Peaks were still just barely visible, silhouetted against a darkening sky. With a Rocky Mountain smile on my face, I absorbed the beauty of our surroundings until the setting faded into darkness.

While in our relaxed states, we scorched our wool socks. We had our feet so close to the flames that we almost barbecued them.

We sat by the campfire reminiscing, recapping the highlights of the day, and thinking up comical scenarios to entertain ourselves. Our favorite comical, fantasy character was a beautiful, well-proportioned young lady named Gretchen. She followed us on all of our mountain adventures. No matter where we camped, she would stroll into our camp wearing a skimpy bikini. Our comical fantasy always started when one of us said, "Look who's walking down the trail toward our camp!"

Comical fantasies were a better way to pass the time than scaring ourselves with bear stories. One night, when we were camped near the remote ghost town of Caribou, we scared ourselves into a sleepless frenzy with a bear story. Our imaginations ran rampant. It was a moonless, pitch-black night. We were the only persons on the mountain. The flickering light from our campfire animated the shadows of surrounding trees. We conjured up the worst-case scenario. We talked about how vulnerable we were. Then we heard a branch crack back in the woods behind our tent. Later, by the time we crawled into the tent, we envisioned a raging grizzly bear charging into our camp. The rest of the night every little noise startled us.

This time we were too exhausted to jeopardize our sleep by cooking up bear stories. Instead, we sat staring at the dancing, hypnotic flames of the campfire until we felt tired enough to sleep. I really enjoyed sitting by the campfire. It made me think about our primitive ancestors. During their times, fire was a life source. They had to have it for light, cooking, warmth and protection. Maybe part of the reason I enjoyed campfires so much was because of the surfacing of primal instincts. We talked by the campfire for about an hour, then crawled into the tent to get some much-needed rest. We had a long trek back over the divide ahead of us.

We made it safely through the night. It didn't rain; the tent didn't collapse; no animals got into our backpacks; and we didn't get attacked by any raging bears. As usual, I was first out of the tent. I enjoyed waking up to the early morning wilderness. It was almost a ritual for me to get the fire started, watch the sunrise and savor the sensations of the mountain wilderness. It was a rush! Listening to the natural sounds was so peaceful. There weren't any noisy cars, ear-piercing sirens, loud jets or loud neighbors. Instead, I heard the harmonious sounds of tweeting birds, flowing water and tree branches rustling in the breeze. It was a very soothing way to start the day.

Craig crawled out of the tent an hour after sunrise. His hair was a tangled mess and he had a day's growth of stubble on his face.

"Guten Morgen!" I said. "Did you enjoy your night in the Pine Tree Inn?"

He mumbled something under his breath. He was probably cursing me, or making a sarcastic reply.

He wasn't the morning person I was.

Then, hardly believing my eyes and ears, I saw and heard three mountaineers clanging down the trail from the high peaks we had crossed the day before. They had a ton of climbing gear stuffed into daypacks. They appeared to be on a serious climbing expedition. I couldn't believe that they were up early enough to have climbed already over the divide. They had to have climbed in the dark.

We exchanged good morning greetings and shared information on the climbing conditions. We told them that we were going back over the pass.

One of them, a lean, bearded man in the lead said, "The snow is hard-crusted. You'll probably need crampons and ice axes."

We thanked them for the information and wished them luck. After they cleared the area, we burst into laughter. There Craig sat, wearing tennis shoes with dangling soles, and these guys told us that we would need ice axes to make the climb. That morning marked the beginning of a tradition of ice axe jokes. From then on, every time that we climbed a snowfield we joked about needing an ice axe.

We broke camp at midmorning and started the trek back up the valley toward the towering granite monoliths of the Indian Peaks. Well into the trek, after we were far beyond the flowing water of Cascade Creek, we drank our canteens dry. We hadn't drunk enough water while we were at camp, and we were getting dehydrated from the hard physical work of climbing. We desperately needed to find a water source.

Later in the morning, we were a third of the way up Pawnee Pass and still hadn't found any water to quench our mighty thirsts. We packed our canteens with snow, but that didn't give us the quantities of water that we needed. We grew desperate for water.

Finally we saw some water! High above our position, a trickling stream of water flowed from an icy avalanche chute. It trickled over some rocks, then disappeared beneath the rock and snow. It would be a steep climb up eroding rock, snow and some ice, but we were thirsty enough to take the risks. It was out of our way as the top of the chute originated from a massive granite wall that would be impossible to climb without ropes. The only time in my life when I had been thirstier was on a hot, dry day when I was stacking hay bales out in a dusty alfalfa field. After his bout with disaster the day before, Craig was reluctant to climb up the precarious chute, but his thirst overcame his fears.

If we slipped and couldn't self-arrest, it would be a 1,000 foot slide onto a bed of rocks. I climbed straight up the chute, facing the mountain, cutting handholds and footholds with each step. My technique was just like the boot camp exercise, "mountain climbers." The climb drained the final drops of fluid from our bodies. We had to have water.

We filled our canteens and quenched our thirst with the icy, pure Rocky Mountain spring water. Even though it was some of the world's purest water, it wasn't worth risking our lives. But we did it anyway. I just can't go very far without water. We balanced ourselves on a thin ledge of snow and ice in the bottom of a warming avalanche chute. Rocks and chunks of ice were starting to break away from the cliff above the chute. We had to get out of the fall path of the debris. We wisely exited the avalanche chute.

On our descent, we crossed the mountain face diagonally back down to our backpacks. Upon reaching our packs safely, we let out a sigh of relief. We were happy to be alive and able to continue the agonizing climb up the west face of Pawnee Pass. Most important, we had full canteens.

The rest of our journey back to civilization was uneventful. We followed the same route back over Pawnee Pass. On the descent down the east face of Pawnee Pass, we made good time by doing some incredible foot glissading down the numerous snowfields along the way back. In fact, we made a very rapid descent from Pawnee Pass back down to our starting point at the Long Lake trailhead.

Amazingly, Craig's worn-out tennis shoes survived the entire trek. I encouraged him to get a better pair of shoes before our next adventure. He agreed. We were both extremely lucky during our trek over Pawnee Pass. We were grossly ill equipped for the journey, and especially thankful that it didn't rain or snow on us while crossing the steep snowfields. It was another valuable lesson in our ongoing education with nature.

Craig still hasn't recovered from the psychological wounds of his fall on Pawnee's east face. He is scarred with the "fear of falling." It is suicidal not to have some sense of fear when climbing. It is equally fatal to be overly worried with the fear of falling. Mountaineers must not let fear interfere with their concentration. When fear overcomes concentration, accidents happen.

If you are interested in backpacking across Pawnee Pass, you'll have to get a permit from the National Park Service before starting your journey. The Indian Peaks Wilderness Area has a delicate ecosystem that must be protected to preserve the beauty of the area. Therefore, there are many backcountry rules that you must follow when backpacking in the Indian Peaks. For more information you can write the Forest Service, Boulder District, 2995 Baseline, Room 16, Boulder, Colorado, 80303, or any other Colorado Forest Service office.

Five Days in the Backcountry

IN THE SUMMER of 1984, Craig and I went on a remarkable five-day, sixty-mile backpacking trek in the Colorado Rockies. We left the comforts and conveniences of civilization for the natural beauty and solitude of the Rocky Mountain Wilderness. For five days, our survival depended on the wilderness and the limited provisions in our backpacks. Our trek took us over the Continental Divide twice, past several alpine lakes and across numerous rugged peaks. We started on the eastern slope of Colorado's Front Range, then crossed over to the western slope, and then ended our journey back on the eastern slope. Specifically, our journey started at the Hessie Townsite, above Eldora, Colorado, and ended in the very familiar Indian Peaks Wilderness Area at Brainard Lake. It is my most memorable backpacking adventure thus far. Likewise, I hope you enjoy reading about our journey as I share it with you.

The success of our backpacking trip was a result of detailed planning, mostly propitious weather and a sprinkle of luck. By luck, I mean that Murphy's Law didn't apply: everything that could have gone wrong, didn't. It wasn't a picnic, but it wasn't a harrowing life-and-death journey either. It was a well-balanced adventure with its share of trying situations and rewarding experiences.

The day before our trek we reviewed a checklist of items to make sure that we had everything we needed in our packs. Every ounce of weight counted, and we only had enough space for absolute essentials. The essentials included food, shelter, clothing, maps, matches, hygiene items, a sleeping bag, an adult magazine and a few other items. The magazine was to keep us from getting tent fever during prolonged rain storms. Suspecting that we would spend a few hours waiting out storms, we also packed a couple of books. Our suspicions were correct; the extra weight proved beneficial. After being pelted by a dozen afternoon thunderstorms, we became accustomed to getting rained on in the afternoons.

Planning our route and estimating our travel time was key to the success of the adventure. Planning is my forte. My adventure partners often accuse me of over planning. However, I can name numerous adventures, including this one, in which careful planning saved us from disastrous consequences. Seated at the kitchen table at home, we charted out our route on the topographic map. We looked for steep climbs, unsurpassable cliffs and other obstacles that might hinder our travel. Except for the first few miles and the last few miles, our trek would be across virgin territory. Day two of our trek would be cross-country travel without any trails. We underestimated many of the challenges of backpacking across the rugged peaks that form the backbone of the continent.

We had to travel an average of only twelve miles per day. That seemed like an easy trek for two young, stalwart men. We envisioned a leisurely hike each day, followed by plenty of time to relax at camp. By the third day on the trail, those visions were shattered.

On the first day, we hiked from the Hessie Townsite to Woodland Land (10,972 feet). On the second day, we climbed a series of peaks over 12,000 feet, as we trekked along the Continental Divide enroute to camp two at Caribou Lake. On the third day, we hiked eighteen miles down to and around Monarch Lake (8,340 feet). On the fourth day, we hiked up to Crater Lake (the un-reached destination on our earlier, aborted trek over Pawnee Pass). On the last day, we climbed over Pawnee Pass and rendezvoused with my dad near the dam at Brainard Lake.

Anything is possible during a five-day journey in the rugged wilderness of the Rocky Mountains. In the final days before start-ing our journey, we thought out the worst-case scenarios. The worst situation that we thought remotely likely was five days of constant rain. We felt that we could survive five days in the rain, although we would be miserable.

The plan was for my dad to drop us off at the Hessie Townsite, and then drive to Brainard Lake to meet us at 3:00 P.M. on day five. He was going to enjoy five days of mountain lake fishing, while we trekked across sixty miles of Rocky Mountain wilderness.

DAY ONE

Craig and I were primed with excitement as my dad drove us toward our starting point. Several days of planning, preparation and anticipation were about to be applied to reality. It was a clear, beautiful morning.

We arrived at the Hessie Townsite at 9:00 A.M. on 14 August 1984. Hessie is the site of a former mining town located just west of Eldora, Colorado, at an elevation of 9,000 feet. Nowadays, it is just a clearing with a few scattered remnants of buildings. High on the surrounding mountainsides, the tell-tale yellow tailings of mines were reminiscent of the once-active mining community.

Dad drove us to a point just short of the townsite, where the jeep trail crossed a briskly flowing creek. It was too rough for Dad's pick-up and camper; our ride was over. It was time for our trek to begin. Craig and I unloaded our backpacks and made a final equipment check.

Dad wished us good luck. "If you're not back by 7:00 P.M. on day five, I'll call for a search party!" he said with his usual sense of humor. He was confident we would make it. After all, he taught me the essentials of backcountry survival.

"We'll see you at 3:00 P.M. in five days," I said confidently. "Have a good time fishing."

Our last contact with civilization left as Dad drove away. There was no turning back. We had five days to reach our final destination at Brainard Lake. For the next five days, our survival would depend upon the wilderness and the forty pounds of provisions that we each packed.

The first, and shortest, stretch of our trek was up a familiar trail. We purposely planned an easy, four-mile hike for the first day. We hoped to set camp at the same site of which we had stopped during our backpacking trek to Woodland Lake the previous summer. The previous summer, we spent three carefree days frolicking around the alpine territory above Woodland Lake. Our camp was a perfect site at the west end of the lake.

We immediately got our feet wet as we crossed the creek that cut across the jeep trail. Ahead of us, beyond Hessie, we would follow Jasper Creek up a valley, then turn west up the trail to the north of Woodland Mountain. The trail cut steadily upward through meadows, forest and along the base of Woodland Mountain. The mountainscape was spectacular. We hiked in the midst of the forested lower mountains and the snow-blotted high peaks.

At first the trail took us through some wet, low-lying areas with lush vegetation. Beyond the jungle-like vegetation of the basin, we hiked through a mountain valley alongside Jasper Creek.

Along the way, I was sidetracked by my curiosity about two piles of tailings slightly above and to the side of the trail. The historical lure of old gold and silver mines has always attracted me to them. I liked to explore the mine sites looking for remnants that provide hints of the mining activities of long ago. Remnants were links to the past.

I scurried up the tailing piles to take a quick look at the two abandoned mines. The entrance to the first tunnel was caved in.

Some rusty iron mining-car tracks led from the buried tunnel entrance to the outward edge of the tailings pile. There were a few other rusty bits and pieces of machinery, equipment, and cables scattered about the site. The second mine was close to the first one, and in similar condition.

Numerous other mines were scattered high on the mountainsides. The bright yellow tailing piles snapped out from the encompassing greenery of the forested mountainsides. The mines were scars on the landscape, but they were small and relatively scarce. They were nothing compared to the devastating strip-mining methods that were recently employed in some mountain areas.

Back on the trail, we came to a fork. The west fork went to Woodland Lake; the north fork went to Devils Thumb Lake. As we started up the west fork, a few puffy cumulus clouds appeared around the peaks. The clouds signaled the possibility that thunderstorms and rain were only two or three hours away. We would be lucky to set camp before it rained.

Our feet were already wet from crossing several streams and marshy areas. Craig wore his traditional tennis shoes. At least I had on waterproof hiking boots. Tennis shoes were fine for short day hikes and excursions, but I preferred the extra protection of hiking boots on long hikes across varied terrain. When forced to traverse a snowfield, hiking boots quickly compensated for their extra weight.

The final two miles to Woodland Lake made a beautiful hike. From Jasper Creek, we climbed from 9,800 feet to 11,000 feet. The trail followed a stream that cut between two beautifully wooded mountainsides. In places, the trail merged with the stream. About ten minutes from Woodland Lake, a clump of dark thunderclouds showered us with a quickly passing thundershower. The sky remained partly cloudy with the threat of thundershowers throughout the rest of the day.

When we arrived at Woodland Lake, we didn't see any signs of other hikers. We were happy to see that the prime campsite at the west end of the lake was available. In fact, until someone else arrived, we had the whole surrounding area to ourselves.

We hiked around the lake and set camp at our favorite site. It had all of the campsite conveniences within just a few yards: a snow bank for refrigeration; the lake for relaxing beside; a stream for washing and fetching drinking water; and trees for shelter and firewood. It also provided a good vantage point for observing the arrival of other backcountry adventurers.

To the west, the ragged-edged Continental Divide formed a monolithic granite wall that divided the watersheds of the eastern and western slopes. Closer to us, a quarter mile to the west and 200 feet above us, was Skyscraper Reservoir. Someone had created the reservoir by building a small stone dam across the mountain stream. At 11,221 feet, without road access, that was quite an accomplishment.

We spent the rest of the afternoon wandering around the sur-rounding mountainsides and relaxing in the soothing high-country environment. We knew that we had a hard day of hiking and climbing ahead of us. We would spend most of the next day trek-king across the rocky peaks on the roof of the continent.

DAY TWO

The night passed quietly without incident. Awakened by the glow of the rising sun, I barreled out of the tent to start the campfire for breakfast. I let Craig sleep for another half hour while I packed my sleeping bag and washed. I finally had to roust Craig out of the tent so we wouldn't get too late a start on the long trek ahead of us. Camp two would be at Caribou Lake. To get there, would have to cross several miles of rugged peaks with only a topographic map, a compass and our senses to guide us.

An hour behind schedule, we struck out for Caribou Lake. During the first two hours of our trek we climbed 1,000 feet to the top of a spur that jutted out eastward from the Continental Divide. Within minutes we were huffing and puffing above timberline. At times, my backpack felt incredibly heavy. Up ahead of us, we saw a herd of deer effortlessly grazing their way up the mountainside. A moment later, they heard us and disappeared into a ravine.

We happened across plenty of drinking water along the way, but we still had to be careful about the water that we drank, especially after seeing a herd of deer in the area. The native inhabitants don't go out of their way to keep the streams pure. In fact, we frequently saw deer, elk and mountain sheep droppings scattered along the banks of streams. The only safe drinking water was purified with tablets or taken right at the source, such as directly beneath a melting snowfield.

To our dismay, dark gray clouds started appearing in the late morning sky. By the time we topped the spur, cloud cover darkened half of the sky. Atop the spur, we took a break to pinpoint our position on the map and to check our progress. As we evaluated our situation, the sky darkened further, threatening to burst with a thunderstorm. The weather outlook for the rest of the day was dismal.

The looming thunderclouds were particularly threatening considering that we had to spend most of the day hiking well above timberline. We would be extremely vulnerable to lightning strikes. At the first sign of lightning we would be forced to retreat to lower territory, and somehow adjust our travel route.

Expecting the worst, we covered our backpacks with rain gear and continued up the gently inclined ridge toward the Continental Divide. Our trail intersected the divide one mile south of the Devils Thumb. The Devils Thumb is a jagged spire just east of the divide. From our position on the backbone of the continent, we saw a panoramic view of the far-away eastern plains, and the sea of mountains to the west. We followed the divide northward toward the Devils Thumb. Despite the fickle weather, the alpine environment and incredible vistas made the trek enjoyable.

As we continued northward, a spectacular view unfolded before us. It resembled poster pictures of the Swiss Alps: grass-covered mountainsides rising up from rustic, sleepy valleys and scattered groves of forest. It was a view I could enjoy staring at all day. It was a sight to behold.

Then the panorama disappeared behind the shroud of a thick layer of clouds pushed by a thirty m.p.h. wind. The picturesque view was smothered by gray mist. The clouds blew across Devils Thumb Pass like smoke through a wind tunnel. It looked like the beginning of a miserably wet and dreary afternoon. Climbing through the clouds, with minimal visibility, we started ascending an unnamed 12,326-foot peak. The climb took us right past the awesome spire of the Devils Thumb.

The distant sounds of booming thunder echoed through the valleys and across the peaks. At a time when we should have been descending, we had to keep ascending higher into the cloud-shrouded perilous peaks. A cold shiver went through my body from head to toe. It was a chilling reminder of how vulnerable we were in the hands of nature.

"If your hair starts to stand on end, crouch down and tuck your head between your knees," I reminded Craig. That was the safest position to assume when in the area of striking lightning. Fortunately, the lightning kept a safe distance from us.

Despite the dreary weather and heavy backpacks, we climbed to the top of a 12,640-foot peak just north of the Devils Thumb. While climbing the peak my pulse escalated to 165, and my heart felt like it was going to explode. Craig's pulse was 180, an amazing three beats per second. We were probably burning fifteen to twenty calories of energy per minute.

Atop the 12,640-foot peak, directly on the Continental Divide, we evaluated our travel route while consuming a tasty can of sardines. After checking the map and looking across the mountainous terrain that we had to cross, we discovered a problem with our original travel route. Our original plan was to follow the divide all the way to Arapahoe Pass and then down to Caribou Lake. That route would take us across a treacherous knife-edged ridge that dropped off hundreds of feet on both sides. With backpacks, that route would be nearly impossible. It would be a hairy nightmare of a challenge, at best. To cross the ridge we would have to perform a balancing act on a narrow, jagged ridge, wearing burdensome backpacks in a thirty mile per hour cross-wind. We opted to avoid the extra risk and time by circumnavigating the dangerous ridge. Our only alternative was to descend 1,200 feet into a cirque, then back up and over Arapahoe Pass (11,900 feet). At least it would be straightforward climbing without any hidden dangers. Or so we thought.

Craig reluctantly mumbled his approval of the alternate route. He was against making the extra descent and ascent. I didn't like having to expend the extra energy either, but the thought of teetering atop a precarious ridge was even less appealing, especially with the constant threat of lightning looming over us. I had been in teeth-chattering situations before by making a wrong decision about a route. Clinging to the steep face of granite cliff, where progress was measured in inches, was an experience that I don't care to repeat.

Dark, ominous thunderclouds rolled across the sky throughout the day. Occasionally, the sun would poke through for a few minutes, but most of the day the sky looked like it could burst with heavy rain at any moment. As we continued northward along the divide toward the rim of the cirque, we climbed in a light spray of mist from the fog.

As we pushed for the south rim of the cirque, the fog thickened and the wind gusted. When we reached the top of the ridge, the wind nearly blew us back down the mountainside. The inside walls of the cirque dropped steeply into the bowl below. It would be a steep, rocky descent, but it still looked easier than tackling the dangerous knife-edged ridge. Provided, that is, that the rain wouldn't turn the cirque wall into a slippery nightmare. The likelihood of rain forced us to stop and reevaluate our options.

A brief break in the clouds revealed the jagged knife-edged ridge that we feared. The side facing us (the west inside wall of the cirque) was a sheer granite wall 400 feet high. The sight of it confirmed our worst fears. After a short break, we started down the rocky mountainside of the southern cirque wall.

A beautiful setting awaited us in the bowl of the cirque. It was a grassy alpine meadow spotted with pools of water linked by a network of streams.

Shortly after we began our descent, a nearby bolt of lightning and boom of thunder rattled our nerves. Our cautious descent quickened into a haphazard survival run! Then our worst fears became reality—the clouds burst in a downpour. Within minutes the mountainside became a slippery obstacle that we had to endure. We were forced to slow our pace and muster all the dexterity that we had.

We had plenty of experience at descending slippery mountainsides, none of it by choice. This was like a recurring nightmare. The slope would be difficult even in dry weather without bulky backpacks. Toting backpacks and fighting the effects of the rain made the descent extremely treacherous. It was a hairy bear! The rocks were slippery; the soil between the rocks was like mud; and many of the rocks were loosened. The rocky slope was like a minefield for ankle-spraining, twisting and breaking. Any of these accidents would prematurely end our trek.

Then, the inevitable happened. In one fluid sequence of events, Craig slipped, fell and bounced back onto his feet. He took a few more strides, then repeated the sequence. The combination of fatigue and poor footing took its toll on both of us.

Concerned that I might end up carrying him off of the mountain, I warned him to slow down. Then I resumed my quick, haphazardous pace down the slope. Shaken by another round of lightning and thunder, I blazed past Craig in a flurry of fear.

Moments later I heard the crashing sound of tumbling rocks behind me, quickly turning my head to see a small avalanche of rocks coming straight at me. I leaped aside just in time to avoid being hit.

Up at the source of the rockslide, Craig was crouched on the mountainside grasping his ankle. I shed my backpack and scrambled up to him.

Craig had slipped and fallen. Fortunately, he only had minor cuts and abrasions. After that brush with disaster we finished the descent at a safer pace.

Finally, after we made it to the bottom, the rain dissipated. The trek across the valley was easy going. When Arapahoe Pass came into view, we knew that the hardest part of the trek was nearly over. Caribou Lake and camp two were only one mile downhill from Arapahoe Pass. Due east of Mt. Neva, we were only two miles up and over the pass from Caribou Lake.

Intermittent sunshine invited us to take a break near a brook in a colorful alpine meadow. We shed our packs and collapsed in the thick grass and wild flowers. We were both exhausted and in dire need of a rest.

After a fifteen-minute rest, we stumbled across the wreckage of a four-seat airplane that had fallen short of clearing Arapahoe Pass by a few hundred feet. It wasn't the first time Craig and I had found airplane wreckage. The highly variable flying conditions over the Rocky Mountains made it difficult for many small planes. Turbulent winds, drastic pressure variations, thin air, dynamic weather and cloud cover made flying over the Rockies dangerous. The wreck was several years old. From the look of the crushed fuselage, no survivors had walked away from the crash.

Interested in our own survival, we picked up our packs and ascended Arapahoe Pass. We maintained a steady pace up and over the pass. On the other side (the western slope), we saw Caribou Lake and a forested valley below. It was a welcome sight. We were starting to drag our feet from fatigue. We were both ready to check into the Pine Tree Inn.

We set camp below Caribou Lake, near Arapahoe Creek. As I drove the last tent stake into the ground, it started raining again. We covered our packs and dove into the tent. Five minutes later we were asleep, oblivious to the pounding rain on the tent.

An hour later it was still raining. I wondered whether or not we would get a hot dinner. I was famished. We had burned many times the number of calories we had consumed during the long day's trek.

The rain didn't stop, but it slowed to a drizzle for about twenty minutes, long enough to start a fire and cook dinner. After dinner, the continuing rain drove us back into the shelter of the tent. There would be no jovial campfire conversations that night. Moments later, we were in dreamland.

DAY THREE

I awoke to the comforting warmth of sunshine filtering through the pine trees and translucent tent walls. It was a relief to see sunshine and blue skies. I started the day with a bath in the icy waters of the creek. It was an invigorating sensation! It felt great to sit in near-freezing water in the diffused light of the rising sun. It felt so good that I spent at least 120 seconds savoring the stimulating experience. I nearly froze my you-know-whats off! Craig was content with the traditional morning head-dunking ritual.

We took time to eat a nutritious, enjoyable breakfast. I even had time to enjoy a refreshing cup of coffee before we broke camp. We had a long trek before us, but it was mostly downhill on a well-kept trail. We would hike eighteen miles before setting camp three. It was all downhill to Monarch Lake, a drop of about 3,000 feet to the lowest altitude that we experienced during our five-day trek.

We hiked down a lush mountain valley of inestimable ecological wealth. It was densely forested and rich with vegetation. The calm air held a piney aroma. The only sounds were the soothing natural sounds of the flowing creek and the singing birds. It was like hiking through a fantasy forest from a storybook. Images of lovely wood nymphs, chubby dwarves and slender elves danced through my head. As we settled into a steady, rhythmic hiking pace, I let my mind float adrift in the magical beauty of the wilderness. In my relaxed state of mind, I expected to see a party of cheerful dwarves appear around the next turn. When I glanced into the woods, I expected to catch a gnome spying on us from behind a log. I told Craig the myths about wood nymphs. If you gaze into the eyes of a wood nymph you will become her eternal slave. Nymphs have a magical charm that make them irresistible to men. They have been known to capture entire adventure parties.

"How would you like to be captured by a band of gorgeous wood nymphs?" I asked.

"It would be like going to heaven," said Craig.

I've heard that young men cannot pass one minute without having a sexual fantasy. I don't remember who made that claim, but I know that it was false. I distinctly remember a time when I went for seven minutes without having any sexual fantasies.

We trekked all morning down the beautiful mountain valley. We arrived at the east end of Monarch Lake shortly after noon. Instead of taking the shortcut trail to the Crater Lake trail, we decided to take a lengthy stroll around Monarch Lake. It wasn't like we hadn't had our exercise for the day. Actually, we were hoping to find a hotdog stand or a convenience store at the other end of the lake. Other than bumping into another gung-ho adventurer and getting caught behind a line of horseback riders, we didn't find anything worthy of our extra time and effort.

We exchanged adventure highlights with the adventurer we met. He made bold claims about spending two carefree weeks climbing and hiking the peaks of the divide. Back on the trail east toward Crater Lake, we got caught behind a line of horses on a narrow section of trail. We didn't dare take our eyes off of the ground while we followed the horses (it wasn't snakes or rocks that we feared stepping on). Finally, the trail widened, allowing us to pass the string of lolligagging horseback riders.

The sky was clear except for a few sparsely-scattered cumulus clouds around the distant peaks. We set camp at the first creek-side campsite we happened upon, just above Monarch Lake, beside Buchanan Creek. We were too exhausted to be particular about our campsite; in fact, we pitched the tent in the creek's flood plain without even thinking about it.

After setting camp, I found a perfect bathing place in the creek. It was a natural whirlpool created by the swirling currents of the tumbling whitewater. I shed my clothes and waded into the deep pool of swirling ice water. Despite my plummeting body temperature, it felt good. I tried unsuccessfully to fool Craig into believing that I was sitting in a hot spring. It must have been the bluish color of my skin that discredited my claim.

After dinner, we sat by the campfire reminiscing about our journey and other experiences in life. Sitting by the flickering flames of a campfire is a favorite pastime of mine. I was happy that we had the time and willingness to enjoy a relaxing evening beside the campfire. We had planned an easy hike to Crater Lake for day four. Our research led us to believe that we needed to get to Crater Lake early to spend some extra time there. From our camp we were six miles and 1,600 vertical feet from Crater Lake—a leisurely day's trek. After exhausting our campfire stories we retired for the evening. Blocking out the crackling sounds of thunder from across the mountaintops, we drifted asleep.

Around midnight, a brilliant flash of lightning and an instantaneous crackle of thunder snapped us awake. It struck within hair-raising proximity! The vibrations of the booming thunder bounced us off of the ground. Shortly afterward all hell broke loose. Pouring rain accompanied by a terrifying series of lightning and thunder kept us awake. As I lay awake, the sole focus of my attention was the roaring sound of the creek getting louder and louder. I was afraid the creek was going to flood. Why did we have to set camp in a low-lying site? Once again, it seemed, nature was about to teach us another lesson on backcountry adventure practices. We lay awake petrified as lightning flashes illuminated the tent and rain gushed down.

Then it happened! Water flooded into and under the tent. The tent floor felt like a water bed. It wasn't flowing fast enough to be the rising creek; it had to be runoff collecting in the low-lying area in which we had pitched the tent. Nonetheless, we were in for a wet night.

Despite the close proximity of lightning, I crawled out into the darkness and driving rain to investigate the situation. Earlier, I had dug drainage ditches around the tent. They were clogged with debris, diverting the water into the tent. I feverishly cleaned the drainage trenches and rerouted the water flow away from the tent. I was wringing wet one minute after stepping out of the tent.

Back in the tent, I found Craig curled up, shivering and complaining of stomach cramps. Bad water was my first thought, but I had adamantly enforced the use of purification tablets in all of our drinking water. Maybe he drank a few drops that didn't get purified, possibly from the outside rim of the canteen. We were at least five miles from any kind of assistance; it would take me at least two hours to find help and return. Craig continued to have stomach cramps, but fortunately, his condition didn't worsen. We didn't sleep very much during the remainder of the night. We were wet, Craig was sick and I was worried.

DAY FOUR

At the first sign of daylight, I crawled out of the damp tent to celebrate the dissipation of the rain. Our sleeping bags, clothes and shoes were soaked. The ground was muddy; the plants were wet. Yet, the clear sky and rising sun brought a cheerful message that things were going to dry out. I strung a line between two pine trees for drying our things. Craig was alive and well, strong enough to resist my efforts to roust him out of the tent.

The day's hike to Crater Lake was short, so we took our time eating breakfast, drying out and breaking camp.

This would be our third attempt to make it to Crater Lake. Our second attempt, the one before, had ended disastrously. We started at Long Lake, on the other side of the divide, at 7:00 P.M., during a momentary break in a thunderstorm. Two miles up the trail, at Isabelle Lake, driving rain, darkness and plummeting temperatures forced us to abort our attempt. In fact, we nearly died that evening.

Neither of us had been to Crater Lake before. Its remote location and unique topography made it very appealing. The name itself conjured up images of an exotic, mysterious place. We planned extra time into our schedule so that we could get there early enough to explore and recuperate for the last day's journey over Pawnee Pass.

On the trail to Crater Lake, we paralleled Buchanan Creek (the creek that had almost washed us away the night before) until Cascade Creek joined it. Cascade Creek flowed with tumbling whitewater from the melting snows of the Indian Peaks. Crater Lake was one of the lakes that fed the creek. Cascade Creek divides two august mountain chains. Two beautiful, green mountainsides rose up from each side of the creek. Once again, the snowcapped peaks came into view, scintillating in the morning sunshine, forming a picturesque mountainscape. The beauty of our surroundings therapeutically healed our feelings of anguish from the miserable night before.

As we continued hiking up into the vivid alpine setting, it became obvious why the creek was named Cascade Creek. We hiked past a series of captivating cascade falls. The dynamic power of the first waterfall forced us to stop and observe it. Pure, white, turbulent water gushed from between two rock walls, then dropped about thirty feet into a pool. At the bottom, we passed through the cool mist created by the falling water.

Along the trail, we passed several other cascading waterfalls. I thought about how fun it would be to ride down Cascade Creek in a small raft or kayak. Maybe we could return to ride the rapids on a future adventure. At about 10,000 feet, we came to the intersection of the Cascade Creek trail and the Crater Lake trail. From there, it was only a mile to Crater Lake. On the return trek, we would have to come back to the Cascade Creek trail to get to Pawnee Pass.

Crater Lake and the surrounding area was spectacularly beautiful, surpassing our highest expectations! It seemed like a secluded, lost mountain paradise. The surrounding mountainsides really do resemble the inside walls of a crater, although the actual origins of the lake was glacial rather than volcanic. In fact, due south of the lake was a glacial cirque filled with compacted snow, remnants of Peek Glacier. Below the cirque and all around the "rim" that encircles Crater Lake, a spectacular array of cascading streams flows down into the lake. The surrounding rock walls were striped with dark water stains. It was the ideal location to culminate our five-day backcountry adventure.

After setting camp on the west bank of the lake, we set out to explore the encircling mountainside. Despite the grueling climb that we had to make the next day, we spent most of the afternoon scrambling around the surrounding cliffs rather than resting. Thunderclouds formed all around the outside of the rim, but the skies above the lake remained clear. It was as if the lake were protected by a magical dome.

That evening, nature treated us to a spectacular sunset, one of the most incredible sunsets that I had ever watched. The main attraction was actually the reflection of the sunset on the rocky peaks to the east. We sat watching in awe as the ragged-edged arete glowed with a pinkish-orange luminescence. The glow grew brighter, peaked, then gradually faded as the sun sank behind the mountains. It was an unforgettable, climactic ending for the last night of our five-day journey. It was a lagniappe from nature: an unexpected, highly appreciated treat, as though the mountains were making amends for the stormy wrath they dealt us during the previous night.

Our last night passed peacefully and without rain, and we got the restful sleep we so desperately needed before making the final day's climb back across the divide.

DAY FIVE

The first rays of diffused sunlight woke me. I sat on a boulder absorbing the rejuvenating sensations of the rising sun and the serenity of the alpine environment. If we hadn't had a schedule to keep, I could have sat there all day. Unfortunately, we had to climb across the 12,540-foot summit of Pawnee Pass before the inevitable thunderstorms formed. We still had ten miles of Indian Peaks Wilderness to cross in order to make our rendezvous with my dad at Brainard Lake.

Reluctantly, we packed our belongings back into our backpacks and set out for Pawnee Pass, vowing to return one day to Crater Lake. Our backpacks were considerably lighter than they had been when we started our trek. We were also lighter and leaner than we had been at the start. But the advantages of climbing with lighter packs were negated by the disadvantages of our decreased energy levels. The ascent of Pawnee Pass would surely consume the last of our waning energy reserves. Our trek would take us up the U-shaped glacial valley, past Pawnee Lake, up and over Pawnee

Pass, down past Lake Isabelle and Long Lake, and down to Brainard Lake.

It was a relatively gentle, low-risk ascent up to Pawnee Lake. From there, we faced a towering granite wall that formed the Continental Divide and contained numerous high peaks. The trail before us zig-zagged up the precipitous west side of Pawnee Pass. It was a craggy, broken mountainside subject to occasional rock slides and avalanches. During the previous summer, on our trek over Pawnee Pass, the rocky mountainside was still blanketed in snow. This time the easy-to-cross snow was gone.

We knew that it would be all downhill after we made it over the pass. Ruled by that positive thought, we started up the narrow trail like two mountain goats. Other than dodging a couple of falling rocks and stumbling a few times, we made it to the summit of Pawnee Pass without incident.

From atop the pass the familiar setting of our favorite Rocky Mountain playground came into view. Since our discovery of the Indian Peaks Wilderness Area, we had explored every mountain, ridge, lake, creek and snowfield in the area. We knew all of the peaks by name, and we frequently referred to them as if they were old friends. In a way, they were old friends. On every climb of every peak, we had a memorable experience that taught us more about the peaks and about ourselves. Six and a half miles away and 2,140 feet below us, we saw Brainard Lake, our final destination. It even appeared that we would make it on schedule by 3:00 P.M.

During our descent, we crossed a couple good snowfields. We took advantage of both of them by foot-skiing down. We had two super runs! The snow was slightly mushy from the heat of the afternoon sun, but it didn't keep us from having a great time.

Once we dropped below timberline, the remainder of our hike went quickly. The lower trails were fairly crowded with numerous day-hikers. After hardly seeing anyone for five days, it was a big change of pace to see so many hikers. We passed more people in thirty minutes than we had during the previous four days. Since the Indian Peaks Wilderness Area is one of the most-visited areas in the Colorado Rockies, it wasn't surprising to see so many visitors. For the first time in five days, I became concerned with my appearance. I had six days of stubble growth on my face (I had quit shaving a day before we started), was wearing smoke-cured clothes, had a dark tan and a tangled rat's nest of hair. We were modeling the alpinist's style of attire, but for some reason I didn't think it would catch on overnight and take the fashion world by surprise.

At 3:05 P.M.—only five minutes late—we met my dad at the Brainard Lake dam. He was amazed to see us on time. Even though I had enjoyed our five-day trek, I was happy to see Dad's smiling face. Likewise, he was happy to see us safely returned. Dad had caught his limit of trout during his five days of fishing. The three of us were tired, hungry, and ready to return to the comforts of civilization—at least, for a while.

Our incredible backpacking trek was over. But, the memories of our five-day, sixty-mile adventure will be with us forever in our treasure chest of memorable experiences. The adventure enriched our spirits and broadened our understanding of the mountains and nature as a whole. We left the mountains with an increased wealth of memories; the only type of wealth that transcends our existence on earth.

That was our last Rocky Mountain adventure for the summer of 1984. The coming of autumn marked the beginning of another school year. It was time for Craig to return to the University of Oklahoma, and for me to return to the University of Wyoming. Once again, we went our separate ways for another year. As the year passed, we knew that the beckoning peaks and the allure of the mountains would bring us back together the following summer.

Δ

Spending five days in the backcountry is an excellent way to relax and enjoy nature's treasures. Backpacking forces you to depend on the wilderness for your survival. It makes you think about human-kind's true dependence on the environment. Craig and I depended on the mountains for our water, cooking fuel (wood), and shelter from wind. The best part of the experience was being able to escape the worries of industrialized life and to enjoy the relaxing wilderness environment.

If you're going to go backpacking you should get in the proper mental state before you leave home. Forget about your worries, and concentrate on relaxing to the rhythms of nature. As you start your trek through the mountains, canyons, forest or other wilderness area, concentrate on listening to nature. Take time to really enjoy your backpacking experiences. Sit on a streambank and think about the natural forces at work while you listen to the soothing sounds of the flowing water. You can expand your feelings abut your environment by simply tracing a stream from its beginning to its end. You will quickly learn how interrelated everything is. The streams, forests, mountains, oceans, lakes, plains, hills, marshes, animals, insects and humans are all interrelated in this complex biosphere that is our environment. Even if you are just going backpacking for recreation, if you enter the wilderness with an open mind, you will probably leave with a greater appreciation for your environment. You may even come to the conclusion—if you haven't already—that we cannot survive if we continue to muck up the natural processes of our one and only planet. When you mentally step back and look at the earth, as from space, you will quickly realize that we are an oasis in a sea of dark, cold emptiness. We do not even know whether another life-supporting planet exists. And if it does, how could we move more than seven billion people? We can't afford to have a throw-away attitude toward our planet. Everyone needs to realize the critical importance of nature's intricate interrelationships. Maybe everyone should be required to take Backpacking 101.

If you are interested in backpacking in the Rocky Mountains, there are hundreds of established trails from which to choose. The first thing you need to do is plan your backpacking trip. Decide where you want to go, how long you want to stay, what you want to see and the degree of challenge that you want. There are so many trails from which to choose that you should be able to find one to meet your customized set of expectations. You should be able to find ample information about backpacking trails at the library, a book store or from the National Park Service. In some areas, such as the Indian Peaks Wilderness Area and Rocky Mountain National Park, you will have to get a backpacking permit and follow specific backcountry rules. The minimal cost of getting a backpacking permit is well worth it.

Always remember to plan your backpacking adventure wisely. Make a checklist of everything that you need to pack; plan for the worst likely conditions; and make sure others know your route and expected return time. The first step to *having* a successful backcountry experience is *planning* your adventure.

6. Caving

Caving is the challenging activity of crawling, squirming and rappelling into a dark, dingy, subterranean passage. There are few logical reasons for surface-dwellers to delve into the depths of caves, but for spelunkers challenge and curiosity defy logic.

W E WERE DEEP inside the bowels of the mountain. We had spent the past two hours crawling, squeezing and slithering deeper and deeper into the earth through the vast network of passages. We were coated with wet clay from the cave floor, and my body started to shiver for the first time. Roni, John and I waited at an intersection of two passages as our guide checked the left passage.

After two minutes passed, we could no longer see or hear our guide. We sat motionless, waiting for our guide to return. "Why didn't our guide know which direction to go?" I thought. My confidence in the guide's ability to get us in and out of this cave began to slip. Roni, my wife, began to shiver. She was also shaken by the guide's indecision over which passage to follow. Our guide, Elrick, was the only one who could get us back to the surface. Our lives depended on his ability to guide us through the labyrinth of passages.

Finally, we saw the light from Elrick's head-lamp as he turned the corner to meet us.

"That passage pinches off," he said. "We'll have to go to the right."

Our goal was a subterranean waterfall. To get there, we had to take the narrow, three-feet high, right passage. Elrick took the lead. Immediately, I didn't like what I heard! Elrick splashing in water. Then I poked my had through the narrow opening before us and saw Elrick on his back, up to his neck in water.

If we weren't wet enough already, we were about to get thoroughly soaked. Roni was ready to turn back, and I would have been, too, if we weren't so close to the waterfall. After some convincing reassurance, we took the plunge. As we slid through the water on our backs, we only had a few inches of air space between the water and the ceiling. It was scary, but we made it safely through the flooded passage.

My confidence was restored when I heard the sounds of a waterfall coming from the passage ahead.

Caving or spelunking is the recreational sport of exploring wild caves. Spelunkers don't take pride in walking through commercialized caves such as Colorado's Cave of the Winds, or Kentucky's Mammoth Caves. Spelunkers specialize in exploring rugged, treacherous, wild caves. They chart their own course, carry their own light sources; and accept the objective dangers. Cavers are adept in dark, wet, muddy, dank, cool, tight, hard, and lifeless caverns. Caving is definitely not an activity for claustrophobics. In fact, anyone with the slightest trace of claustrophobia should stay away from caves.

Caving is more demanding than most non-cavers realize. Maneuvering through caves requires the use of nearly every muscle in your body. Sometimes you have to crawl, climb, chimney, swim, squirm, and squeeze. It is very beneficial to be in good physical condition before embarking on a caving adventure. You'll feel much better the day after.

As with every recreational sport, caving also has its share of extremists. There are plenty of extreme opportunities for caving in the Rocky Mountain region. It's easy to find extremely challenging obstacles within the vast domain of the Rocky Mountains. Scuba-spelunking is one example of extreme caving. In fact, a high percentage of spelunking-related deaths are attributed to scuba-spelunking. Scuba-spelunking can be done in any flooded passage. Because of heavy spring runoff, many cave passages in the Rocky Mountains become subterranean rivers—ideal places for extremists to get their feet wet.

By now you should know I am not an extremist. I get ample satisfaction and challenge without going over the edge. The caves I have explored have been challenging enough to satisfy my appetite for adventure. I enjoy caving for many of the same reasons that I enjoy other recreational adventure activities. I enjoy the challenge, personal triumph, and exhilaration of participating in outdoor recreational activities. Some people enjoy feeding the ducks at the city park. I enjoy exploring and adventuring in the Rocky Mountains.

Al, a college friend, gets the credit for introducing me to caving. Al is an experienced spelunker and past president of the University of Wyoming Student Grotto (caving club). After Al told me about caving, I was ready to try it. Al even knew about a small, "introductory cave" within an hour's drive of campus. It was the perfect cave for me to get my feet wet.

Al is a serious caver and amateur speleologist. He has the skills to get into and out of caves, and he can identify many of the speleological formations inside the caves. He is adept at many of the skills necessary for spelunking, such as descending and ascending ropes to get through vertical sections, keeping one's head above water through partially-flooded passages, shimmying through tight cracks and adjusting to the cool, dark cave environment. Al taught me almost everything I know about caving. And I had some exciting caving adventures while I was learning.

The two caving adventures that I have included in this collection occurred at Coal Chute Cave and Cave Creek Cave. Coal Chute Cave was my first caving adventure. Cave Creek Cave is a twofold adventure of first finding the cave, then exploring it. The first part of that adventure could be titled: "The Map-Reading Mishaps of Three College Students."

Coal Chute Cave

ON THIS ADVENTURE, we discovered a small cave in the Sherman Mountains between Laramie and Cheyenne, Wyoming, in an area known as the "Gangplank." The Sherman Mountains, the Gangplank and the Vedauwoo rock formations are all in the Laramie Range. The Laramie Range contains several small caves, including Table Mountain Cave, Horned Owl Cave, the Bates Creek Ice Cave and a few other small, difficult-to-find caves.

After a forty-five minute drive through southern Wyoming's rolling hills and mountains, we pulled to the side of the sleepy two-lane road. Brent and I relied on Al's memory of the cave's location. Al was the only one of us who had ever been to the cave, and that had been over a year ago. In fact, among the three of us, Al was the only one who had caving experience; Brent and I were pure greenhorns. Coal Chute Cave was to be our first caving adventure.

The three of us were students at the University of Wyoming. Brent and I were in engineering, and Al was studying computer science. It was mid-semester, and we were all suffering from midterm burnout and dormitory fever. Brent and I sat in the dormitory room trying to conjure up something fun to do on the upcoming weekend. We stared out the large sliding windows of our sixth-floor dormitory suite, looking east across campus toward the Laramie Mountains.

"Let's drop a rope out the window and rappel down the side of the building," joked Brent.

"All right," I said, "where shall we tie the ropes?"

"We can tie them off to the back of the bunk bed frame," he said, continuing the joke.

"We better wait until dark. We could attract some unnecessary attention at this time of the day."

I felt guilty for even thinking of such an act. A stunt like that would get us both thrown out of college. We left it as a wild thought. However, a day of rock climbing and rappelling at Vedauwoo sounded like a good way to spend a Saturday. As we were about to make our decision, someone banged on the door. It was Al.

Al stood six feet tall, was large framed and had a beer belly in the early stages of development. He had an oval face, light skin and straight, short, blonde hair. He served with the Wyoming Army National Guard, but his military bearing was rarely noticeable. His weight and haircut pushed the limits of military regulations. As a clean-cut, spit-and-polish former Marine and then Air Force Reserve Officers Training Corps (ROTC) cadet, I had always harassed him about his relaxed attitude toward meeting military regulations.

Al swung the door open, walked across the room and sat down on my bunk. He had come over for a social call. Knowing that Al was a caver, I asked him where the closest cave was. Al told us about a small cave in the Sherman Mountains east of Laramie. He hadn't been there in over a year, but he thought he could remember how to get there.

Al had our full attention as he described the cave. The images that Coal Chute Cave brought to mind convinced us that we had to explore it. Being a member of the University of Wyoming Grotto, Al said that he could get us the necessary hard hats and head-lamps for the adventure. To Brent and me, Coal Chute Cave sounded like an ideal beginner's cave. We anxiously waited for Saturday to arrive.

Finally, after waiting several days in anxious anticipation, we made it to the Gangplank, a hilly area where Al thought the cave was located. Actually, Al wasn't very confident of the location where we pulled off of the road, but it was his best guess. He remembered more than he led us to believe. We parked the car, slung our daypacks across our backs and set out on foot to find the cave's entrance.

The local terrain was rolling hills, rounded mountains, gullies and shallow canyons. The vegetation consisted of bristly sagebrush and sparsely scattered pine trees, with occasional bare rock outcroppings. The foothills stretched to the horizon in every direction. It was a wild, rugged and lonely landscape. I loved every part of it.

The search for the cave's entrance began, and we spread out to comb the hills. All we knew was that the entrance was a hole in the ground or in the wall of a gully, but there were numerous gulches, gullies and canyons in the surrounding area. It might take all day to find the entrance; it could be hidden by rocks, trees or groundbrush.

Determined to be the first one to find the cave, I jogged to the nearest gulley. I imagined what the cave entrance might look like; it had to be near a rock outcropping. From the edge of a steep-walled gulley I scanned the walls for a black hole set within some sort of outcropping. Brent and Al split up and fell back to search other potential areas.

I anxiously ran down the gulley wall to investigate a suspicious-looking bedrock outcrop in the gulley floor, but it was just an exposed section of bedrock. Following the streambed upward toward the head of the gulley, I looked behind every suspicious-looking clump of rocks. Nearing the gulley's head, I casually scanned the top edge of the gulley, not really expecting to see anything. Then I saw something peculiar. There it was! I saw a black circular opening or some kind of indentation in a sandstone cliff at the rim of the gulley. It had to be the entrance to the cave.

"I found it!" I yelled back to Brent and Al. "It's up here!"

In the rush of adrenalin that followed, I ran full speed up the gulley's headwall, dodging between boulders and brush. Brent and Al jogged around the rim of the gulley to see what I was so excited about. I scrambled up the loose debris at the base of the cliff, then climbed up into the niche that contained the dark opening. Sure enough, there it was: an oval opening about five feet high and two and a half feet across. A large boulder blocked most of the entrance; it had obviously been lodged into the entrance to keep common, everyday adventurers out. There were only two small gaps above and below the boulder, just large enough for determined adventurers to squeeze through.

While I analyzed the entrance, my fellow adventurers climbed down to the opening. Al confirmed that the opening was indeed the entrance to Coal Chute Cave. A look of determination appeared on Al's face. He was getting serious. He dropped his pack and donned his caving gear. Not really knowing what to do, Brent and I imitated Al. First, he tested his carbide head-lamp to assure that it had proper mixture of water and carbide. Brent and I had battery-powered head lamps, with bulky and cumbersome battery packs strapped to our belts. We also carried flashlights, butane lighters and matches. The cargo pockets of my camouflage fatigues were perfect for storing extra gear. We didn't intend to be in the cave for more than two hours, so we left our water, extra clothes and snacks outside with the packs.

Al, the experienced gung-ho caver, dropped to his stomach and started crawling head first under the boulder. When he was up to his shoulders in the entrance, he changed his mind about his approach, and turned around and made a second attempt feet first. He slipped in easily up to his shoulders, and after some struggling, he squeezed through and disappeared into the cave.

Watching Al squeeze under that boulder made me a little wary. My shoulders were broader than Al's, and my chest was deeper. My broad-framed muscular physique would be a hindrance in this situation.

Taking advantage of my reluctance, Brent quickly slithered his slender, trim body under the boulder.

After Brent made it into the cave, it was my turn. I passed my battery pack and hard hat down to Brent. Feet first, on my back, I squirmed back and forth, working my chest and shoulders through the opening. After exhaling all of my air, I finally slid beneath the boulder with my arms stretched above my head. Inside, the passage sloped steeply downward, and gravity was a great help on the way in. It would be just the opposite on the way out and I immediately wondered how I would get back out again.

Inside it was dark and muddy. Before I could react, I started sliding helplessly into the cave's throat. I couldn't see or hear anything. I scratched at the walls and floor for anything to grab, but there was nothing. Then, several feet into the cave, I rammed into a stone wall. It was a median between two passages. Hitting the wall feet-first saved me from injury; my legs absorbed the impact like springs. After recovering from the mishap, I looked around for my partners. There was barely enough light to see by. I heard Al off to my left. I looked just in time to catch a glimpse of his feet sliding over the edge of a dropoff. Off to my right, Brent was working further into the main passage; his head was stuck into a restricted passage as he probed for the best route into the depths of the cave.

Before going any farther, I went back up to retrieve my hard hat and head lamp. The entrance passage was just high enough to allow me to stand upright. After fetching my gear, I returned to the "Y" to help explore the cave. The light from my head lamp was dim, but it was enough to see by.

Brent and Al attacked the cave like two groundhogs sniffing for food. Brent was buried up to his waist inside the constricting main passage, and Al had slipped off into a pit a few feet down the left passage. I thought Al might be injured; he had been in a precarious position the last time I caught a glimpse of him. On my hands and knees, I crawled down the constricting left passage to see what had happened to him. I stopped at the edge of a circular pit and peered over the edge. Al was standing safely in the bottom of the pit. The passage dead-ended there. Al's headfirst approach to the pit amazed me; it was at least six feet deep. After thoroughly searching for leads (continuing passages), we returned to the main passage to join Brent.

Brent was energetically pulling loose rocks from the blocked main passage. He looked like a badger digging a burrow. At that point, the passage was only two feet in diameter, blocked by debris that someone had intentionally rolled into the cave to block the passage. Someone didn't want adventure-seekers like us in that cave.

We spent an hour re-opening the main passage. Most of the debris was manageable-sized rocks. We dug them out and stuffed them into cracks alongside the passage.

After opening the entrance, we faced another tight passage with a ceiling height of eighteen inches. Single file, we crawled on our bellies through the compressed passage. Frightening thoughts flashed through my mind while I was sandwiched between the massive, cold slabs of stone. I felt uncomfortable being in such a tight place. I don't know which scared me the most, the fear of being crushed, or the fear of being entrapped. I wasn't claustrophobic, but the small space was getting to me. I hoped I wouldn't have to crawl much farther.

I overcame my fear by thinking pleasant thoughts. Then I wormed my way into a small chamber on the other side of the restricted passage. Two passages continued from that chamber: one of them was like a two-foot diameter pipe that snaked back and forth, tapering narrower and narrower; the other lead went straight a few feet, then dropped off into an uncomfortably narrow bottleneck passage. Neither of the two leads looked very promising. Brent and I pushed down the snaking lead as far as we could until it tapered down to an impassable diameter of about six inches. We couldn't turn around, so we had to crawl backward back to the last chamber. That left only one other passage, which we hoped would continue. We were having fun in the mud, and were getting our hearts into the mucky, messy fun of caving. We weren't ready to quit yet.

With hopes high, we pushed on down the last passage. At first it looked good, but soon it turned for the worse, tapering down into an impassible bottleneck. But there was a glimmer of hope beyond the bottleneck; the passage appeared to widen, then turn out of sight. The bottleneck walls were made of a sand and clay mixture. With some digging tools, it might be possible to widen the passage enough to get through.

Unfortunately, we didn't have the time or equipment to initiate a worthwhile digging effort. So, it seemed, the lower chamber would be the end of our Coal Chute Cave adventure. But there was a grain of hope for a future return expedition. The passage might open up into a large passage beyond the bottleneck. We could discover a whole new section of cave! It would put us into the book of cave explorers. That glimmer of hope was enough to charge us with the motivation to make a return trip.

Before returning to the surface, we shut off our lamps and experienced total darkness. A nyctophobe would have gone insane. It was a strange, unique experience to be in total darkness with our eyes wide open. Aside from the sound of our breathing the cave was also completely silent. It was very strange. I wondered what it would be like if we had to find our way without lights. A few minutes of silent darkness was enough for me. I was too accustomed to sensing constantly sights and sounds. I sighed with relief when our head lamps flicked back on.

Brent and Al crawled out of the cave ahead of me. The dreaded squeeze under the boulder lurked ahead. I knew that I would need help getting past the boulder. It was a tight squeeze up a steep, slippery incline.

Brent slipped out almost effortlessly. Al had some trouble, but managed to get out without help. I started out all right, then I started slipping. I couldn't get any leverage to propel myself upward. I couldn't even get far enough to see daylight. Luckily, Brent and Al were there to pull me out by my arms. It felt good to see natural, abundant light again. Coated with mud, we looked like mudmonsters from the bowels of earth.

Back at the university, Brent and I couldn't get our minds off Coal Chute Cave. We wanted to go back in to enlarge the bottleneck passage. For the next week our minds ran wild with imagination. I conjured visions of a new network bigger than any other cave system in Wyoming. Through the bottleneck passage we would tap into a great cave system filled with subterranean wonders. Images of subterranean waterfalls, great chambers, walk-through passages with cathedral ceilings, underground rivers, hot springs and amazing stalactites and stalagmites danced through my thoughts. And above all, I hoped to tap into a stream of endless adventure!

By the end of another week of studying, taking tests and listening to lectures, it was time to get out of the stuffy academic environment. Saturday night we met in Brent's and my room. Al showed up with a green military duffel bag full of gear and a new recruit named Rich. We quickly checked the equipment inventory before departing for the cave.

During the hour drive, we talked about the relatively small cave as if it was something really big, fully charging our motivational batteries. By the time we parked the car, we were primed for adventure. I thought we would sprint to the entrance the instant the car stopped. It wasn't quite that dramatic; we hiked briskly to the cave.

We quickly slid under the boulder and slithered into the depths of the dingy cave. Once down in the chamber, we went straight to work on the bottlenecked passage. It was only wide enough for one person to dig at the front end. Brent volunteered to take the first digging shift.

It was tedious, time-consuming work. Brent worked upside down on his belly, with barely enough space to breathe. He passed the soil up an incline back to me. I, in turn, took the dirt from Brent and relayed it back down the tight passage to Rich. At the end of the line, Al had it the easiest. He was able to stand upright in the comfort of the chamber. For two hours we worked like miners digging for the mother lode, taking turns digging, passing and dumping the muck. Curiosity was the fuel that kept our flames burning so intensely.

Of course, there wasn't a mother lode down there. The only remotely possible reward for us would be to find an additional passage. Then we would be able to explore more cave. If we were really lucky we would discover two or three new passages, and would be the first to explore those virgin passages.

At first we made some progress and removed buckets of dirt. But the bottleneck was longer than we had thought. Instead of opening up beyond the bottleneck, the narrow passage continued and digging only revealed more narrow passage. We would have to enlarge the entire passage to continue. Our meager progress transformed into futile madness. We found ourselves digging our own cave, rather than simply tapping into a new passage. Finally, our fires flickered out. Soaked in muddy sweat, exhausted and discouraged, we finally abandoned our digging operation. The small passage continued on, but how far? It might make a turn and end. Or, it might make a turn and open into something bigger. Whatever lay beyond that point was out of our reach. It would have to remain a mystery.

Our efforts that evening—sane or insane—were fueled by the shared desire to explore the unknown, to go where no one else had been, to see something that no one else had seen, and—if we were extremely lucky—to find a new cave network. We left Coal Chute Cave that evening with nothing to show for our efforts. We went back to campus with sore muscles and memories. The muscles recovered in two days, but we will always have the memories.

Δ

Even though our efforts that evening were in vain, the experience was worthwhile. My memories of that crazy evening in that dingy cave are still clear. I will always remember the spirit of adventure that brought us together to face unknown challenges.

Exploring Coal Chute Cave added caving to my mountain adventure repertoire. Caving allows me to venture into the insides of mountains, giving me an even better understanding of the mountain environment. Mountaineering and caving are clearly distinguished as separate recreational activities, yet they have many similarities. Many caves are located in mountainous areas, and many of the same skills used in mountaineering are also used in caving. Since the focus of this book is on mountain recreational activities, I felt compelled to include mountain caving. So be it. For now, I will return the memories of Coal Chute Cave to my Rocky Mountain adventure memory file, and I will open up the Cave Creek Cave file.

Cave Creek Cave

CAVE CREEK CAVE was the second cave in which I ventured. It was much more challenging than Coal Chute Cave, and was a good second step up in spelunking experience. Compared to other caves of the world, it is not a highly difficult or very large cave. But, for me, it was a good advancement.

Cave Creek Cave is nestled in the Shirley Mountains of south-eastern Wyoming. The Shirley Mountains are an island of mountains, surrounded by a sea of rolling, sagebrush-covered hills northwest of Medicine Bow, Wyoming. The North Platte River separates them from their mother range, the Granite Mountain Uplift. They are neighbors to numerous other scattered Wyoming mountain ranges, and one of about twenty-seven separate mountain clusters and ranges that are randomly distributed across Wyoming.

Our spirits were high when we left the university on that crisp, cool October morning. After six weeks of studying, we wanted to get off campus, and into the mountains. We made the drive in my blue 1967 Ford Fairlane. A jeep would have been ideal. And my roommate's four-wheel drive would have done better. He even offered to let us take it. I wish that we had. But somehow, my old low-sitting car made the journey across sagebrush, snow and mountain.

Three of us went on the adventure: Al, Brent and myself. Al was the only one who knew how to get to Cave Creek Cave; he had delved into its depths several years before. Cave Creek Cave would be Brent's and my advancement from Coal Chute Cave; it was the test cave to see if we were ready to advance from greenhorn to recreational caver. We were aching to venture into a more challenging cave. We were also in dire need of some relief from classroom fever. We were long overdue for a healthy taste of the great outdoors.

Al told us all about the cave during our three-hour road trip. Cave Creek Cave was, and continues to be, carved by rapidly flowing water. Every spring, melting mountain snow swells the nearby creek and floods the cave. Cave Creek once flowed into the cave; several years ago it was diverted away from the entrance sink by a man-made canal. Even so, a substantial head of water collects in the sink and floods the cave annually. Heavy snowfall in fall, winter and spring often buries the sink entrance.

The Shirley Mountains had already received a mid-fall snow, but snow or no snow, autumn is the prime time to explore the cave. The entrance is buried by snow in the winter and spring, and during the summer the cave is subject to flooding from heavy thunderstorms.

We prepared for the worst. We were well accustomed to the fickle weather of the Rocky Mountain region. An early blizzard or a heavy thunderstorm was a distinct possibility during October. I packed a daypack with a heavy coat, a sweatshirt, extra socks, gloves, a raincoat, water, food, two flashlights, matches and a hardhat with a head lamp. We also carried maps of the cave (mapped by the Vedauwoo Student Grotto in 1969 and 1973). Al held the all-important topographic map showing the cave's location.

The sky was cloudless, the air cool, and the ever-present Wyoming wind blew across the high plains as we drove north on highway 287. Driving across the wide-open Wyoming plains was extremely exciting. The territory between Laramie and the Shirley Mountains is very desolate. In one ninety-mile stretch we passed through three towns whose combined population was 1,500. Between the towns we drove across vast stretches of sagebrush-covered hills populated by herds of cattle and antelope. The hills rolled on to the horizon in every direction.

If the landscape was harsh, barren and rugged, the climate was equally harsh and relentless. The dynamic weather patterns could turn a clear sky into a stormy sky in thirty minutes or less. Thick-stemmed sagebrush plants exemplified the ruggedness required to survive in the harsh environment. Sagebrush stems are so tough that cowboys and pioneers have used them for firewood.

Caving

Wyoming's high plains bridge the gaps between numerous scattered mountain ranges. The high plains provide the base from which the mountains majestically rise, and a distinct contrast sets the mountains apart from the plains.

After two hours on the highway, we had passed six cars and a thousand antelope. The Shirley Mountains were in sight. They stood majestically apart from the plains, providing the focal relief my eyes needed desperately. The road leading to the mountains was a bump-riddled gravel road. It wound steadily upward through the foothills to the base of the mountain range.

I had camped in the Shirley Mountains on several trips with my parents. They had taken me on a hunting and camping trip there when I was a young tyke. My memories of that trip are just fuzzy images of our campsite; my clearest image is of Mom cooking breakfast on a portable gas stove. We were huddled around the stove, wearing coats, gloves and stocking hats. Dad and I slept in a pup tent, and Mom slept in the car, because she didn't want to sleep on the hard ground. I remember one night when I snuck up to the car window and growled like a bear. Mom screamed! She was really scared, until she saw that it was me. I dashed back to the tent and slid in next to Dad.

Dad and I camped in the Shirley Mountains on two or three other hunting trips. I was older then, and I remember more of those later trips. I especially remember how much I enjoyed camping out. I enjoyed the camping, climbing and exploring much more than the hunting. I liked looking for the ideal campsite and setting camp. I looked for campsites that were surrounded by trees, near a stream and close to large boulders or cliffs. The instant Dad parked the pickup, I would bolt out the door to scout the area. To receive my approval, a campsite had to have trees to hide behind, a stream to listen to and rocks to climb. I timed my exploring excursions so that Dad had most of the camp-setting chores done before I returned. At night, I enjoyed listening to howling coyotes. I enjoyed it most when I was safely snuggled next to Dad in the camper. Those are still fond memories. The Shirley Mountains will always have a special, sentimental meaning to me.

It had been nearly a decade since my last trip to the Shirley Mountains. As we neared the mountains and I began to recognize landmarks, my joyful memories of those times with my family resurfaced, and I enjoyed them as we bounced up the deteriorating mountain road.

The Shirley Mountains support a unique environment, distinctly different from the surrounding plains. Their towering height allows them to capture more precipitation to support a lusher environment than on the plains. The pine trees, diverse wildlife and unique geographical features contrast beautifully with the surrounding plains.

Even though we found the mountains, we were far from finding the cave. The Shirley Mountains cover a large expanse of Carbon County. Our only means of finding the cave were Al's fuzzy memory and a topographic map. First, we had to find something on the map that we could correlate with the actual landscape in order to pinpoint our location on the map. Then we could proceed toward the cave. That was much easier said than done. Brent and I had assumed too much when we assumed that Al could at least get us to the right topographic quadrant.

My faith in Al's memory waned as we bounced along the rough road in a state of bewilderment. The further we went, the more confused we became. Al couldn't recognize any landmarks, and Brent and I couldn't match the topography with anything on the map. It was stop and go for several miles. We would stop, study the map, examine the terrain, then continue on. The only thing we could confirm definitely was that we were in Wyoming. At times we doubted what county we were in.

Finally, Al recognized a crossroad that led up into the mountains. He was sure that it led to the cave. Coincidentally, that road was the same road that went to the campsite of my childhood memories. The road conditions didn't look good; less than a half mile up, the muddy, steep road was buried in snowdrifts. We made it far enough to see my childhood campsite, but that was it. The studded snowtires quickly lost traction and spun helplessly on the slippery, steep road. The snow was too deep even for a four-wheel-drive with chains. We were forced to retreat back to the loop road.

Al was positive, however, that the road led to the cave, and swore it was the road he had taken to the cave on a previous trip. But that didn't help us. According to the map there was another road to the cave; we just had to find that road. Unfortunately, there were several roads and jeep trails that matched the map's description; many of them were not shown on the map. With a detailed topographic map, the cave should have been easy to find, but it wasn't.

Al was still the only one who knew what the terrain surrounding the cave looked like. Unfortunately, the entire mountain range looked like the terrain surrounding the cave.

After driving west much farther than we realized, we turned off on a jeep trail that looked like the other way to the cave. We followed that trail as far as we could with the car. Three miles into the mountains the car spun-out on a steep incline. We were forced to strike out on foot. We were sure that the cave would be just up the road a mile or two.

With canteens strapped to our waists and our essential gear stowed in daypacks on our backs, we struck out to find the cave. We still couldn't positively pinpoint our position on the map; every time one of us found a discrepancy between the surroundings and the map, another of us countered it with a peak or stream that seemed to correlate exactly with the map. We played an ongoing game of rationalizing the certainty of our location. Each time we convinced ourselves of our location, we went a little farther. There were enough similarities between the map and the surrounding terrain to keep us hiking most of the day.

Then we found a creek that we thought was Cave Creek, so we followed it up a valley, hoping to find the cave along the way. We hiked through some remote wilderness. Along the way we came across the ruins of an old ranch. Part of a cabin was still standing, and rusty machine parts were scattered about the site. No one had lived there for many years. We guessed it was an early 1900s homestead.

The creek flowed swiftly with ice-cold, clear water. While crossing it, we saw a school of rainbow trout swimming upstream. They were beautiful, as their silverish scales glimmered in the sunlight.

Anxiously searching for the cave, we hiked and hiked deeper into the unfamiliar wilderness. It was as if we were hiking under the influence of a bewildering trance. Despite being unable to pinpoint positively our location on the map, we wouldn't admit that we might be lost.

Finally, after hiking several miles, we stopped again to compare the map with the surroundings. We each admitted to being temporarily dumbfounded. We looked at each other in a stupor, then concluded that we were in the wrong topographic quadrant. We were possibly ten or fifteen miles west of Cave Creek Cave. We were disgruntled, hungry and wasting precious daylight. On a grassy knoll, between two converging streams, we broke for lunch.

We kept our composure and maintained a sense of humor about the whole affair. Brent and I jokingly made Al the scapegoat, but each of us was partly responsible for our mishaps. We were all equally guilty of improperly reading the topographic map. There was nothing to get mad about. There were other, more immediate problems on which to concentrate.

Suddenly, the early afternoon sky began to darken with clouds. They could bear snow or rain in a wide range of quantities; anything from a blizzard to a crackling thunderstorm could hit us before we returned the car. Then, a cold gust of wind blew a subliminal message across our faces; the message told us to "get moving." My instincts said the same thing.

Without delay, we finished our lunch and backtracked toward the car. The clouds quickly merged together. The sky grew darker, and the temperature dropped steadily. The colder it got, the faster we walked. The air felt cold and moist, like before a snow.

When we were two miles from the car, it started snowing. We had crossed the creek and were climbing the valley wall. The descent into the valley was easy, but the ascent proved to be a vigorous cardiovascular workout. The harder it snowed, the faster we climbed. It was an uphill race to beat the weather.

The sky was white with falling snowflakes, and a thin layer of

Caving

white covered the ground. The snow fell steadily. As we topped the valley, the steady snow transformed to flurries. One minute it was snowing and the next minute it quit. The snow flurries continued throughout our hike back to the car.

Shortly after we reached the car, the clouds dissipated. Within minutes the sky began to clear. Rays from the late afternoon sun pierced the scattered clouds.

That bright sunshine pierced our tired souls and instilled a new glimmer of hope inside of us. Disappointed and chapfallen, we drove back to the main road. The sun was low in the sky behind us. It seemed as if our quest for Cave Creek Cave was going to end in failure. We were on the main road, driving toward the highway back to Laramie, when the full effects of the rejuvenating sunshine started to sprout inside of our spirits. Until that magical moment, our spirits had been crushed; our bodies were tired, and we hadn't set foot in the cave. Then, like a growing fire, our spirits began to rage with new-found hope.

We each had similar feelings. We couldn't go back without exploring that cave. Quitting meant accepting defeat. We couldn't quit! We had too much time invested in our weekend excursion. Unfortunately, we hadn't solved the problem of finding the cave.

Then, in a flash of intellectual amazement, Al got a brilliant idea! He said, "Let's go to a ranch and ask one of the locals how to get to the cave."

I slammed on the brakes, slid the car to a halt and turned around. We had just passed a ranch house a few hundred yards back.

Brent and I stayed in the car while Al walked to the house to ask for directions (something we should have done to start with). While we waited for Al to return, we told jokes about our fiasco. After thirty minutes passed, we were sure that Al had been invited to stay for dinner. Finally, Al emerged from the ranch house.

After he returned to the car I asked him. "How was dinner?"

"Didn't have any," he said.

"How was the cake and coffee?" I ribbed.

"Didn't have that either."

He had had a friendly chat with the rancher. The rancher not only knew about the cave, he had been in it. He gave Al directions for another road to the cave. It had recently snowed several inches, but this west access road normally didn't collect as much snow as the other road.

We drove back around the base of the mountains, past the campground access road, to the west access road. The road began at the base of the mountain as a narrow, double-rutted jeep trail across a grassy pasture. From there it gradually went up into the Shirley Mountains. It was marked by an abandoned two-story house east of the jeep trail near a creek. It was dusk when we started up the rugged road.

It was a very rough road for a four-door passenger car to endure. Near the beginning of the road there was a large hump that high-centered the car. We had to find two sturdy boards to use as a ramp to get over the hump. Fortunately, we found the boards and made it safely over the obstacle. Rocks scraped underneath; sage brush scratched the sides; and the tires were scarred by sharp-edged rocks. The grade was steep, but not steep enough to stall the car. We drove as far as we could, until we were stopped by a waist-high snow drift across the road at the edge of a forest. By then it was dark, but we were confident that we were on the map. We were about one mile from the cave. Once again, we gathered our gear together and struck out on foot into the nighttime mountain wilderness.

Starlight, reflecting off of the snow-covered ground, provided enough light by which to travel. In most places the snow was only a few inches deep; the large drifts were in the lower areas, like on the road. By hiking on higher, windswept ground, we kept our feet dry. According to the map, the road passed right by the cave entrance. The surrounding vegetation consisted of a natural blend of aspen and pine trees. Along the way we hiked through a shallow glen. For once, the actual topography correlated with the map. We were hiking in the right direction. We were within a half mile of the sinkhole cave entrances.

After our day of misadventures, I was very excited to be about to

Caving

find the long-sought cave. I hoped that it was worth all of the effort.

Then, after hiking for a while along Cave Creek itself, we came to a sinkhole in a grove of aspens on the other side of the then-dry creek. The sinkhole was about twenty feet in diameter and fifteen feet deep, with several fallen trees lying criss-crossed in it. The sides consisted of loose rock and soil, except for the south side (at the mountain base), which was a granite wall with a few indentations, crevices and a wide, crack-like opening at the bottom. That opening was the main cave entrance!

I was the first one to slide down the sides of the sink into the ankle-deep snow on the bottom. I stepped into the entrance and peered inside. It was cold and coal black. I could only see a few feet into the narrow, granite-walled passage. The passage sloped downward. Streaks of ice filled cracks and crevices where water had flowed down the cave walls.

Brent was equally excited to get into the cave. He was on my heels right into the entrance. Al, the veteran caver, wasn't as excited. Brent crowded past me as I looked for a place to stow excess gear. Brent quickly donned his hardhat and turned on the head lamp. While he was exploring the entrance passage, I donned my hardhat and prepared to explore the cave. For backup lights, I stuffed two flashlights in my pockets.

After double-checking our equipment, we started into the cave. Al led us inside where the narrow width of the passage forced us to proceed single file. The ceiling height started at a comfortable seven feet, then quickly tapered down to a mere two feet.

We could see our breath in the faint light from our headlamps. The first section of the passage was like a walk-in freezer hewn from granite and ice. We had to walk cautiously to avoid slipping on the spotty patches of ice. As the ceiling height decreased, we were forced to crawl, on elbows and knees, along an ice-covered floor. In places the cave walls were also coated with white sheets of ice.

Knowing a little about caves and the earth's temperature, I knew that it would warm up as we went farther into the cave. I was so sure that it would warm up that I wore only a double layer of long-sleeve shirts. A coat would be too bulky to fit through the tight squeezes that Al warned we would have to negotiate.

The cave walls, ceiling and floor were very irregularly shaped, vastly different from a man-made mine or tunnel. It was a small, wild cave; very different from the commercialized caves with guided tours, such as the famous Mammoth Caves of Kentucky, or Colorado's Cave of the Winds. The passage width and ceiling height varied continuously as we ventured through the cave. There were only a few sections high enough to walk through upright. We spent most of our time crawling on elbows and knees, or, in the worst cases, on our stomachs.

Thirty feet into the cave and four feet below the entrance elevation, we came to a four-way intersection. The three intersecting passages were too tight to enter and appeared to peter out, so we pushed onward through the main passage. The next stretch of passage was tall and narrow, a vertical fissure between two gargantuan slabs of granite, and we had to walk sideways to get past.

I was fortunate to have a hardhat. It was difficult to see the numerous protruding rocks in the dim light that our head lamps provided, and I already had dinged my head against the hard walls and ceiling twice since we began. The light from the headlamps flickered and danced against the irregular shapes of the walls, casting strange shadows that played tricks with my eyes. Even if we had had brighter lights, the frequent jogs and twists of the cave made it impossible to see more than twenty feet ahead.

About a hundred feet into the cave, we came to a chaotic intersection of several passages on two different levels. Some of the passages led away at the same elevation as the main passage, and some split off at an upper level. Several of the leads showed potential. We agreed to check them on the way out. Beyond the multiple intersection, the ceiling of the main passage tapered down again, and we were forced to crawl on our stomachs, like worms.

Sandwiched between two layers of cold, damp granite, I inched forward. The floor had painfully sharp ripples carved into it, probably from the eroding effects of flowing water over thousands of years. The rough surfaces scraped and bruised my knees. Knee pads would have been very beneficial; Al, of course, was the only team member to have such a thing. He had forewarned Brent and me to get some, but we had failed in our efforts at scavenging or borrowing them. On penniless college-student budgets, we couldn't even afford to buy any equipment. Hence, we had to bear the pain of having unprotected knees.

Midway through that tight section, while sandwiched between two slabs of granite, I almost lost my composure. A moment of normally subdued, subconscious claustrophobic fear surfaced. Suddenly, I became concerned about being deep inside a mountain beneath a million tons of rock. I became preoccupied with horrifying thoughts of escaping, flooding and earthquakes. I felt trapped and confined. What if I had to get out fast? There were no quick exits to the outside. Unlike exiting a building, I couldn't just walk down a corridor or ride to the surface in an elevator. What if I got stuck? My pulse quickened, and I nearly worked myself into a state of panic. I desperately needed some openness. I had to get out of that dreadfully tight section to calm myself. For a few minutes my mind ran wild with claustrophobic thoughts driven by the extreme confinement of the cave.

Al squirmed along quickly. He was far ahead of Brent and me. I couldn't hear him or see the light of his carbide head lamp. Brent lagged a few feet behind me. He was busy satisfying his irresistible curiosity; he crawled into every intersecting passage that he could. But he and I had to be within about twenty feet of each other, because I could still hear him.

Squirming faster and breathing harder, I shouted ahead, "Al!"

I heard a faint and muffled, "What?"

"How far until I can stand up?"

His muffled answer reassured me: "Not far, I am standing now."

That was enough to help me recover from my minor attack of claustrophobia. On my belly, with my arms stretched in front of me, I feverishly inched across the painfully jagged cave floor toward higher ceilings and relief.

My sense of direction was gone. Directions, relative to myself—

front and back, left and right, up and down—were the only ones to which I could relate. The downward slope of the cave was too gradual to notice in most places. From the map, I knew that we were about twelve feet below the entrance elevation.

Al was gone by the time I made it to the stand-up area. I was relieved to get off of my stomach for a while. Al had forged on ahead. He went through the cave like water through a pipe, despite having a small beer belly.

Beyond the tight passage, I took a few minutes to recover. I noticed another passage intersecting the main passage. According to the map, it connected with the second entrance sink. Before Brent could catch up with me, I pushed forward into the next section. Then the three of us were about twenty feet apart.

The high ceiling of relief quickly tapered down again, and I was forced to crawl on my hands and sore knees. Again, the cave floor was jagged and relentlessly hard. Water stains on the walls revealed that the cave recently flooded.

Then I entered another vertical crevice-like section, whose narrow width forced me to walk sideways. It was barely wider than the depth of my chest, but the ceiling was 18 feet above. At times, I had to exhale to get my forty-two inch chest through the passage. Beyond that vertical squeeze I came to the Crossroads: an intersection with two upper passages at right angles to each other. The Crossroads were shown on the map as not fully surveyed passages. They definitely had potential. They might or might not lead to other sections of virgin passage.

At that time I was not interested in exploring the Crossroads. Instead, I pushed onward down the main passage. Along the way there were several passages splitting off from the main passage. Many of them were unsurveyed. Most of them were too tight to crawl through, but a few of them had potential.

History Hall offered the first real relief. It was the largest chamber in the cave. It was roughly thirty feet wide, two hundred feet long, and twelve feet high. The walls of History Hall were scratched with the names and dates of past visitors. Some of them dated to the early 1800s, when Wyoming was just a territory.

We regrouped in History Hall. We also rested and checked our equipment. Al recharged his carbide lamp with carbon and water. Brent and I checked the wiring on our battery-powered head lamps. Without head lamps or flashlights, it would be next to impossible to get out of the cave. Matchlight would only be slightly better than wandering in the dark. Makeshift torches would probably work if we could keep them burning long enough. Unlike the movies, we wouldn't have conveniently prepositioned torches to use either. Without any light, we would probably die of exposure before finding our way out.

Before leaving History Hall, Al warned, "Be careful not to step in any water. Pools of water are hard to see."

His advice was well taken. I, for one, did not want the nagging discomfort of wet feet. Either inside the cave or outside in the snow, wet feet would be extremely uncomfortable. It would also increase our chances of contracting hypothermia.

We continued in single file. Al pointed out a water pool at the far end of History Hall. It proved his point. The water was so clear and calm that it was almost invisible; I had to touch it to believe it. We maneuvered around the pool and left History Hall.

The passage became wet and narrow. Moments later we were stopped by a seemingly unsurpassable obstacle. The passage before us was partially flooded! We couldn't tell how deep it was. Wading wasn't a rational option anyway. The passage walls above the water were steep and jagged, and zigzagged and curved out of sight. The condition of the passage beyond was unknown. The water posed an interesting challenge. Our only reasonable alternative was to chimney along the passage walls, above the water, but one slip or misplaced foot would spell disaster.

Al straddled the flooded passage first, followed by Brent, then myself. Mud, from the bottoms of our shoes, made the rock walls especially slippery. Handholds and footholds were scarce, and our faint lights compounded the difficulty of finding good holds.

Then, midway through, I heard a splash in front of me! Brent had slipped. He struggled to keep from falling completely into the water. Fortunately, only one foot slipped into the cold water. His other foothold and two handholds kept him from falling farther. A fall by any of us would force us all to abort the expedition and return to the car. A good adventure team or climbing team never jeopardizes the safety of a team member for the sake of reaching an objective. Our body temperatures were already dropping, due to the constant cool temperature of the cave (about fifty-five degrees Fahrenheit). In relatively dry clothes with constant movement, we kept warm; with wet clothes, our body temperatures would rapidly plummet. If we got soaked we would have to go quickly to a source of heat, such as the car's heater.

Finally, after chimneying for several minutes, we made it safely over the flooded passage. From there the passage became a tall, narrow crevice again. A new challenge confronted us. The passage precariously split into an upper and lower level, one on top of the other. A narrow gap in the floor of the upper passage dropped down to the lower passage. Despite the hazard posed by the gap, the upper passage was more appealing because it was wider. I straddled the gap, and crawled through the upper passage. If we slipped, we would fall eight to ten feet onto the rocky bottom of the lower passage.

Midway through the treacherous bi-level passage, we came to another unsurveyed passage that split off to the west. It continued as far as we could see, at least fifteen feet. It could open up and continue as another good passage. We wanted to explore it, but it would have to wait until after we finished the main passage. At that juncture, Brent decided to take the wetter, lower passage while Al and I continued on the upper level.

Exploring the subterranean world was a unique experience. There was no natural light, no plants, no wind and no weather. It was profoundly quiet. Occasionally I heard a squeaking bat, some dripping water or a falling rock. It was peaceful, yet eerie. We were now sixty feet below the entrance and separated from the outside world by a mountain of granite and hundreds of feet of snaking passage behind us. We were crawling deeper and deeper into the bowels of the mountain, farther and farther from our native environments on the surface.

Caving

I began thinking about how powerless we were against the awesome forces of nature. One cave-in could entrap us; a freak thunderstorm could flood the cave and drown us; a driving blizzard could leave us stranded to freeze to death; a slight tremor could crush us. But facing unpredictable risks is what separates adventure from the norm. Caves, mountains, rivers, forests, canyons and other natural features are all potentially fatal attractions. They all hide dangerous challenges and risks behind their enticing beauty. Adventurers who rise up to meet the challenges and surpass the risks are rewarded with personal satisfaction and unforgettable memories.

Below us, Brent emerged from the Dead Marsh Land of the lower passage. The passages converged back together. Then we walked into the Tokyo Philosophers Room, named for the Japanese writing scratched on its walls. This was to be the end of our journey. The cave continued, but recent flooding had blocked the connecting passage with mud. The mud-filled section was a natural siphon. It could contain tons of mud. There was no way to continue without initiating a major dredging operation. We discussed the possibility of making a return trip to try digging our way through the mud-filled section, but the discussion served more to satisfy our delusions of grandeur than to consider a plausible option.

We stopped for a much-needed rest. Al seized the opportunity to pull some grub from his knapsack. He broke out a can of pudding and spooned it into his mouth. It was like a picnic for Al; a regular outing. Why didn't I think of packing something like that? There we sat, enjoying our Saturday evening in a dingy, dark cavern sixty feet below the entrance and over one thousand feet into a mountain. Our clothes were coated with mud. We were tired, and still had to make the return journey. As Brent's and my stomachs growled, Al calmly slurped down his can of pudding.

Al looked entirely too smug, and I was compelled to rattle him. I asked him about a dreadful scenario that I had thought of. "What would you do if it was pouring rain outside, and a growing stream started gushing through the cave?"

Of course, Brent and Al said that they would make a gallant effort to get back to the entrance. We might have a chance if we followed the highest routes. We were silent for a while, as we thought out the terrifying scenario. We could probably make it back to the tight section with the two-foot ceiling. There, we would face a wall of gushing water with no way around it. We let it end at that.

Next, Al convinced Brent and me that we needed to experience total darkness and silence. So we shut off our lamps and kept quiet. Instantly, we were engulfed by pitch-black darkness. It was strange to have my eyes wide open and yet be unable to see anything. This was the cave's natural state. It was very different from our active world of sights and sounds. I concentrated on "listening" to my other senses. The air smelt musty, and the rock that I sat on felt cold, rough and hard. Few creatures were capable of living inside such an uninviting environment.

What if our lights wouldn't click back on, I thought. Without light, we would be hopelessly lost; it is doubtful that we could find our way back to the surface. We would have to wander through too many branching passages, dead-end passages, rises and falls and zigzags.

My fears subsided after we clicked our lamps back on. They still worked. We weren't living some nightmare in which everything went wrong. It was further proof that Murphy's Law didn't always apply. Thank God.

We stayed a while longer. We sat in a triangle and rehashed the day's events and blunders. We laughed at ourselves for a few minutes, then we adjusted our gear and started the journey back to the surface. There were several unmapped leads that we wanted to push, but it was getting late. Time always seemed to work against us. We were concerned that our friends back at the university might get worried about us and call the authorities to search for us. Brent's girlfriend, Gayle, was probably concerned about our whereabouts, especially since we were supposed to be back before nightfall.

The return journey went faster or seemed to go faster. There were several tempting leads branching off from the main passage, but we would have to wait for a return trip to explore them. Brent and I were optimistic that those branches opened up into new unexplored passages. From past experiences, Al knew that most of the leads pinched off.

The return journey was uneventful. We retreated from the cave's depths as quickly as possible. As we neared the entrance, the air became colder—a sure sign that we were almost back to the surface. We emerged from the subterranean world, into the familiar sink. The Wyoming wind blew across the pine tops, barely rustling the branches. The sky was clear and dotted with a spectacular array of stars. The starlight, reflecting off of the snow-covered ground, provided enough light by which to travel. It felt good to see the stars and walk upright again.

On the trek back to the car we made plans for a return visit the following year. We wanted to explore those unmapped leads. And maybe the spring runoff would flush the siphon clean, opening access to the remaining third of the cave. We looked forward to returning to Cave Creek Cave.

Even though the day started out terribly and almost ended in complete failure, our relentless determination for adventure made the day a success. Satisfied with the adventure, we left the Shirley Mountains in good spirits. We had plenty of things to talk about during the tiresome drive back to Laramie.

Δ

The following fall, we returned to Cave Creek Cave. We took three newcomers with us, including my wife to be. To our disappointment, the siphon was still plugged with mud. Brent and I crawled into every lead we could find and pushed them as far as we could. As anticipated, most of the leads pinched off and became too narrow to explore. Brent and I were last to emerge from the cave. The others weren't as enthusiastic. After crawling up out of the sink, we found everyone else napping on the ground. They were mud covered and baking in the warm sunshine. They were starting to look like adobe statues.

Now I am 1,600 miles from Cave Creek Cave, wondering if I will ever see the Tokyo Philosophers Room again. I certainly hope so.

Caving or spelunking is another Rocky Mountain adventure activity that I enjoy. Caving is not solely a mountain sport. In fact, caves are abundant in many parts of the world. Nearly every state in the United States has at least one cave. After moving to Georgia, my wife and I explored a cave in the Blue Ridge Mountains. There are many caves in Georgia and the surrounding states. No matter where you live, you are probably near some caves.

There are 265 known caves in Colorado, alone. There is also an assortment of lost, treasure and undiscovered caves, offering a wide range of opportunities to everyone from the first-time caver to the extreme caver. For instance, the Cave of the Winds, near Manitou Springs, Colorado, can be enjoyed via a guided walking tour; on the other hand, Marble Mountain's Spanish Cave is very dangerous and requires rope work, wet work and extensive chimney work. The entrance to Spanish Cave (also known as *La Caverna Del Oro*—The Cave of Gold) is above 11,000 feet. It is a very intriguing cave with a mysterious history. It is also a very deadly cave.

Before embarking on any Rocky Mountain adventure activity, you should learn as much as you can about the surrounding environment and attain the necessary adventure skills. Go to the library or bookstore and read about the activity. Talk to an expert. Take a course. Learn the techniques you will have to use. Buy, borrow or rent the necessary equipment. Finally, plan your adventure in as much detail as possible.

Bookstores and libraries are your best sources for additional information on the caves of the Rocky Mountain region. The National Speleological Society is another good source of information. Some of the caving books include directions and maps. Whether you're an armchair enthusiast, an avid caver or just thinking about going caving, your curiosity will inevitably lead you to sources of higher adventure.

7. Exploring

The desire to explore forgotten realms
is in the heart of every adventurer.

NOT KNOWING WHERE we are going, nor what we would encounter, we continued hiking up the wooded mountain valley. This time, we weren't looking for anything in particular, we were just exploring new territory in the Rocky Mountains. We carried daypacks with the bare essentials: food, water and extra clothing. Since we were hiking through Colorado's gold country, we half expected to find the remnants of a mining camp or at least an abandoned mine, but it didn't really matter whether we found anything or not. We enjoyed simply hiking through the wilderness, enjoying nature's unexplored treasures.

After two hours of hiking, we struck paydirt! We found an abandoned cabin, adjacent to a gold mine. It was similar to hundreds of other such sites scattered about in the Rocky Mountains. It dated back to the late 1800s. All that remained were the cabin walls, a few rusty pieces of mining equipment and the mine shaft. At one time, six or seven hardy miners probably lived in the cabin while working the mine. The dream of finding the mother lode kept them returning to the dangerous labors of the mine. If they were like most miners, they probably labored extremely hard and barely found enough gold to keep them going.

Exploring can be a passive or active adventure, depending on what you are exploring. Oftentimes, a passive exploring adventure turns into a dangerous, highly active exploring adventure. Poking around a ghost town or mining camp can be dangerous in itself. Many of these old mining centers are boobytrapped with partially hidden or buried mine shafts. Additionally, the old structures are often shaky from a century of neglect and decay. Even though I have enjoyed many hours of childish fun by exploring abandoned mining camps and mines, I don't recommend that any of you participate in similar adventures. There are plenty of other safe wilderness areas to explore, without exposing yourself to the man-made risks that exist in and around mines. If you are interested in visiting some of the Rocky Mountain mining sites, I highly encourage you to visit some of the ghost towns and restored mining towns. There are many places in the Rocky Mountain region where you can visit and tour mining towns and mines without exposing yourself to unnecessary risk. Some of my favorite places in Colorado are Central City, Idaho Springs, Fairplay, Silverton, Ouray, Leadville, Georgetown and Estes Park. The other Rocky Mountain states also have safe places to explore passively ghost towns and mines.

Aside from exploring ghost towns and mines, it is also fun merely to explore new wilderness areas and features, such as glaciers, remote snowfields, alpine lakes, waterfalls, geysers, hot springs and so on. By explore, I mean to venture into areas that are new to you. With over five billion persons on earth, there are few places that remain undiscovered. Die-hard adventurers can still find undiscovered places, but in another thirty years they will also be hardpressed to find any undiscovered places on earth. At present growth rates, the world population could reach eight billion by the year 2015, within the lifetimes of most of us. So, if you have a burning desire to explore the undiscovered, I suggest that you do it soon.

There are still some opportunities to explore totally undiscovered places, caves, hidden valleys, lost treasures, mother lodes, lost cabins, secluded springs, buried mines and a few other undiscovered attractions dispersed in the vast Rocky Mountain region. However, finding any of those undiscovered places will take more than a passing interest. You will have to do your homework and spend some considerable time looking for your undiscovered item of interest.

Most of the things that I have explored are in the category of "previously discovered attractions." I have happened across some remote cabins and aging mining camps that were quite complete, and relatively untouched since they were abandoned over a century ago. If any others had passed through, they did so without disturbing the sites. We made at least one authentic discovery: Sean and I uncovered the entrance to a mine that had been buried for a questionable period of time, probably since it was originally closed and hidden (more about that later). Considering that the mine was buried, in remote wilderness and surrounded by forest, I consider it to be an authentic discovery. However, most of my exploring amounts to poking, snooping, investigating and photographing ghost towns and remnants of mining camps and mines.

The gold and glory of most of these places are gone. Only the legends, history, and a few remnants remain as hints of the past. While there are a few well-preserved ghost towns, most of them are in ruins. If you decide to "explore," or simply visit these historic sites, don't be discouraged by their deteriorating condition. There are still enough remnants to allow you to recreate a picture of the past. Let your imagination reconstruct the buildings, towns and spirit as they once existed. If you refresh your history before embarking on your exploring adventure, you'll be able to create a better vision of what life was once like in the boisterous mining towns.

There is a vast amount of historical significance contained within the decrepit structures and decaying equipment of the once-booming mining towns. It wasn't until after I saw some ghost towns first-hand that I developed a burning interest in the history of the Old West. During my school days, I hated history; the past seemed insignificant and unimportant. I specifically remember how I dreaded reading about Baby Doe during a junior high school class.

Now I realize how Baby Doe Tabor's life was so representative of the life and times of Colorado's booming gold mining days. She was a millionaire mining queen who experienced boom and bust. History was boring to me because it was taught through words in a book, without any physical link to the past. But after visiting a few historical sites, I began to see the links to the past. I saw how contemporary society evolved from the past. Once I could see some of the things that I read about, it added a physical dimension to the words in the history books. Now, I can't find enough history books to satisfy my curiosity. The more I read about the colorful history of the Rocky Mountain states, the more I like it. If you are a history teacher having problems getting your students interested, I highly recommend taking your class on a field trip to a historical site. Likewise, if you are a history student finding it hard to get interested, I recommend visiting some historical sites.

Although I have explored many areas other than ghost towns and mines, those are the two areas that I selected for this collection. Since I am not yet a world-class explorer with a history of exploring exotic places, I concentrated on two topics that I think you will find the most interesting. Furthermore, I included ghost towns and mines for their historical significance. It is also a good lead-in to the chapter on my prospecting adventures. Hence, this chapter contains two sub-chapters: Ghost Towns and Mines. In the first sub-chapter, you will learn what makes ghost towns interesting and worth exploring. In the second sub-chapter, you will learn about the appealing features of mines, and I will narrate a few of my mine-related adventures.

Ghost Towns

GHOST TOWNS, abandoned mining sites, crumbling timber cabins and other remnants from the colorfully painted gold rush days are gateways to the past. With just an inkling of imagination, the careful observer or explorer can drift into history upon the aura of the ruins. To the passing observer, ghost towns are just crumbling wooden buildings in various states of decay. But, for the curious observers who stop for closer looks, ghost towns are lasting parts of history. They are remnants of past lifestyles. By linking the remnants together with some historical knowledge, the ghost town explorer can take a trip into the past.

Ghost towns were boom towns that sprouted from the rich resources buried in the ground beneath them. The towns played important roles in the discovery of gold, silver, copper, iron and other precious metals. They provided places for the miners to get supplies, to cash-in their gold and to relax from the hard labors of mining. Wherever a series of gold strikes were made, a mining camp or town sprang up shortly afterward. Numerous ghost town books are available at libraries and book stores. These books tell some of the history of the towns, where they can be found and the state in which they are located. Of course, many of those towns are still in existence today. Not all of the boom towns busted. There are many Colorado boom towns that are still full of life today, and some of them are still mining towns. A few of these are Central City, Black Hawk, Jamestown, Ward, Leadville, Cripple Creek, Fairplay, Silverton, Idaho Springs and Georgetown. Some of Wyoming's boom towns that are still alive are Encampment, Albany, Centennial, South Park City and Jelm. These towns, and the many other former mining towns, offer a taste of the past with the comforts of the present. They are good places to visit and gather information about life in the gold rush days. Today, most of these towns survive because of tourism, skiing and their recreational wealth; most of the gold played out many years ago.

Central City is in the heart of Colorado's richest gold district. It was once publicized as "the richest square mile on earth." While there is still some gold trickling from the surrounding mountainsides, Central City's colorful history is its primary resource today. Annually, thousands of visitors crowd into the small mountain town to see the mines, walk the streets, shop in the stores and get a feel for the town's past. Many mountain towns offer mine tours, scenic train rides, horseback riding and gold panning lessons. Believe it or not, there are still many places where you can pan for gold and find some, but don't hold your breath expecting to strike it rich. Most of today's gold panners do it because they enjoy it, not to make a living doing it. I'll tell you more about that in the chapter on prospecting.

While the modern towns are fun to visit, they are not as exciting to explore as ghost towns, which have an aura of the past about them. The architectural remnants, mining relics and serene mountain settings contain information about the past. Some ghost towns are better preserved than others, but, regardless of their conditions, they all have a story to tell to anyone who is willing to listen.

There are three basic types and conditions of ghost towns: restored, protected and natural. Restored ghost towns are very authentic and in excellent condition. South Park City, Colorado, near Fairplay, is a well-restored historic town. Protected ghost towns are in their natural states, but visitors are not allowed inside the structures. Natural ghost towns are unprotected and in their natural states. As you can imagine, natural ghost towns are not in very good condition, but they are the only ones that adventurers are free to explore. By explore, I mean to walk among the structures and look, not touch. High country explorers must be careful not to disturb historical sites; throughout the years many natural ghost towns have been damaged by careless explorers and vandals. Anyone visiting natural ghost-town sites should be sensitive to their historical significance. During my numerous explorations I have discovered many relics that would be nice to have, but for the sake of preserving the sites I have refrained from taking them. Most of the remaining relics are either too big to carry off, or small worthless items such as rusty nails, tin cups and metal plates.

You may wonder why the natural ghost towns aren't protected. The two foremost reasons are because some of them are in remote locations and some of them are already too deteriorated to protect. The remoteness and natural state of the sites are the qualities that attract me and other adventurers to the sites. It is an adventure just getting to some of the abandoned mining sites and ghost towns.

Sometimes you can roll several adventure activities into one while getting to and exploring ghost towns. Reaching some of the sites requires one or more of the following means of transportation: hiking, backpacking, jeep or motorcycle.

The difficulty involved in getting to some of these locations provides insight into the arduous lives that the miners had: they had to carry their provisions and equipment across rugged, mountainous terrain using horses, donkeys and wagons. The roads to these places are often the original, crude roads first made by the miners. The roads are steep, rocky, rutted and dangerously slick after a rainfall. During the winter, traveling to and from remote mining camps was compounded by deep snow, strong winds and freezing temperatures. Rocky Mountain winters, for the old timers, were very demanding.

When exploring a natural ghost town or visiting a restored ghost town, put yourself in a historical mindset. Try to draw a sense of history from the old buildings and rusting machinery that you see. Take a walk through history. The typical passing tourist just marches through, takes a couple pictures, then leaves. Exploring a ghost town is a chance to experience and see part of history. It is an experience that cannot be fully obtained from a dusty history book.

Ghost towns are rooted in the silver and gold mining operations that occurred in and around their perimeters. To get a good understanding of gold rush life, it is imperative to see the places in which the miners worked. Take a commercial tour of a mine. Try your hand at gold panning. There are many Rocky Mountain towns that offer mine tours and gold panning lessons. At the Argo Gold Mill, near Idaho Springs, Colorado, you can tour a restored mine and gold mill. You can see how the gold ore was mined from the mountain, then processed in the mill. From mining the gold ore, to getting the gold out of the ore is basically a fourteen-step process. At the Argo Gold Mill, you can take a self-paced walk-through tour of the entire fourteen-step process.

If you take a walk-through mine tour, you will get a sense of the arduous lives that the miners had. The mines are narrow, with low ceiling heights. They were carved through solid rock with picks, shovels, hammers and dynamite. Tunneling ten to fifteen feet per day was considered good progress. That required breaking up and removing 300 to 450 cubic feet of rock, weighing between twenty-six and thirty-nine tons. Each ore-car held about one ton of rock or ore. If fifteen ounces of gold was produced from 2,000 pounds (one ton) of ore, that was considered a very good gold mine. Of course, very few mines yielded gold in such high concentrations. Most miners yielded five ounces of gold or less per ton of ore. However, that was very good compared to modern yields. Gold production in a modern mine is measured a fraction of an ounce per ton of ore.

Gold panning was also difficult work that typically yielded meager quantities of gold (I say that from experience). Contrary to common beliefs, few gold panners struck it rich. Most of them worked long days just to maintain a simple existence. The high costs of food and provisions made the store merchants and business persons in the boom towns wealthy, but depleted the profits from the average prospectors.

My greatest ghost town and mining camp exploring adventure occurred on a late-spring afternoon in a remote mining district near the Collegiate Peaks of Colorado. My experience was amplified by the Rocky Mountain springtime setting. Sean, Craig and I were relaxing at base camp, after a harrowing experience on Mt. Princeton the day before, when we made a spur-of-the-moment decision to go exploring. From the time that we left camp to the time we returned, our entire experience was accompanied by a pleasantly mysterious, magical feeling. Something in the mountain air made our adventure exceptionally special. It was almost as if time had stopped for us to explore the past. It seemed as if we were the only three persons in the mountains. At times, I felt like I was in the twilight zone (no, we were not under the influence of drugs or alcohol, just pure Rocky Mountain air).

After an exhausting, harrowing day on Mt. Princeton the previous day, the three of us were rested and ready to get out of camp for a while. On the spur of the moment we decided to explore some of the ghost towns and mining camps to the west. Under partly cloudy skies, we drove westward up a rough gravel road, and along the way we stopped and investigated every mine we passed.

We were high (above 9,000 feet) in the Rocky Mountains of Colorado's beautiful Sawatch Range. The setting was spectacular! We were surrounded by rugged granite peaks, spotted with patches of snow and forested mountainsides. Occasionally, we caught a glimpse of the roaring white water creek that paralleled the road.

The gravel road was bumpy, rutted and generally rough from the onset, and it got worse as we went, but it was nothing that my 1967 Ford Fairlane legacy couldn't handle. The tempo was set by the sighting of the first mine. I parked the car and ran into the trees to investigate. More than anything, I just wanted to see what remained at the old abandoned mines. I searched in hopes of finding the mine shaft, a rusty ore-car, the ore-car rail, a miner's cabin, or any other remnants. At the first stop, Sean and Craig looked at me with reservations, but by the second stop they wholeheartedly joined in the spirit of exploring.

The first stop was rather disappointing. The mine's entrance was caved-in and there weren't any remnants lying around. From one site to the next, we gradually made our way higher and higher into the mountains. We stopped at several mines. Most of them were nothing more than a tailings pile with a collapsed mine shaft. We were more interested in exploring some out-of-the-way, unvandalized ghost towns, so the paltry discoveries at the mine sites did not upset our high spirit of adventure.

Generally, following directions from a Colorado ghost towns book, we knew which roads to follow, but the roads were crude and unmarked. Eventually, the gravel road that we followed transformed into nothing more than a nice jeep trail. The trail was riddled with mud puddles, pot holes and ruts. We followed the trail as far as possible. We passed some ghost town sites on the way up, but waited to stop at them on the way back. We were finally stopped by a drift of waist-deep snow across the road. We turned around and coasted the Ford back down to the nearest ghost town site.

The first ghost town that we explored was south of Romly, Colorado. The architecture was depicted by rustic, weathered wood buildings topped with steep-pitched, rusting corrugated sheet-metal roofs. Other typical roofing materials of the late 1800s and early 1900s were wood shingles and asphalt-type sheets and shingles. The buildings that we explored were primarily gold mills and cabins. The first building that we explored was precariously situated on a steep mountainside, near the road; a small landslide or avalanche could carry it right onto the road.

We thoroughly explored the site. We found the mines that kept the small mining community alive. We carefully walked around the site, trying to preserve what remained. In the robust mountain setting, it was easy to let our minds drift into the history of the mining community. In the distance, we saw the same majestic views that the old timers saw: towering, snowcapped granite peaks across a forested valley. The steep-sloped mountainsides kept us constantly aware of gravity, and its effect on mountain life. Everywhere we walked we had to either climb or descend the sloping mountainside, just as the miners had to do. As we explored the site, it also became evident how the elements influenced life in the mining community. The melting snow fed streams and made the ground muddy. It also flooded the mines, making pumping a necessary part of mining. Even in late May, the wind carried cold air from across distant snowfields. Just by exploring the site, it was evident that the miners had to be strong willed, determined, highly motivated and hard working. I wondered if they took time to see the beauty of their environment, or if they were too obsessed with looking for the mother lode to notice. It would take a strong case of gold fever to keep me working inside a dark mine, with the outside lure of the scenic beauty.

It was so peaceful and quiet that we decided to coast the car down the road to the next ghost town so that we didn't disrupt the serenity. We coasted to a stop at Romly, Colorado. Romly was a true ghost town, south of St. Elmo, Colorado. The first building that we looked at was a three-story, rusty, metal-clad gold mill owned by the Murphy Gold Mining Company. It was a tall timber structure, sheathed with sheet metal and covered by a gable roof.

We decided to hike up a mining road that went east from Romly. It was a refreshing hike up a rocky trail. The thin air and mesmerizing scenery toyed with my imagination. I decided to help it by thinking about images of mining life in the late 1800s. For a few moments I drifted in and out, here and there. As we approached a curve in the road, I half-expected to see a prospector ambling toward us, leading a donkey. Or possibly we might see a small mining community overflowing with the jovial spirit of past prosperous times. Other images from the past danced from my stimulated imagination: prospectors panning gold down by the creek; miners traveling to and fro on horses and in wagons; the ricketing sound of cable-stayed trains carrying ore down from the big mine; and shouts from those who had struck it rich. The aura of past lives still hung mysteriously in the quiet mountain surroundings, and around the remaining structures and rusting equipment. Maybe ghost towns really are inhabited by ghosts.

Although the trail continued up the mountain, toward the mines, we stopped to explore a small mining community. We saw a couple of cabins, a small horse shed and a few remaining traces of a tram system that once carried ore from the mine to the mill. I captured an instant in time with a photograph of Sean and Craig in the windows of the rustic cabin. Sean peered through the second-story window and Craig was captured peering through one of the ground-story windows. The cabin was a link to the past.

After thoroughly exploring the site, we hiked back toward the car under a darkening sky. We wanted to hike farther up the mining trail, but the threatening weather and fleeting daylight warned us against it.

The ride back to camp was a mysteriously pleasant journey. Without starting the car, we coasted quietly and harmoniously down the mountain road. We glided through the forest for nearly ten miles. Craig and Sean sat on the trunk while I steered the car slowly down the winding mountain road. It was like skiing. Quiet, serene and refreshing. Then, the magic of the moment was enriched by a light snow that gently floated down to the ground. We were all overtaken by the delightful experience that we shared;

it was one of the best Rocky Mountain highs of my life. Sean was ecstatic! He rolled onto his stomach on the car trunk, and imitated a gliding bird. His hair blew freely in the wind, and he jubilantly laughed all the way down the mountain. Likewise, Craig thoroughly enjoyed the passing forest scenery as we peacefully glided along.

Midway back to camp, Craig took the steering wheel so that I could ride on the trunk. Sean was having so much fun that I had to join in the fun. It was a blast! It was like gliding through the forest on a blanket. The snow continued to float to the ground like glitter. It was one of those rare experiences that I wished would never end. It felt wonderful just to concentrate on watching the magnificent passing scenery. The pinnacle of our experience came when we saw a herd of elk foraging at the edge of the trees alongside the road, not frightened by our presence. We looked at them as we rolled by, and they looked at us. I felt a supreme feeling of peace and harmony; we had a truly wonderful ride back to camp at the base of Mt. Princeton.

As the sky darkened with the advancing night, our magical afternoon in the mountains passed into history. We spent our last night together talking about our adventure while seated around the crackling glow of a campfire.

Δ

That last Rocky Mountain afternoon together was like a grand farewell from nature. To date, that was the last day that the three of us were together for an adventure. Shortly after that grand day, I moved to Atlanta, Georgia, to work as an architectural engineer for the Air Force, Sean stayed in Colorado to attend flying school, and Craig moved to Puerto Rico to explore new territory there.

Some say that the riches, treasures and gold are long gone from the Rocky Mountains. I disagree. The natural wealth is still there, for those who know what to look for and how to look. There is still gold in them hills, but the natural beauty is the greatest remaining treasure in the Rocky Mountains. The treasures are locked in history. The only way to find the key to those treasures is through knowledge, an open mind and genuine concern. Mix your Rocky Mountain explorations with history. Visit some ghost towns and mines, then read about their colorful history. Or read about the history, then visit the sites. As you explore a ghost town, walk softly and quietly so that you can hear the sounds of the past. Walk carefully so that you don't awake the ghosts that guard the treasures.

As previously mentioned, there are many books about ghost towns in the Rocky Mountain region. Some of the books contain detailed descriptions of the ghost towns, their conditions, history and how to find them. If you are serious about exploring ghost towns, I encourage you to learn as much as you can about the history of the areas that you intend to visit. It can be a bundle of fun! To get to the area that we explored, around St. Elmo, Colorado, you can take Highway 24 to Nathrop, then turn west toward Mt. Princeton Hot Springs and St. Elmo. The road is paved part of the way. St. Elmo is a protected ghost town. Be courteous to the few residents who live in the St. Elmo area. Most importantly, have a fun, rewarding experience that you will be proud to share with your family and friends. You will undoubtedly return from your adventures with many treasures to share and remember.

Mines

MINES, LIKE GHOST TOWNS, are remnants of human history, not a part of the majestic beauty of the Rocky Mountains. Yet they are more than scars on the mountainsides; they are reminders of the destruction of which humankind is capable. But they are also remnants of a romantic time in Rocky Mountain history. The mines that I am writing about are abandoned gold, silver and copper mines made during the late 1800s and early 1900s. They were carved by human muscle and primitive blasting powder; compared to modern strip mines, the old mines are relatively insignificant marks on the mountainsides. The only visible part of the mine is the entrance, the tailings pile and possibly a wooden structure or two. Today's strip mining operations literally remove large parts of or entire mountains. Those mountains will never be restored to their natural states; they are gone forever. The two most appalling strip mines with which I am familiar are at Climax, Colorado, and six miles east of Idaho Springs, Colorado. Although there are hundreds, if not thousands, of abandoned mines from the gold rush days, they can be easily covered up and removed from the landscape; covering up modern strip mines is not so easy. Although some areas, such as Central City, were overmined, most areas are simply spotted with a few mines here and there on the mountainsides. The old abandoned mines are not environmental threats, but reminders of human impact and history in the Rocky Mountains.

The biggest threat that the old abandoned mines pose is a safety hazard. They are very dangerous! They are old tunnels that are partially supported by timber columns and beams, and in many cases the timber supports are rotted. Some of the mines are partially buried, posing a danger to passing hikers. Nearly every year several persons are injured or killed in old, abandoned mines. Sometimes it is their fault for going in or near the mine, and sometimes it is purely accidental. Because of the danger of these mines, many Rocky Mountain states are trying to seal permanently the entrances to all of the mines that they can locate. That task is expensive, time consuming and difficult. Throughout the Rocky Mountains, there are thousands of mines in various conditions. Some are right along major highways, some are miles deep in the wilderness, some are lost treasure mines and some may never be found. Nevertheless, some states are making progress toward sealing the entrances to dangerous abandoned mines, especially in the more visited areas.

Like ghost towns, mines also have an air of mystery to them. You have probably heard stories about lost gold mines, the mother lode and buried treasures. If you haven't heard of them, there are many books written about them. In most cases, it is not known whether or not the stories are fact or fiction. They are probably a mixture of fact and fiction, with a higher percentage of fiction. Every Rocky Mountain state has its share of lost-gold-mine legends. To name a few of Colorado's lost mine legends, there is Murdie's Lost Gold Mine, the Lost Mine of Stevens Gulch, the Lost Mine of Big Baldy and the Lost Pitchblende Mine. I'm sure that some of the lost mine stories are true. Since the mines were originally lost, they may have been buried by avalanches, landslides, new forest growth and flood activity.

Thus far, I have not gone on any treasure-seeking adventures. Some people are obsessed with looking for lost treasures, and they do it full time, a necessity to be a successful treasure hunter. The easy-finds were found a long time ago. To be a full-time treasure hunter, you have to be independently wealthy, retired or living by some other means of support. I don't fall under any of those categories, therefore I am a part-time explorer, not a treasure hunter. My interest in exploring mines is due to history and curiosity.

Old, abandoned mines are undoubtedly dangerous. Unlike caves, mines are man-made. Mines are not formed through millions of years of natural processes; mines are tunnels that were blasted and dug in a relatively short time. The abandoned mines have deteriorated under the natural forces of the mountain environment. The timber supports are rotted and broken, repeated freeze-thaw cycles have cracked the rock walls, some mines are flooded, some entrances have been buried or partially buried by avalanches and new forest growth, and the wooden ladders into vertical shafts are damaged and weak. Other hazards include pockets of toxic gases, deep vertical shafts, slippery walls and floors, falling rocks and cave-ins. The kicker is that there is nothing to gain from exposing yourself to those inherent pitfalls. These mines were not hastily abandoned; the owners removed anything of value before abandoning their mines. Unless you have found a bonafide lost mine, you are foolish to explore any abandoned mine. Caves are much safer and offer the same basic environment. I admit that

I acted foolishly on my mine-exploring adventures. Learning from mistakes can be a dangerous, if not fatal, way to learn. Yet, that is how I gained my experience. I strongly advise you against exploring mines.

The safest and best way to explore a mine is on a tour of an active or commercialized mine. There are many places in the Rocky Mountains where you can take a safe tour of an old gold mine. The advantage of taking a tour is that you normally get to learn about the mine and its history through a guide or brochure. The sensations of being inside a mine are very similar to the sensations of being in a cave.

Despite the hazards, risks and dangers, I have explored abandoned mines. My curiosity and will to face a new challenge overpowered my fears. I liken it to any other thing that we know is dangerous, yet we still do it. We all do things that are dangerous, despite warnings that tell us otherwise. Smoking is dangerous. Driving without a seatbelt is dangerous. Everything that we do has a certain degree of risk associated with it. In the end, every risk that we take comes down to a personal decision. You have to ask yourself if the risk is worth the satisfaction or potential benefits, and you can reduce the risk by preparing yourself before participating in a dangerous activity. We all do things that seem irrational when looked at from different perspectives. When I made the decision to venture into the mines, it seemed like pure fun. Now, in retrospect, it seems like exploring mines was a stupid, foolish thing to do. Enough said.

I have three short mine-exploring adventures to share with you. The first one is about my first mine-exploring experience in Wyoming. The second one is about a mine that Sean, Craig and I explored in Colorado. And the third adventure is about Sean's and my discovery of a hidden mine in Wyoming.

One day, while riding motorcycles in the copper-rich Sierra Madre Mountain Range, south of Encampment, Wyoming, Brent and I discovered a vertical mine shaft atop a small mountain. It dropped vertically down into the core of the mountain, lined with decaying timber and wood siding. Our first thoughts were that it would be fun to rappel into it. From then on, that idea was planted in our minds. After our discovery, we later returned with our ropes and rappelling gear.

Our first task was to calculate whether or not our rope would reach the bottom. Our rope was 120 feet long. The shaft was too deep to see the bottom adequately. Being industrious engineering students, we estimated the depth of the shaft by timing the fall of a rock. We dropped a rock, actually several rocks, and timed how long it took to hit the bottom. Using a standard physics equation, based on the acceleration of gravity, and by subtracting off the speed of sound (the time that it took the sound of the rock to travel from the bottom up to our position at the top rim of the shaft), we estimated the depth at 110 feet. It appeared that our rope was long enough to reach the bottom.

We had to overcome another problem. We didn't have anything in which to tie the rope. The entrance to the vertical mine shaft was uncovered on a bare mountaintop, so we searched lower on the mountainside and found two large diameter logs to lay across the entrance. We tied the rope around the logs and dropped it down the shaft; the rope appeared to reach the bottom, but the dim light inside the shaft made it difficult to confirm.

I strapped on my rappelling sling, connected it to the rack, weaved the rope through the rappelling rack and lowered myself into the throat of the shaft. A few feet into the shaft, I got an eerie instinctive feeling to abort the rappel. I became uneasy and nervous about the descent. I felt that something was going to go wrong if I continued down into the shaft. The feeling was so strong that I couldn't ignore it. I decided to abort the attempt and let Brent rappel into the shaft. Yes, I whimped out, but I always listen to my instincts. Sometimes instincts are the difference between life and death, or safety and danger. I have read many stories about climbers who got into trouble because they ignored their instincts.

Brent wholeheartedly accepted the challenge. He hooked into the rope, positioned himself over the shaft and lowered himself down without hesitation. I anxiously peered over the shaft's edge, watching my good friend drop straight down the throat of the old mine shaft. It became obvious that the shaft was not perfectly vertical. Midway down, Brent touched the side of the shaft, because it was slightly slanted to one side.

He kept descending and descending. I began to wonder if the rope was long enough, for it seemed to take a long time for him to rappel down. Either the shaft was deeper than it appeared, or he was just being extra careful.

"How far from the bottom are you?" I yelled.

"Still another sixty feet!" he said.

Amazing, I thought. It didn't look that deep.

"Is the rope touching the bottom?"

"Yeah," he replied, "but barely."

He continued down for another five minutes. After taking so long to reach the bottom, I knew that it would take him a long time to ascend back up the rope. After all, we didn't have mechanical ascenders. We planned to ascend by the rope using the prusiking method (a common method used by mountaineers to ascend out of crevasses). Prusiking is a method of tieing into the rope with three prusik knots and alternately sliding them up the rope. It was a technique that Al explained to us, but neither of us had ever tried using it.

Finally, Brent touched bottom. It was just under 120 feet. The rope was barely long enough. Brent unhooked from the rope to explore the mine.

My depth perception was tricked by the narrow walls of the mine shaft. He didn't appear to be 120 feet away, but he was. Judging by eyesight and sound, it appeared to be about half as deep, but we could hear each other fine.

In the bottom of the vertical shaft, Brent found two horizontal tunnels leading in opposite directions away from the main vertical shaft. It was too dark for Brent to see anything. I pulled the rope up, tied a flashlight to the end, then lowered it down to him. One of the tunnels ended in a pit that appeared to be another vertical shaft that had collapsed. The other tunnel went outward toward the mountainside, as if it might connect with a horizontal entrance. At one time, it probably was another entrance, but it had collapsed. Brent's hopes of finding anything eventful were crushed; it hardly seemed worth his effort, but he was already thinking about the long rope ascent back to the top of the shaft. Looking up at the tiny rectangle of light, he knew that he faced an awesome physical challenge.

Like a true adventurer, he started inching up the rope using the prusik knot method. It was his first time at using the technique and at ascending a free hanging rope. He was held to the rope with a prusik knot at the chest and one for each foot. It was primitive but adequate.

It took him forty-five minutes to ascend the rope. After that, I lost my appetite for exploring the mine. Brent explored the unknown; he stole the mystery of exploring the mine. After all, I didn't have any desire to spend forty-five minutes ascending a rope.

I haven't returned to that old mine; Brent, however, has rappelled down into it at least two more times since we discovered it. Something about it appealed to him. Maybe he discovered something down there that he didn't share with me. Then again, he probably just enjoyed the challenge.

Δ

Under the sunshine of a beautiful Rocky Mountain afternoon, on 28 May 1987, Craig, Sean and I found a mine into which we could delve. We had just recovered from a harrowing experience on Mt. Princeton the day before, and we were out looking for more adventure. We were exploring some of the ghost towns in the area when we were sidetracked by the dangerous lure of an abandoned mine.

After poking our heads into the entrances of several other caved-in mines, we finally found one that was still open. We climbed up the yellow-brown tailings pile to the mine's entrance, where a set of ore-car tracks went into the mine. With flashlights in our hands, we ventured closer to the entrance, framed by three large timbers, one on each side and one across the top. One by one, we cautiously entered the mine. Just inside the mine, the tunnel floor was covered by a sheet of ice, two feet thick. It looked very dangerous.

Venturing further into the mine, we slid across the ice-covered mine floor. Our curiosities guided our actions. Common sense was subdued. We had to see what was around the next bend. Then the next. We followed the ore-car tracks. Farther into the mine, the temperature rose above freezing and instead of slippery ice, we had to contend with cold water. The rails of the track and the floor of the mine were submersed in knee-deep water. We balanced on the rails, then waded into the frigid water. We were concerned that a vertical shaft might be hidden beneath the water, but we reasoned that we were safe if we stayed atop the rails of the track.

We made it safely across the water, then the mine sloped slightly upward and we were back on dry land. We ventured another fifty feet into the eerie depths of the abandoned mine and heard distant sounds of dripping water, or perhaps it was the sounds of Tommy-knockers warning us of danger. Then we reached the end of our journey; the tunnel was blocked by a heap of large rocks from a cave-in. We couldn't determine whether it naturally caved-in or was intentionally caved-in to keep intruders (explorers) out.

The entire time we were in the mine I felt a spooky sensation, cold, like death. I knew that we didn't belong inside that dangerous old mine. It was almost as if the spirit of an old miner (possibly a Tommyknocker) was telling me to get out. Maybe a miner was killed in the mine, and his spirit still haunts the mine or warns intruders to beware. Whatever my sensation was from, it scared me out of the mine in a hurry. A wave of relief went through my body after I returned to see and feel the sunshine, and I was happy to make it safely out of the ghost mine.

We satisfied our curiosities and were content with our mini-adventure, exploring the mine as far as possible. We had no inclinations to explore any more mines that day. Instead, we turned our attention to the beauty of the high country and spent the rest of the day frolicking in the high country and exploring ghost towns.

Exploring

Δ

None of my mine-exploring adventures have turned up anything exciting. The relics, antiques, gold and treasure have long since been looted or removed. Curiosity is the only thing that drew me toward mines. Most of the time, the yellowish tailing piles get my attention and spark my curiosity. In fact, I enjoy simply exploring around the entrances of mines, without stepping foot into them. Even that is dangerous: the risk of falling into a buried shaft is always present. The soil surrounding vertical shafts is often unstable, and every year a few people are killed by falling into a mine shaft.

The excitement of exploring comes from venturing into the unknown, making new discoveries and increasing your knowledge. You don't have to discover a new pyramid to enjoy your experience. To enjoy your exploring expedition, all you have to do is discover places and things that are new to you. On 15 June 1986, Sean and I made an exciting discovery in the Sierra Madre Mountains of southern Wyoming.

We were in Encampment, Wyoming, to attend Brent's and Gayle's wedding. Shortly after their wedding, we strapped our backpacks across our shoulders and struck out into the remote Wyoming wilderness. Encampment is situated in a basin between two mountain ranges. The population is about 600. Today, it is primarily a lumber producing town, but it spawned from the copper mining industry. If you ever visit Encampment, make sure that you visit the Encampment Museum and restored historic buildings. Before much of Encampment was destroyed in a tragic fire, it was about to become the capital city of Wyoming.

The wilderness surrounding Encampment is remote and teaming with wildlife. Brent can tell deer and bear stories for hours. He and many of his relatives have had a few close encounters with bears and other wild critters.

Sean and I left Encampment at 2:30 P.M. By 3:00 P.M., we were breathing hard and dripping with trail sweat. The warm afternoon sunshine siphoned the water from our bodies as we hiked into new territory. We planned to hike as far as we could before nightfall; our goal was simply to enjoy the wilderness.

As we hiked up the canyon, we passed several abandoned mines. We poked our heads into the ones that were relatively close to the trail and found some blue copper ore in one of the mines. The worst part of our trek was contending with the plentiful wood ticks. They were at their peak! That was the worst tick-infested wilderness through which I had never trekked. The thought of sleeping with ticks in the tent was already sending chills up and down my back. The last thing either of us wanted was a case of Rocky Mountain Spotted Fever.

Shortly before dusk, we found a level forested area, an appealing campsite near the river. Before bedtime, we stripped and carefully checked ourselves and our clothes for ticks. Despite our scrutinizing efforts, in the morning I found a tick on Sean and one next to my sleeping bag.

Other than the usual array of strange noises in the dark, the night passed uneventfully. We broke camp early so that we could explore the territory farther up the canyon before returning home. We had a good breakfast, topped by a cup of camp coffee, then stowed our packs and struck out to explore the area.

A short distance up the canyon, we hit pay dirt. We found a huge tailings pile with a small one-room cabin next to it. The large size of the tailings pile was a telltale sign that we were near a large mine. The trail was carved in the canyon wall. On one side of the trail the mountainside dropped steeply down to the river, and on the other side the mountainside rose steeply upward. The mine had to be on the side toward the mountain. We thoroughly searched the area but failed to find anything. We couldn't even find a hint of a mine shaft. There had to be a mine somewhere. The tons of rock in the tailings pile had to come from somewhere, so we explored the area a second time.

Fifty feet from the trail, I found a strange-looking rockslide behind a clump of trees. It didn't look like a buried mine entrance, but I knew it had to be there. I told Sean about my suspicions, and we decided to dig for it. We feverishly started heaving, tugging and pulling large rocks from the suspected entrance for several minutes without finding anything; it seemed to be merely a talus pile. After a rest, we attacked the rocks again.

Then, we found it! Eureka! A hole opened up at our feet. If it had been a vertical shaft, we would have become mining fatalities. The hole dropped straight down a few feet before leveling out into a horizontal mine tunnel. We enlarged the entrance by feeding the rocks down into the entrance. We heard water splash as the rocks tumbled into the mine. It swallowed the larger rocks that we heaved into it. After the dust cleared, we saw the horizontal tunnel. It was flooded and too deep to wade into. We gauged the depth with a branch and found it was four feet, probably, becoming much deeper farther in.

Since wading wasn't an appealing alternative, we tried to build a foot bridge with rocks. For several minutes we diligently pushed rocks into the water. We made very little progress; the water was too deep and consumed the rocks as we shoved them in. It would take us forever to build a rock path into the tunnel. The mine was flooded as far as we could see into it. We needed a raft, or a way to drain the mine.

The most exciting part of our find was not knowing how long it had been buried. Did the original owners close it after they left? If so, it may have been untouched for eighty years or more. It was an authentic discovery. Finally, after a gallant effort, we accepted the fact that we couldn't go any farther into the mine. We decided to re-bury the entrance, in hopes of returning with more gear at a later date.

We left the mine as a mystery. During the hike back down the canyon, we talked about returning to the mine to explore it, but, in reality, it probably wouldn't be worth the effort. Unless it was abandoned in haste, everything of interest was probably removed by the people who originally closed it. Other than collecting more wood ticks, the return trek was uneventful.

Δ

My best advice for you is to stay away from abandoned mines. The best way to explore a mine is to take a commercial tour, and the best way to learn about mines is to read. Curiosity was the only thing that drew me into the ghost mines. It was a potentially fatal curiosity. I never have found anything of significance in a mine. Caves are much safer, and much more interesting.

My main purpose for including this chapter is to urge you to stay away from mines. My mining adventures were foolish. Quite frankly, I'm lucky to be alive to share my experiences with you. Mines are not worth your time. Instead, choose to spend your time exploring the beauty of the high country.

8. Prospecting

Prospecting is the adventurous activity of digging, scratching, panning and otherwise searching for glorious gold.

M OST OF TODAY'S prospector's are adventurers and romanticists. They aren't seeking to get rich or even to earn a living. Their enjoyment stems from the challenging process of looking for gold. Except for a few infrequent strikes, the gold rush days in the Rocky Mountains are history. Even with the high price of gold, it is very difficult to earn a living by prospecting. Brazil, Australia, Alaska and a few parts of Canada are among the only remaining places on earth that still yield enough surface gold to make prospecting a feasible career.

However, there is still enough gold or "color" in the Rockies to keep prospecting interesting. In fact, it is still possible to find gold nuggets. It isn't very likely, but it is possible. Recently, while in a souvenir shop in Central City, Colorado, I was looking at some of the gold nuggets that were for sale. Some of them were found in the Colorado Rockies, but I was surprised to hear that most of them were from Australia. The shop owner bought them from an Australian prospector. Today, if you find even a pea-sized nugget anywhere in the lower forty-eight states, you are very fortunate. Cherish your find by mounting it on a ring, display it or keep it in a safe place. Whatever you do, don't sell it at market price. Gold nuggets are much more precious than market gold. If you choose to sell your nugget, you should be able to sell it for at least triple the market price of gold. Most of you who try prospecting or gold panning should be pleased with finding gold flour, or if you're lucky, gold dust. Finding your first flake of genuine yellow gold is an exciting experience. If you have panned for gold, you know what I mean. No matter how easy it sounds in a "how to" book, or how easy it looks on television, it isn't easy! You may find "color" on your first attempt, or not until your tenth attempt.

The process of panning for gold is amazing. It is incredible that you can start with a panfull of sand, weighing three to five pounds and, if you're lucky, end up with a few tiny flakes of gold in the bottom of your pan. If you get in a hurry or don't use the proper technique, you will wash the gold right out of the pan with the sand. Gold panning is easy once you understand the physics of the process. First of all, gold is very heavy. It weighs more than most of the other things that you will shovel into your pan. Therefore, if there is gold in your pan, it will naturally tend to settle to the bottom of the pan. Second, you have to agitate the material in your pan to get the gold to settle to the bottom. Gold dust or flour will sit on top of the sand and gravel if you don't vigorously shake the pan. Forget about swirling the pan like actors often do in movies. That will only help to swirl your gold out of the pan. Mentally imagine the gold tumbling downward as you shake the pan back and forth. You can practice gold panning with BB's or small bearings; if you do it right, they should be at the bottom of the pan after the rest of the sand is gone.

I learned how to gold pan by reading, practicing, and from the Mining Engineering department at the University of Wyoming, which gave demonstrations on how to pan for gold. The graduate student who taught me had spent a summer panning gold in Alaska. He wore his largest find on a finger. It was a gold nugget a little larger than the eraser on a pencil. The things that he taught me with his demonstration were my most valuable lessons in gold panning.

In addition to learning how to pan for gold, you have to learn how to get the gold out of your pan. When, and if, you do find some gold, it will probably be in the form of gold flour, dust or flakes. Gold flour is the smallest form of gold that is recoverable by panning and is essentially specks of gold so small that they will float, if you're not careful. It is important to keep the oil from your hands from getting into the water in your pan. These specks of gold are so small that you can get them on the end of a toothpick. In fact, one way to recover them is to stab them with a toothpick. Gold dust is a little larger than gold flour. Gold flakes are a little larger than gold dust, and will typically settle to the bottom. Gold flakes can be retrieved from the pan with tweezers. My gold panning kit includes a gold pan, a small shovel, an empty film case, a syringe with a flattened needle, a toothpick and a pair of tweezers. After I pan as much of the lighter material out as possible, I use my tools to get the gold into a film case. Unless you are very fortunate, don't worry about getting an ounce of gold dust in the bottom of your pan. Instead, you will probably have six to twenty specks of gold mixed with a batch of dark material, primarily carbon and iron particles. By gently swirling the remaining material in the pan (not over the edge), you can get most of the gold to collect in one spot. Once the gold flour is concentrated, I use a syringe to suck the gold particles out of the pan. Then I simply eject them into a film case or a small test tube. Occasionally, I find sand-sized gold flakes that I can extract with tweezers. Some day, I hope to find something that I can pick out with my fingers, but I'm not holding my breath waiting for that day.

Since this is not a "how to" book, I will not go into all the details of gold panning. Gold panning is adequately covered by many other books that you can find in a library or book store. The two most important things that you need to learn about gold panning are how to do it and where to look. If you don't find any color in your first try, you should try a new location. Gold is almost everywhere. It is a natural element. It exists in the ocean, the desert and probably in your backyard. But to find any appreciable quantities of gold you need to prospect in areas where surface gold is concentrated. You need to learn a little about the geology of gold.

I started prospecting for the pure enjoyment of passing time in the mountains. Gold panning filled a void. I didn't always have the energy to climb or hike, so I looked for something that I could do while relaxing on the bank of a mountain creek. Gold panning can be active or passive. You can move from place to place looking for better gold deposits, or you can stay in one place all day. It just depends how ambitious you are feeling.

Besides filling a void, I also became interested in prospecting through my interest in history at the same time that I started reading about ghost towns, and I acquired a mild case of gold fever. After purchasing my first gold pan, I rushed to the mountains to try my luck. Just like many other first-time prospectors, I had visions of finding vast amounts of gold. My grand visions were quickly dispelled after I panned my first dozen pans of sand and gravel. After a back-breaking, disappointing day of gold panning, my spell of gold fever was cured for a while.

My mom used to look for gold by flipping rocks along the banks of creeks. She came to Colorado with my dad from the farming community of St. Francis, Kansas. She thought that she could find gold nuggets like hunting for Easter eggs. I knew that it was harder than that, but my hopes of finding gold were just as grand as hers when I first started gold panning.

In the 1800s the mountain valleys echoed with the sounds of prospectors searching for gold and finding it. The first push to find and process gold in the United States started with its discovery in 1801, on Meadow Creek in North Carolina. From there, the search for gold gradually moved westward over the span of a century. America's first major gold rush began in 1828 with the discovery of gold in the Blue Ridge Mountains of Georgia, near Dahlonega. After the echoes of gold hushed in the eastern states, James W. Marshall discovered gold at Sutter's Mill, California, in 1848. In 1858, the gold rush shifted to Colorado after Green

Russell discovered gold on Cherry Creek, near the present location of Denver. In 1896, prospectors rushed north to Alaska to search for gold. Since then, gold has been discovered in every Rocky Mountain state. Gold was big news during the 1800s. Today, gold production is monopolized by large mining companies. The high market price of gold keeps big mining operations in business. They typically extract a fraction of an ounce of gold for each ton of ore processed. To be profitable, they have to process tons and tons of low-grade gold ore every day.

Finding gold for the first time is an exciting and magical experience, even if it's only a speck. Gold's brilliant yellow luster distinguishes it from everything else. Once you have found gold for the first time, you will always remember what it looks like. Its bright yellow luster is unique. It is easier to see against a black background, hence having a black pan is an advantage. If you happen to find fool's gold (iron pyrite) the first time that you think you have found gold, don't be ashamed. Being fooled by fool's gold happens to many. Fool's gold doesn't "pan out" under basic tests. The properties of fool's gold and gold are quite different. In fact, their colors under direct sunlight is about the only similarity. Fool's gold may look like gold in direct sunlight, but it loses its gold luster in the shade. Gold is bright yellow in the shade and in sunlight. Fool's gold may rust after you get it home, it is hard and breaks in planes. Real gold is soft and malleable. Unfortunately, I didn't know all those things the first time I rushed out to pan for gold. I had plenty of book knowledge but little practical experience. Even I was fooled by fool's gold the first time I panned for gold.

My fiasco is best described by my diary entry of 4 May 1987: "I found more gold today! I even found enough to save in a tiny test tube. I also have some fine sand with small quantities of gold dust in it. Everything I found came from a one-gallon bucket full of sand found below a mine's tailings, about one-half mile west of . . . "

Guess what? It was all fool's gold. How did I find out? It was simple. Two days later it started rusting! I wanted to believe that I had found a secret placer deposit. I brainwashed myself into believing that I had found gold. The rust was indisputable evidence that I had been fooled. I couldn't force myself to rationalize that gold rusts. For the record, that was the goldest iron pyrite I have ever found.

My first two prospecting adventures were fun, but I didn't find any real gold. I returned to the library to research a better place to prospect. Deciding on a place to look wasn't easy. Every mountain county in Colorado has some history of gold discovery. I finally decided to go prospecting in the "richest square mile on earth." I planned a prospecting adventure for Russell Gulch in Clear Creek County, the heart of Colorado gold country. I hoped to find the vaccine for my reoccurring spells of gold fever.

The following two prospecting adventures describe experiences of modern day prospecting in the Rocky Mountains. The first story, "Russell Gulch," is about the first time that I found real gold. The second story, "Pay Dirt," is about a surprising gold discovery that yielded the most gold of all my prospecting locations.

Russell Gulch

EVERY TIME I GO prospecting, I still feel some of the same excitement that the old time prospectors probably felt. However, their goals differed drastically from mine. They depended on their findings to survive. I am in it purely for the recreation (and the remote possibility of striking it rich).

After my disappointing fool's gold experiences above James-town, Colorado, I was anxious to find some real gold. I decided to go prospecting somewhere with a proven history of prosperous gold discoveries. My research led me to Clear Creek County. Being the adventure-minded person that I am, I wanted to find a place where I could enjoy the serenity of the mountains without the buzzing of cars in the background. Also, I wanted to camp near my prospecting site. Russell Gulch met my criteria. I planned a three-day excursion that just happened to coincide with one of Roni's visits. At the time, we were long-distance dating. She was studying education at the University of Wyoming, and I was at home awaiting my active duty reporting date and spending as much time as possible in the mountains.

Early in the morning of 16 April 1987, Roni and I set out on a three-day prospecting excursion. My veins flowed vibrantly with the excitement of gold fever as we drove higher and higher into the mountains. Roni wasn't as enthusiastic as I was; it was her first gold-panning adventure. Camping and the associated inconveniences didn't suit her very well. She was more of a day-hike, picnic and trail-ride person. But we were normally so happy together, that we enjoyed each other's companionship no matter what we were doing.

After getting off of the nice, paved roads, we skirted into the backcountry via rough, narrow, gravel roads. Since Roni was not a good map reader, I had to navigate and drive at the same time. The abundance of creeks and gulches in Clear Creek County made it difficult to pinpoint Russell Gulch, named after the man who received credit for discovering gold there. He migrated to Colorado after his prospecting played out in Georgia. As we drove through the rugged terrain in the comfort of my Ford Fairlane, I thought about the difficulty of getting around in the mountains during the 1800s. It had to have been a tremendously difficult undertaking.

About midmorning, we found Russell Gulch. It was a narrow briskly flowing stream. It was a tributary stream that fed Clear Creek. As the temperature climbed, the snow-fed stream grew larger.

With a shovel in one hand and a gold pan in the other, I trotted down to the stream bank to try my luck. The first pan of sand came right from the streambed. I patiently squatted at the water's edge and panned the sand. After a few minutes I finished. No color. There was a substantial amount of heavy black metals in the pan, so I knew that my technique was good. I filled the second pan with sand from the material deposited on the inside of a bend. Gold was more likely to settle anywhere that the velocity of the current is slowed, such as the inside of bends, behind and under boulders, and in deep pools. Highly concentrated gold deposits on the inside of bends are called placer deposits. When looking for placer deposits it is important to realize that the course of rivers continuously changes and ancient deposits will not necessarily be in the same location as recent deposits.

Roni sat in the sunshine watching as I patiently panned my second pan of sand. After all of our adventures together, she was accustomed to my goofy ways of enjoying the outdoors. She knew that it didn't take much to keep me happy in the mountains.

The material in the bottom of the pan grew darker as I panned the lighter materials over the edge. Then, in one swift swirl, the black minerals unveiled an accumulation of brilliant yellow gold!

"Pay dirt!" I shouted. "I finally found some real gold!"

It wasn't much, but it was a start. The bright, yellow gold contrasted beautifully against the other dark materials in the pan and created an attractive, colorful display. Captivated by the brilliant display, I marveled at it for several minutes. This time it was real. It passed the telltale property tests; it was a memorable moment in my history.

I definitely wasn't going to get rich from my findings. It was just a few specks of very fine gold flour. I used my ingenious syringe extraction method to recover the gold. Then I ejected the gold into a small test tube. I saved it as a memento to be shared with my future children and grandchildren. At market value it was a few cents worth, and if packaged and sold for a souvenir, it was worth five dollars.

My accomplishment shouldn't be downgraded too much. Finding that amount of gold was actually an amazing feat of astronomical proportions. There aren't many ways to recover a few specks of gold from five pounds of sandy material. It was an incredible challenge. My first monumental challenge was to find a panfull of material with any gold in it. Clear Creek County covers a vast area of mountains. You can't just stick your shovel in the ground anywhere and expect to find gold. It is a matter of continually reducing and refining your search until you eventually have some gold to take home. Anyway, I was happy with my meager find.

Roni strained her eyes trying to see the gold, but she finally saw it. She wasn't as impressed as I was and didn't understand the full magnitude of my find. But, she didn't have gold fever either.

We hiked up the gulch in search of a better deposit. I thought that the concentrations would be better, closer to the mother ore. Somewhere, farther up the gulch, there had to be some gold mines. The surrounding area was "freckled" with mines. There was a mine two hundred feet from our campsite. In fact, I was tempted to poke my head into it later, maybe after I found some more gold.

I quick-tested several samples of sand on our way up the gulch. I checked behind boulders, on islands and on the inside bank of every bend. Nothing panned out. It appeared that most of the gold was deposited farther downstream. We returned to camp empty handed.

Between prospecting, we went on an exploring hike far up the gulch. I carried my gold recovery kit, gold pan, shovel, camera and canteen. A couple of miles up the gulch we found the remnants of a colossal mining operation, several deteriorating buildings and mines on both sides of the gulch. On the way back to camp, we took a shortcut went through a minefield of mines. It was very dangerous territory, probably off limits to hikers, but we didn't see any signs. We hiked up and over several mine-covered mountains. On a couple occasions we stumbled precariously close to deep vertical mine shafts without any warning; we really had to watch our step and hope that we didn't step on any buried or hidden shafts. We also walked past several old claim stakes that probably dated back to the 1800s. That area had the highest concentration of mines that I ever saw, not a good place to let children play hide and seek. I wouldn't take a moonlight stroll around there, either. We managed to dodge the pitfalls on our hike back to camp.

We camped on a mountainside terrace safely above the gulch. We noticed the water level in the gulch drop as the temperature cooled. It was very peaceful; we didn't see anyone else all day. The weather remained favorable. The only real annoyance with which we had to contend was an abundance of wood ticks, typical for April and May.

The next day my curiosity compelled me to explore the mine near our camp. Roni protested my actions, but I forged onward. With a flashlight in hand, I scurried up the tailings pile to the entrance. At first glance, it appeared to be a short horizontal tunnel, damp, cool and dark. I crossed two piles of rock that had fallen from the ceiling, and, after that, I lost sight of the entrance. I was about 200 feet into the mine. Then, without warning, I came to the edge of a vertical shaft. It looked very deep, and the opening covered the entire area of the tunnel floor. A narrow ledge was the only way around the pit. It momentarily petrified me, and I carefully backed away from the edge of the shaft. I tossed a rock into the hole, which fell for a couple of seconds, then splashed into water. The tunnel continued on the other side of the shaft, but I wasn't about to try skirting around the edge. My instincts told me to get out, and that is exactly what I did. Walking up to the edge of that deep shaft sent frightening chills through my body and reminded me of the dangerous nature of abandoned mines.

I quickly put a comfortable distance between myself and that dangerous mine shaft. After emerging from the spooky mine, everything looked great again. The light of day looked beautiful! Russell Gulch looked beautiful. Roni looked beautiful. It is amazing how everything looks so much better after a bout with danger or after a frightful experience. Once again, my instincts gave me good advice. There were times in my life that I would have been more tempted to try getting around that mine shaft. My instincts have pulled me back from the edge of disaster on many occasions. I have learned to listen carefully to my instincts, a gift from nature; they are like having a sixth sense.

Back in the gulch, Roni anxiously awaited my return. Together, we returned to the bank of Russell Gulch to pan for some more gold. Before leaving the gulch, I taught Roni the art of panning for gold. She was somewhat reluctant about the learning experience, primarily because it seemed like so much work for such meager results.

During our three days in Russell Gulch, I found a hundredth of an ounce of gold flour and one flake of gold dust. Needless to say, I wasn't in a hurry to get to the assayer's office to cash in my findings. I was content with taking my findings home to keep as a memento of our prospecting adventure.

As we left Clear Creek County we passed dozens of weekend prospectors panning for gold along Clear Creek. The high value of gold had obviously convinced a few people that this could be a worthwhile pastime; it looked like a mini gold rush. The high numbers of gold panners didn't upset me, but the few destructive gold diggers did. I was appalled by the destructive methods that some of them employed. There were places where they had carved into the canyon walls without respect for the environment. They were probably capitalist urbanites from the plains who didn't care about anything except fattening their bank accounts. Their interest in the environment was limited to keeping their backyard clean. To the weekend gold diggers, the mountains are just a place to spend a few hours. Afterward, they retreat to the sanctity of their urban homesteads. To mountaineers and other outdoor enthusiasts, the mountains are their sanctuary, their backyards.

Δ

Russell Gulch was the vaccine for that spell of gold fever that I had, but since then, I've had a tinge of gold fever flowing through my veins. Now, every time I go to the mountains, I pack my gold panning kit. It only takes a few minutes to check a stream for color. That tinge of gold fever will always be with me and keep me wondering where and if I will ever find pay dirt.

Pay Dirt

SINCE THE FIRST DAY gold fever invaded my blood stream, my gold panning kit became an almost permanent part of my regular mountaineering gear. It isn't on my list of top ten essentials, but it's close. Obviously, I don't carry it on climbing expeditions or while rappelling off cliffs or while crawling through a cave. But when it isn't with me, it is as close as base camp or the car, and I frequently carry it with me on day hikes. I usually carry a black plastic pan on hiking excursions and keep a sturdy steel pan in the car. Gold pans also make great sleds for sliding down snowfields.

One afternoon, while hiking in the Medicine Bow Mountains west of Laramie, Wyoming, I was particularly happy that I had a gold pan with me. My experience that afternoon was like a story out of a lost mines and treasures book. It followed the story line in which the characters blindly stumbled onto a lost gold mine or buried treasure. In the typical "lost treasure" story the characters experience hardships that cause them to lose or forget where their treasures were hidden. Fortunately, I didn't forget where my secret find was.

It was a beautiful Wyoming afternoon when Roni and I started our hike up the mountainside. The sky was mostly clear with a few afternoon thunderclouds starting to form. We didn't have any high aspirations for our little hiking excursion. We just wanted to take a hike together and enjoy the serenity of the mountain environment. I carried a daypack with the normal essentials in it and a gold pan attached with a string that I slung diagonally across my shoulders and chest.

We were hiking in one of Wyoming's many forgotten gold territories. Few of Wyoming's gold mining events received much recognition during the hoopla of the Colorado gold rush. There were at least ten gold, silver and platinum mines in the area in which we were hiking. There were also three places that major placer deposits were discovered. The mines were all abandoned, ghost mines. Their best ores were poor compared to some of the high yielding Colorado mines. They yielded one to five ounces of gold per ton of ore, compared to over ten ounces per ton with some of Colorado's mines.

It was really a blessing that Wyoming didn't receive the public-ity and development that Colorado did. The unexploited nature of

Wyoming gives it a uniqueness that few other states have. Wyoming was the last frontier of the lower forty-eight states. It was the only state with more pronghorn per square mile than persons (not really). Everytime I visited Wyoming I felt like I was visiting the last real wilderness outpost in the contiguous United States. Being in Wyoming always elevated my spirit and made me feel great. Wyoming and Alaska are the last of the unspoiled states. I hoped that Wyoming's secrets would never be discovered, but I was sure that future demands for land and resources would eventually destroy Wyoming's sanctity. It would be nice if Wyoming and Alaska could remain the same for future generations to enjoy.

We hiked up the trail toward the first of several mines. The trail gently cut diagonally up the forested mountainside. The vegetation was typical for the 8,000- to 9,000-foot range, groves of pine trees accented by intermixed aspens. We were both familiar with the terrain, but for Roni our excursion was like a hike through her backyard. She spent her childhood and teenage years riding horses, hiking, playing and growing up in Centennial Valley (in the foreground of the Medicine Bow Mountains and Snowy Range).

The trail was not well maintained; few hikers used it. In several areas the vegetation attempted to reclaim the trail. Brush grew high along its sides, and we frequently had to step across fallen timber. We crossed several streams along the way, and I stopped at each one to test for color. As each try failed to yield any yellow, we continued hiking up the trail.

After a relatively short hike, we arrived at the first mine. It was marked by a few closely spaced log buildings in varying states of ruin. A few yards off the trail stood a three-room miner's cabin with a collapsed roof. Farther up the mountainside, hidden in the pines, was the caved-in mine entrance. The mountain was slowly reclaiming the short-lived mining community. The logs were gradually decaying, and the vegetation was slowly creeping in on the log walls that still defined the perimeter of the buildings. Eventually, only the hidden mine shaft would remain as a clue to the arduous lives that the miners once lived.

Farther up the trail, we passed an iron boiler tank and a heavy stamping device that was once used to crush gold-bearing ores. Then we came to the site of the second mine marked by a huge tailings pile and a three-story log structure. Like the other mine, the entrance to this one was also caved-in. By the large size of the tailings pile, the mine had to go deep into the mountainside, and we spent a few minutes exploring the mining site.

Jokingly, I told Roni, "With a little digging, I bet I could reopen that mine."

While exploring the area I found a trickling stream. It was only three feet wide and a foot deep. Still, it was big enough to pan gold! I scrambled down the mountainside through some trees to a small clearing on the stream bank. From a small pool in the stream, I scooped a few handfuls of sand into my gold plan. Then I went to work.

A few minutes later I yelled, "Roni! Come here! I hit pay dirt!"

After panning most of the sand over the edge of the pan, several specks of gold four were grouped together on the bottom of the pan. It was the most concentrated gold deposit that I had ever found.

Roni wasn't as impressed as I was; it was just a few specks of gold. To me, it was my greatest find. It was pay dirt! If I wanted to, I could probably sell it for $10 or $15 at a souvenir shop. Maybe when I'm eighty years old I'll have a worthy collection.

Realizing that it wasn't enough to make us rich, we abandoned our efforts after panning a few pans of sand. Before leaving, I meticulously examined the area so that I would remember how to get back to my secret gold deposit. I didn't want my find to become a "lost treasure" as has happened to so many others.

Δ

If you're thinking about packing the car and driving to Wyoming to find this deposit, don't. Even if you could find it, it wouldn't be worth your time and effort. After all, it certainly didn't make me rich. Now, it is just a special place that I will always remember, like a favorite rock, tree or hideaway.

Although there is still "gold in them there hills," my experience has proven that the real riches are buried between the covers of history books and preserved in the beauty of the mountains. You can explore the colorful gold mining past by reading about it and exploring the beautiful riches of the mountainscape by visiting it. If you're interested in prospecting in the Rocky Mountains, I urge you to learn how to do it, then by all means try it. But don't be disappointed if you don't see the yellow glitter of gold in the bottom of your pan. Instead, be satisfied by the natural beauty that will surround you during your prospecting adventures.

Where should you look for gold? Everywhere. With the right type of equipment you can find traces of gold almost anywhere, including your backyard. However, if you're going prospecting with a gold pan and shovel, your best bet is to look in places it has been found before. A little research at a good library will probably give you the information that you need to get started. There are many places in the Rocky Mountain states where you can find gold. In Colorado, I have found gold in Russell Gulch, Clear Creek and in the South Platte River below Montgomery Reservoir. In Wyoming, there are several areas that have yielded gold in the past, but my recent prospecting experiences failed to yield any. The Douglas Creek District in the Medicine Bow Mountains of southern Wyoming have yielded gold nuggets and dust during past mining operations. If you are interested, you might try gold panning at Douglas Creek, Pelton Creek, Muddy Creek, Beaver Creek, Dave's Gulch, Moore's Gulch and Lincoln Creek Gulch. Although Muddy Creek reportedly has some gold, I didn't find any along its banks after a full day of prospecting. For other possible prospecting locations in Colorado, Wyoming and the other Rocky Mountain states you should do some library research. Research and planning is a fun part of any adventure. That is when you can imagine what your adventure will be like before you start.

Have fun and enjoy whatever prospecting adventures, you may partake. Please remember that the real treasures are in the history and scenic beauty of the Rocky Mountains. Every autumn, anyone can find a scenic treasure by driving into the mountains to see the golden aspen leaves. The Rocky Mountains are infinitely abundant with scenic treasures.

9. Miscellaneous Adventures

After surviving a near fatal experience,
every facet of life sparkles in grand splendor.

THIS CHAPTER INCLUDES a potpourri of adventures that don't fall under the categories of the other chapters. It is a mini collection of hair-raising, gung-ho highlights from other Rocky Mountain adventures. I will take you on six exciting high country adventures including a quick descent down a snowfield, a near fatal shortcut down the Chalk Cliffs of Princeton's south face, a futile hike in a frigid rainstorm, clinging for life on a wet rockface, getting trapped on a summit during a nasty hail storm and a day of carefree rock climbing and scrambling.

Twenty-Second Descent

CUTTING LOOSE AND getting wild in the high country seems natural. Frolicking in high alpine meadows and skipping along mountain ridges rejuvenates the spirit and strengthens the body.

Twenty Second Descent is a story about one of many splendid summer days that Craig and I spent following the whispering calls of the mountains. It was a character-building day, rather than a day for serious mountaineering.

This is a story about a twenty second glissade down a 1,000-foot snowfield. Glissading, or sliding down a snowfield without skis, is the second fastest way to descend a snow-covered mountainside. A solid spring snowfield is a dream come true for mountaineers who enjoy glissading.

My descent from Apache Peak was my most exhilarating glissading experience. I can still picture the frightening steep view from the top edge of that long snowfield, the first section steeper than the most difficult ski slope that I've skied. It was a fifty to sixty degree slope I felt a little heroic on the day that I stepped out onto that slippery summer ski slope. In fact, it was an extreme glissading event. However, on that July day in 1985, it was just a few moments of a midsummer's day of fun in the mountains.

After an early morning start from the 10,600-foot trailhead, we reached Apache Peak's 13,441-foot summit in the early afternoon. Every mountaintop offers a different perspective—a different reward—and those simple, self-satisfying rewards are always worth every calorie of energy that it takes to make it to the top.

Seated comfortably on the rocky summit, we ate a light lunch. During lunch, a pair of squeaking pikas curiously watched us from a distance. Hoping to satisfy their curiosities (and silence their high-pitched shrills), I tossed them some crumbs that they snatched and with which they scurried away beneath the rocks.

After lunch we lay down to recuperate from the climb and to absorb the sensations of the majestic summit. Even though I rested upon a bed of rock, the soothing effects of the warm sunshine and "thin" air relaxed me. Breathing deeply, I drifted into a comfortable state of relaxation and sensed a closeness with nature. My back touched the earth, my stomach touched the sky and my thoughts swirled in the breeze.

Lasting for about fifteen minutes, the serenity nearly put me to sleep, but the chill of a passing cloud interrupted my state of supreme relaxation. The temperature felt as if it had dropped ten degrees as the cloud shaded the sun. I opened my eyes to a much whiter sky than before. Thunderclouds were rapidly growing into ominous, towering stacks. It was Mother Nature's subtle way of telling us that it was time to descend to lower ground. In another hour her warnings would turn into orders enforced by lightning bolts.

We wanted to stay longer (we always did), but years of experience told us not to. Time after time we used to stay on the peaks too long. And time after time Mother Nature punished us with wind-blown rain and hail and threatening bolts of lightning. After a few too many hard-learned lessons I came to heed to nature's warning signals.

Like two boys unwilling to quit playing, we slowly stuffed our gear back into the daypacks. Before starting our descent, we walked a large circle around the summit charging ourselves with a final view of the panorama. Without saying a word, we started down the mountainside.

Looking for the easiest way down, we angled toward a snowfield that we saw during our ascent. From the valley below Apache Peak, the snowfield looked dangerously steep. In fact, we didn't think that we could use the snowfield during our descent, but it wouldn't take any extra time to swing by to examine it. It could shave forty-five minutes from our descent which would otherwise follow a precariously rocky slope.

Foot skiing or stand-up glissading is a blast! Whenever possible, I took advantage of foot skiing during descents. Occasionally it was more dangerous than simply downclimbing a mountainside, but the joy and time savings were usually worth the added risk. The danger variables are the steepness of the slope, the depth of the snow, the condition of the snow and the skill of the glissader. But, like everything that we do in the wilderness, we have to know our own limits and abilities in addition to nature's laws. As my mother frequently reminded me during her protective lectures, "People are always getting killed doing that. Just last week, three people were killed while sliding down a snowfield." They were killed because they went too far. They went beyond their limits in nature's arena; they made a fatal mistake.

A few hundred feet below the summit, we stepped up to the top edge of the impressive snowfield. The upper part of the snowfield was "as steep as a cow's face." It bridged the narrow gap between two walls of an avalanche chute. The lower part of the snowfield wasn't visible from our vantage point because it made a wide turn and disappeared behind the mountain; however, the snowfield leveled out some, as it turned near the start of the lower, hidden section. It appeared to have a safe runout at the bottom. But the full runout wasn't visible because the snowfield curved behind the mountain. It looked steeper than an advanced (black diamond) ski slope, and it contained additional hazards that weren't typically found at local ski areas. There were a few boulder hazards directly in line with our most likely travel path. The snowfield was bound by rocks on every side and spotted with an assortment of small to large rocks exposed by the summer melt. In addition to the visible hazards, there were also some potential hidden hazards: rocks just beneath the snow surface, cavities around rocks and cavities formed by flowing water beneath the snow's surface. Of course, we couldn't determine where the hidden hazards were or if they even existed. And we could only hope to steer around the visible hazards. Ice axes would have been nice amenities to aid in steering, slowing and stopping, but we didn't have any with us.

It looked hairier than a hairy bear. Standing at the top of that vast snowfield reminded me of standing at the top of my first difficult ski slope. I looked at Craig, looking for a decision.

Craig shook his head and said, "No way!"

The longer I stood there, the more frightened I grew. I stood there for a few more seconds waiting for the victor of an internal tug of war between common sense and craziness. Opposing thoughts zipped in and out of my conscious mind like electrons through a conductor.

In an instant of insanity, I leaped out onto the snowfield, instantly accelerating down the steep, icy surface. There was no turning back. Within moments I accelerated to a dangerous speed which made stopping impossible. I quickly switched my mind from decision-making mode to survival mode. Meanwhile, my heart moved toward my throat. Acting on my actions, Craig followed in my footsteps. I suspected that he would follow my lead.

The snow was great: hard enough to support our weight but soft enough to get some traction for switching directions. I stayed afoot for the first 100 feet. Then I lost my footing and fell smartly onto my rear; that is how I stayed for the remainder of the run. After that, the incline proved to be too steep, probably for the best. I had more control and stability from a seated position. A third of the way down the chute, Craig flew past me also sliding on his seat.

The next thing I was aware of was that I was on a collision course with some boulders. Somehow, I had to alter my course enough to dodge them. Attempting to slow my ever-increasing speed, I dug my heels into the snow; the action barely slowed my descent, and I was blinded by spraying snow which was kicked up from my heels. Switching tactics, I tried to dig my bare hands into the snow, but I couldn't penetrate the crust which scraped my hands like sandpaper. When the spraying snow momentarily cleared, I saw the mound of rocks directly in front of me. In a flash of disaster, I saw myself smashing into the rocks, splintering my legs and busting up my body. I estimated my speed at fifty miles per hour. I was in grave danger and had to act quickly. In a final fury of actions, I dug my heels in and pushed to the right with my hands. My efforts seemed futile. I was sliding too fast and couldn't get any leverage from the snow. I desperately scratched my hands and feet across the snow. Just in front of the rocks, my desperate actions worked; I veered past the rocks within arm's reach of them. Moments before me, Craig also passed dangerously close to the rocks.

Just beyond the rocks I sighed with relief as my speed slowed. As suspected, the slope had a safe, gentle runout. Through the lower stretch I maintained a steady, comfortable speed. I happily shifted my mind from survival mode to enjoyment mode. Although not as breathtaking, the lower part of the snowfield was certainly more enjoyable. The snowfield ended in a rock bed of weathered, fallen boulders from the eroding peaks. Under control, I popped back up onto my feet before sliding off the snowfield. White faced and shaking slightly, Craig awaited my arrival. Apparently it had been as good for him as it was for me. We took a few minutes to recount our experiences and to recover. We slid 1,000 vertical feet in twenty seconds.

Relative to that bear of a slope, the rest of our foot skiing action that day was cake.

Many would call our actions senselessly stupid. I call it character building. My mom calls it "taking unnecessary risks." Every time before I left the house she warned, "Don't take any unnecessary risks." I always obeyed my mother. It's just that her definition of "unnecessary risks" is different from mine. I figure that my chances of getting killed in the mountains are less than my chances of getting killed crossing a street or driving a car, even if I take some "unnecessary risks." None of us knows when our clocks are going to stop ticking. When my time expires, it will expire, regardless of where I am or what I am doing. It could happen while I'm crossing a street, driving a car, climbing a mountain or foot skiing down a steep snowfield. I just hope that there are mountains in Heaven.

Many authors would tell their readers not to go out and try the same thing. While that is an admirable thing to say, I will not offer any such advice for glissading. Everyone has a right to enjoy his life as he sees fit, providing he doesn't violate the rights of others. It is up to you to use your own judgment. If statistics are part of your judgment, you should know that every year many people are injured and killed in the mountains. Regardless of skill, intent or ability, death is always a possibility. The more experienced mountaineers often try greater, more dangerous challenges. Intermediately skilled mountaineers sometimes try to go too far too fast. Beginning mountaineers are still finding their limits. Many good mountaineers are killed as a result of trying to reach beyond their limits. Some mountain fatalities are purely foolish or caused by an act of nature. For everyone, experience, training, education, common sense and knowing your limits are the best safeguards while playing in the wilderness. For those of you who are not so adventurously inclined, don't worry about it; your natural instincts have already told you what is best for you.

In the Rocky Mountain wilderness everyone must measure their limits against nature's risks. Before embarking on any alpine adventure you should ask yourself: are the rewards worth the risks? Before glissading down a snowfield, of any magnitude, you should at least learn the proper techniques and how to recognize the pitfalls. I suggest starting on a very small hill or gentle incline and working up to more challenging snowfields.

Death-Defying Descent

THIS IS A STORY about a grueling descent that never should have happened. It is about our perilous descent down the south face of Colorado's Mt. Princeton (14,197 feet), otherwise known as the Chalk Cliffs. The Chalk Cliffs are actually composed of crumbling white quartz monzonite, which is unstable and steep. It was a shortcut that quickly turned into a nightmare.

The original objective of our May 1987 climbing trip was majestic Mt. Harvard, Colorado's third-highest peak. Mt. Harvard and Mt. Princeton are both in the Sawatch Range, located almost in the dead center of Colorado. They are also part of a smaller subdivision of peaks known as the Collegiate Peaks.

Craig, Sean and I planned to make the climb on 27 May 1987. During the adventure-planning stage Sean was still at graduate school in North Dakota and Craig was still at Oklahoma University. After the climbing trip, Sean and Craig returned to their respective universities for summer school. I had orders to report to Sheppard Air Force Base, Texas, for active duty in June. Hence, our climbing trip was a reunion followed by a departure.

It was one of those trips that almost anything that could have happened did. First, it was late in the day by the time we all joined together to get started. Craig had the least time to acclimate to the altitude: we had to leave for the Sawatch Range the same day that he arrived in Denver from Norman, Oklahoma. Our base camp was 7,000 feet higher than Norman's elevation. It was late in the afternoon when we arrived at the base of the Collegiate Peaks and started searching for a way to access Mt. Harvard. Mt. Harvard was apparently blocked by private land on the east side. After searching for as long as we could, we abandoned our primary objective for Mt. Princeton. We didn't have any problems finding a good base camp at the southern base of Mt. Princeton. We settled on a campsite that was a quarter mile from Chalk Creek.

The last-minute change in plans added a few complications to our climb. The topographic map that we had was, of course, for Mt. Harvard. We would have to route find our way up to Mt. Princeton by sight alone. Since we hadn't studied Mt. Princeton at all, we didn't know where the dangerous features were. We didn't know what its subpeaks looked like. And we certainly didn't know about the perils of the Chalk Cliffs.

The stresses that we accumulated earlier in the afternoon while searching for an access to Mt. Harvard faded away after we set camp and ate dinner. Sometime during the excitement of seeing the awesome Collegiate Peaks, we missed a turn, a sign or something. But, we had to put that behind us to concentrate on our new objective: Mt. Princeton.

During our initial approach, from Highway 24, Mt. Princeton looked incredible. Aesthetically, it is a beautiful mountain. From the east it looks like a pyramid, towering above its neighboring peaks. Even though there were higher peaks in the area, the lure of Mt. Princeton won our hearts; reaching its summit would be an honorable accomplishment.

On the morning of 27 May 1987, we awoke at sunrise. We started the day with a hot breakfast cooked over a campfire. We dined in high country elegance in the relaxing forest environment. The day began peacefully and quietly. The rising sun was starting to chase away the morning chill as we left camp.

We dressed in layers and packed daypacks with the typical essentials required for Colorado mountain climbing. I packed water, extra clothes, food, sunscreen, sunglasses, matches, a compass, a knife, a camera, and a few other miscellaneous items. I layered undergarments beneath a sweatshirt and wool pants. Craig wore a sweatshirt, sweatpants and hiking boots. Sean started the climb wearing a wool shirt, blue jeans and hiking boots.

After a gentle ten-minute hike, we started our ascent up Mt. Princeton. We lost sight of the summit as we started the climb. Our pulses rapidly rose above 100 and stayed there most of the day. After ten minutes of climbing I wished that I had trained harder for the climb. I'm sure that Craig and Sean were thinking similar thoughts. Craig barely got his feet on the ground when we picked him up at the airport and hauled him up into the mountains. I was at least partially acclimated to the altitude from making several mountain excursions during the previous five months.

We chose a direct route up the south mountainside. We didn't have a trail or map to help us. Early in the climb we were fortunate enough to find a deer trail which helped speed our ascent. We followed it upward along the edge of a small, steep ravine. A gushing, white water stream flowed through the bottom of the ravine, providing a soothing background sound. As the trail skirted along the nearly vertical edge of the ravine, I wondered if we were following a mountain goat trail rather than a deer trail. We were forced to do some rock climbing but nothing serious enough to require a belay.

While skirting along the edge of the ravine, we were treated to a very rare encounter with a mountain goat. We noticed him when he was drinking from the stream, about thirty feet below us. It was the first time any of us ever had seen a mountain goat in the wild. He was dressed in a white, longhaired winter coat. His beard of white hair hanging from his chin gave him a very distinguished appearance. He calmly watched us for a few seconds then effort-lessly climbed up the other side of the steep ravine. He was well equipped for the rugged mountain terrain with thick muscular legs. After topping the ravine he disappeared into the cover of the forest. The encounter boosted our spirits and got the climb off to a spectacular start.

Farther up the mountain we happened across an abandoned mining community that consisted of a few log cabins. Other than having a few holes in the roofs the cabins were in relatively good condition. We poked around the remnants of the small mountainside mining community for a few minutes. We also found a sluice box along the banks of a dry steambed. They must have had a good reason for building in such an inhospitable location. I felt sorry for the pack animals that had to lug their provisions up the mountainside. We left the cabins as we found them and continued our ascent.

After reaching timberline, we got our first glance of Mt. Princeton's summit since leaving camp. At least we thought we were looking at Mt. Princeton. However, after looking at it for a few minutes, I suspected that it wasn't high enough to be Princeton. It only looked to be about 1,500 feet above timberline; that would make it about 13,000 feet, rather than 14,197 feet. It was probably a subpeak. Regardless of what it was, it appeared to be the direction to proceed.

The best route happened to be a steep-sided ridge that connected with the summit, jagged, narrow and restricting movement to two directions: frontward or backward. We had to rock climb again. Fortunately, there were many short, stair-stepped pitches that didn't require belay or rope work. A long steep pitch would seriously jeopardize our chances of reaching the summit. Even if we had carried ropes, we wouldn't have time to use them. The high altitude and tedious ridge climbing were already putting us behind schedule. I began to realize that we should have started an hour before sunrise. That extra hour of sleep might cost us the summit.

A chilling breeze whipped across the mountaintops forcing us to stop to add an extra layer of clothing. We took advantage of the stop to rest, take a drink and eat a snack. We breathed hard from the vigorous exercise in the thin air; we were more tired than we should have been. That was yet another signal that we might be prevented from reaching our objective.

We used brief rest stops every ten paces, the remainder of the climb up the summit. As suspected, the summit that we topped was just a subpeak of Mt. Princeton. From the 13,273-foot subpeak we were still well below and nearly a mile east of Princeton's summit. It looked like 100 miles to my tired body. Actually, it was heart-breakingly close.

Our fatigue could be overcome; it was the ominous white thunderclouds that had us concerned. The sky grew darker by the minute. Mt. Princeton's summit was the last place that we wanted to be during a thunderstorm. I then realized that our extra hour of sleep had cost us the summit.

We contemplated the situation while eating lunch and staring at the spectacular perspective of Mt. Princeton. We knew that it would be dangerous to attempt the summit beneath the rapidly deteriorating weather conditions. A cold thunderstorm on top of our fatigue would be a very dangerous combination. It was only a hike across a saddle then up a spur to the top. It was very tempting, but hard-learned lessons from past climbing experiences told me not to continue. The memories of being caught on a barren, rocky summit were deeply etched in my lessons-learned file.

The forming thunderstorms helped us forget about attempting the summit. The weather was deteriorating so rapidly that we became concerned about making a safe descent. Our first concern was to get off the subpeak as quickly as possible. The route that we followed up would be very time consuming to down-climb.

Instead, I pointed out a more direct route down the south face. It didn't look any worse than numerous other rocky slopes that I had climbed. Farther down the mountainside, there were some snow-fields down which we could glissade. Craig and Sean agreed with my shortcut recommendation.

Without delay, we started the descent. We instinctively strung out into a zigzagging pattern to decrease the chances of being hit by falling rocks. Ten minutes into the descent I realized that the composition of the slope was weaker than other rocky slopes that I had descended. The slope consisted of crumbling, loosely piled bowling-ball-sized rocks. It was very unstable. With every step we dislodged mini rockslides that threatened to grow into avalanches. It didn't take us long to realize that we were flirting with disaster.

"It's looking hairy! Shall we turn back and take the other way down?" I said.

"Ah, it isn't that bad," said Sean.

"Are you sure? This stuff is really loose," I said. "One wrong step or accidental fall could bring the entire mountainside down."

"We're already committed," added Craig. "Climbing up this stuff would be harder than continuing down."

With me in the lead, Sean in the middle and Craig following above and behind, we cautiously continued down the precarious rock slope. Every step jarred rocks loose; some of them rolled to a quick stop, others hundreds of feet down the mountainside. Every step required delicate placement. Below us were scattered cliffs, steep gulches and a steep walled canyon. The worst part of it was that self arrest was nearly impossible. There was nothing solid to grab onto, just more loose rocks.

As I worked down the rocky slope, I wondered if I would dislodge the key rock that held the mountainside in place. One bad step could put all of us beneath a million tons of rock, but we certainly wouldn't suffer very long. The rolling rocks would pulverize us almost instantly. It was like walking across a lake, wondering if your magic was going to wear off before you made it to shore.

As we neared the snowfields that we hoped would lend some relief, we found that they were too steep to glissade down and almost impossible to reach. Murphy's Law definitely applied to our situation. We were still 1,500 feet above the nearest glimmer of relief. The ever-darkening sky threatened to rain or hail on us at any moment; I only hoped that it wouldn't start to lightning and thunder. The reverberations from a booming thunder could start an avalanche.

We angled toward the only glimmer of hope for relief within sight: a patch of scattered trees on a mountainside knoll which looked like an oasis amidst a vast slope of barren rock. Anything that was rooted to the mountain had to be safer than the loose talus on which we were dancing. However, we still had three formidable obstacles to deal with: the knoll was another 1,500 feet below our position, there was a deep ravine between us and the knoll and we would have to cross a very steep snowfield.

We were at the mercy of the mountain. There was really little that we could do to self arrest if we started to slide or fall. Everything that we grabbed onto moved. Every time a rock tumbled down the mountainside I knew the same thing could happen to me. With three of us moving there was always at least one rock in motion. We tried to stay out of the fall line of each other, but sometimes it couldn't be avoided.

Sean was fifteen feet above me when I heard the crashing sound of a larger than normal rock. It rolled, then it started to bounce. I didn't even have to look back to know that it was bounding directly toward me. I had to make a split-second decision. Judging by the sound of the rock, if it hit me it would seriously injure me and probably knock me down the mountainside. On the other hand, by trying to avoid the projectile I could start an avalanche. I acted on the immediate threat. I leaped to the side as far as I could, desperately trying to spread my weight among the rocks evenly. I clung to the rocks and lay flat against the slope, praying that the rocks beneath me stayed put.

The rock bounced into the air whizzing by my head through the space where I had been an instant earlier. It bounced and rolled several hundred feet down the mountainside.

Then the rocks beneath my feet dislodged, causing me to slide. At that moment, seemingly like eternity, I thought it was all over. Fortunately, the mercy of the mountain was on my side. I only slid a few inches before coming to rest. The rocks that I dislodged tumbled to a stop without starting anything major.

Sean and Craig were still frozen in position. They helplessly watched the entire ordeal that lasted three or four seconds. It happened so fast that I was in motion before Sean screamed, "Rock!" I stayed motionless for a few minutes trying to put myself back together.

Then the silence was broken by a crackling thunder that echoed back and forth between the mountains and valleys. What next, I thought. We had to get moving again. We at least had to try to reach the knoll before it rained. Thinking about rain forced me to realize how easy we had it. The danger would be doubled or tripled by a wet mountainside.

Next, we arrived at the bloody ravine. Actually, it offered some stability to our descent. The ravine walls were solid slabs of granite. It was the same stuff that was all around us, but it hadn't broken up yet. From farther down, the ravine's walls probably resembled the other "chalk cliffs" that gained recognition in Mt. Princeton's history. We had to down-climb the cliff carefully, one by one. It was difficult, but safe enough to justify down-climbing it without a belay.

At the bottom of the cliff, inside the ravine, we were back on the rocks. The ravine dumped us back onto the vast rocky slope after a short distance. Minutes seemed like hours. I seriously began to wonder if we would survive our ordeal. The green knoll was still far away across a vast stretch of rocks and a steep strip of snow. I thought about all of the time that I spent in school preparing for the real world, and whether or not I would live to use my education.

After crossing another hairy stretch of the rocky slope, we came to the edge of the snowfield. It was too steep to glissade down, and it ended in a rocky field without flattening out at the bottom. It was a 200-foot snow slide that we had to traverse. One slip would certainly be fatal. It was much too steep for any type of self arrest.

That was the first time during the climb that I felt we really needed some climbing equipment. To cross the snowfield safely, we should have had crampons, ice axes, rope and secure anchors. Unfortunately, we had none. Our hard-soled hiking boots were the only help we had.

Before stepping onto the slope I tossed a rock out onto it to test the snow condition and slope. It dented the snow then rapidly slid down the slope and smashed onto the rocks below.

"That's exactly what will happen to us if we slip," commented Craig, the acting team psychologist.

Before making the final decision to cross, we thoroughly discussed our limited alternatives. Going around the snowfield would expose us to the rocky danger longer and increase our chance of getting rained on. Crossing the snowfield was the quickest way to get to the knoll of relief.

Feeling responsible for getting the team into the predicament by suggesting the route, I took the lead across the snowfield. If anyone was going to die, it should be me. From the rocks, I carved my first step into the treacherous snowfield. Carefully carving footsteps and handholds I slowly worked across the snowfield. I focused my complete concentration on making each move. I had no way to stop myself in the event of a fall. One mistake could end everything that I wanted to achieve in life.

After what felt like eternity, I made it safely across. The rocks didn't offer total comfort, but they were much safer than the steep, slippery face of the snowfield. It was the most dangerous situation I had ever experienced. A safe distance from the snowfield, I sat down with my knees pulled against my chest to regain my composure. The blade of Death's scythe nicked my soul.

Using my footsteps and handholds, Craig and Sean made it across with relative ease.

Craig and Sean continued descending the hairy talus while I took a few extra moments to shake the gloom from my stunned body. The stressful descent was wearing on our patience. Each of us just wanted to get off the mountain as quickly as possible. Craig and Sean were just brightly colored dots far below when I continued the arduous descent; however, the relief of the grassy knoll was getting closer. Craig and Sean reached the oasis a few minutes before I did. They collapsed onto the firm footing of the grassy knoll. Finally, we were able to relax mentally and physically. We lay in the intermittent sunshine until the roaring of a thundercloud reminded us of our still-vulnerable position. We were still above timberline and surrounded by more of the same type of talus that haunted us all afternoon.

As we descended over the knoll, our luck took a fortunate change. We found a ride to refuge. It was a way to get through the last portion of hairy talus, a snow-filled avalanche chute that ended at timberline. Even though the snowfield that filled the chute was spotted with protruding rocks, we still decided to chance glissading down it. We were so exhausted by the grueling descent that we were willing to do anything to get us off of the mountain faster. One after the other, we sat on our rears and slid down the chute. Sean was the first to get stung by a rock hidden just beneath the snow surface. Craig was next in line for punishment. He dinged his knee against a protruding rock. Somehow, I made it safely to the bottom of the chute without any rocky confrontations. At the bottom, we slid into the firmness of the forested mountainside.

Our traumatic bout with death was over. The remainder of the descent was through the comfort and security of the forest. I kissed the ground, and thanked the Lord for delivering us to safety. Everything about life glowed by the light of my renewed appreciation. Everything meant more: the pine aroma of the forest, the texture of the trees, the chirping of the birds, the rumbling of the river in the valley below and the dreams of my future.

We dragged our feet into base camp in the fading glow of the setting sun. Craig and Sean went directly to the tents and collapsed for siestas; I ambled down to Chalk Creek to relax by the soothing sounds of the bubbling white water. From a rock out in the creek, I immersed my thoughts in the soothing sounds while the sun disappeared behind the mountaintops and darkness encroached upon the landscape. I was deeply grateful still to be alive to enjoy the wonderful sensations of life.

Δ

A better title for parts of this book might have been "The Trials and Errors of a Beginning Mountaineer." But even advanced mountaineers make mistakes and take risks that get them into hairy situations.

Unless you want to spend an afternoon running from the Grim Reaper, I suggest that you stay away from the Chalk Cliffs of Mt. Princeton's south face. However, I would recommend climbing Mt. Princeton. As we later discovered, there is at least one trail to the summit and another route that is better than the one we chose.

To get to the trailhead, follow U.S. 285 eight miles south of Buena Vista to Colorado 162. Follow Colorado 162 about eleven miles; the trailhead will be on the north side of the road. You will pass Mt. Princeton Hot Springs and Cascade Campground before getting to the trailhead. The other popular route is to climb the southeast ridge by making a direct assault up Merriam Creek. To get to Merriam Creek, follow Colorado 162 west four miles, then follow Chaffee County 321 north for about a mile. For either route be prepared for foul weather and give yourself plenty of time to make the climb and enjoy the scenery.

Mt. Antero (14,269 feet) is another impressive peak due south of Mt. Princeton. The trailhead for Antero is another mile west of Princeton's trailhead on the south side of Colorado 162. If you're an aggressive weekend climber, you could climb one of the peaks on Saturday and the other on Sunday; or for a three-day excursion you could give yourself a day to relax between climbs. Both peaks are admirable goals to add to anyone's climbing accomplishments.

Night of Misery

SOAKING WET, in a mountain downpour at 11,000 feet, we struggled to pitch our tent. It was rapidly getting dark, and the mountainside was coated with a sheet of flowing water. It was cold; the wind relentlessly drove the rain into us. We were miles deep in the Colorado backcountry, and our situation was worsening.

The deteriorating weather was only the beginning of our problems on that cold, wet night in the Rocky Mountains. Before the weather went bad we were enroute to a remote destination on the other side of the Continental Divide. We didn't expect to make it over the divide on the first day; we had visions of hiking as far as we could before nightfall, then setting a peaceful camp somewhere just below timberline.

Our destination was Crater Lake on the west side of the Continental Divide in the Indian Peaks Wilderness Area. Our route
would follow the well-established trail from Long Lake, past Isabelle Lake, over Pawnee Pass, down past Pawnee Lake and on to
Crater Lake. A month earlier we made our first attempt to make it
to Crater Lake. We made a gallant effort trudging across snow-
covered mountains and valleys and wading through waist-deep
snow. We fell short of Crater Lake by a mile and a half.

We were determined to make it to Crater Lake on our second
attempt. The only problem was that the weather wasn't cooperating. It rained all morning and afternoon on the day that we
intended to start our trip. We piddled around all day waiting for the
clouds to break. The day was 14 August 1983. It was our last high
country get-together before going our separate ways back to college. Craig would be starting his sophomore year at the University
of Oklahoma, and I would be starting my sophomore year at the
University of Wyoming. This would be our fourth Rocky Mountain adventure for the summer. We spent a full week enjoying the
Indian Peaks Wilderness Area, our favorite Colorado adventure
area; the Crater Lake trip was intended to be a three-day backpacking excursion.

We treasured getting together for high country adventure and
relaxation during the summers. As soon as I had wheels and a
driver's license, we started spending as much time as we could
afford in the Rocky Mountains during the summers. After high
school, during college, the summers were like Rocky Mountain
reunions for Craig and me. Earlier in the summer of 1983, we
climbed Caribou Hill (10,505 feet), hiked over Pawnee Pass,
camped at Woodland Lake, climbed Rollins Pass, hiked to King,
Betty and Bob Lakes and then spent a night of misery making a
futile attempt for Crater Lake. Two days after our night of misery
we recovered enough to climb Mt. Toll (12,979 feet).

When it was still raining at 3:00 P.M., we should have forgotten
about backpacking to Crater Lake; it was a hopeless situation.
Unfortunately, our desire clouded our judgment. Due to time
constraints, we had to start the trip on that rainy day or forget

about it until the following summer. Our backpacking excursion to Crater Lake was going to be the highlight of our week. We thought that if the rain lightened, we could still get a good distance up the mountain before it became dark.

The rain showed some weak signs of letting up, but not enough to get excited. The rain stopped long enough for us to cook dinner, but that was about it. After dinner it resumed drizzling on us.

Against all common sense, we weatherproofed our backpacks, strapped them to our backs and stepped off up the trail to Isabelle Lake. Darkness was only two hours away; the trail was muddy and dotted with mud puddles. Brief, intermittent flashes of blue sky kept our hopes alive, but the continuing light rain threatened to get heavy again. Somehow, under the influence of our clouded judgment, we thought that we could find a dry patch of ground to pitch the tent. As we trekked up the trail in the light rain, wishful whims replaced rational thinking.

Then, a mile up the trail in the fading light of dusk, the sky burst into a downpour. In places the trail looked more like a stream. Unimpeded by the saturated ground, the water rapidly flowed downward to the valley bottoms. That was when we should have turned back. Foolishly determined, we continued to slosh up the trail as if our lives depended on getting to Isabelle Lake. Contrary to our determination, not getting to Isabelle Lake would have been better for our health. Nevertheless, we steadily climbed higher and higher into the darkening mountain wilderness. The higher we went, the more hostile the mountain environment grew. An increasingly strong wind intensified the effects of the steady, heavy rainfall. We would be lucky (we hoped) to make it to Isabelle Lake before it was pitch dark.

Isabelle Lake (10,868 feet) was just below timberline; however, the surrounding terrain was more alpine-like than forest-like. The only substantial protection was provided by a few patches of krummholz (or elfin wood) and a few stands of stunted pine trees. Most of the surrounding area was barren, windswept tundra. When we arrived at Isabelle Lake, the mountainsides were draining into the lake in sheets of flowing water.

We couldn't go any farther. We were forced to bivouac on the mountainside north of Isabelle Lake. It wasn't a planned campsite, but we had to get out of the rain. As nightfall drove the temperature lower it also threatened to do the same to our body temperatures. The conditions were ideal for the onset of hypothermia.

The wind-driven rain battered us as we pitched the tent. The end result was a sagging tent soaked inside and out. Inside the tent water flowed across the floor as in a streambed. Our sleeping bags were our only hope of keeping dry. Air mattresses would have been beneficial (at least they would float), but we only had foam pads which soaked up water like sponges. By the light of my trusty Boy Scout flashlight, we unrolled our sleeping bags on the wet tent floor.

As we tried to get comfortable within the restricted confines of our two-person pup tent, our situation worsened. The steaming vapor from our breath hung in the air, creating an eerie environment inside the tent. As we shed our wet clothes and crawled into our sleeping bags, I felt like we were inside a coffin. Even though I had a good polyester mummy bag which would retain its insulative value when wet, I had a ghastly premonition about spending the night there. By 5:00 A.M. it would be unbearably cold. Craig's cheap cloth sleeping bag wouldn't be able to keep him warm and dry throughout the night. I feared that neither of us would see the light of day if we stayed on that mountain.

After ten unsuccessful minutes of trying to convince myself that it was safe, I told Craig that we had to get back to the car. We could at least dry out and keep warm in the car. We would have to make an emergency descent back to the car, parked below the Long Lake trailhead. It was only two miles, but the mountainside was slippery, it was dark, windy and raining, and we were under stress.

We hastily abandoned camp. Our sleeping bags were the only big items that we took with us; we left the tent and backpacks behind. Craig wore shorts and wrapped a blanket around himself. After emerging into the black, seemingly hostile wilderness, I realized the full value of having a working flashlight. That flashlight was a lifesaver.

Our first obstacle was just getting back to the main trail. We had to skirt around the slippery mountainside north of the lake and cross two streams that were almost steep enough to be waterfalls; the way was rocky and muddy. Conditions were ideal for ankle injuries. There were no safe places to step; we just had to try our hardest to stay afoot. Sharing the light of one flashlight also proved challenging.

We were in a near-panic situation. I mentally reviewed the survival rules as we traversed the slippery mountainside. Don't panic and keep your head clear were the two survival rules that I kept repeating to myself. Even though we were familiar with the area and had hiked to Isabelle Lake over a dozen times in daylight, I knew that we could still get disoriented and possibly lost under the trying conditions. At the east end of the lake the trail split into several lesser trails at the steepest part of the hike. It was the result of numerous hikers taking shortcuts.

Then, as we neared the east end of the lake, the flashlight dimmed, threatening to quit working. I fixed it with a couple of vigorous shakes. We lost the trail as we started down the steep slope back into the forest. At the time it didn't bother me because I knew the general direction that we had to travel to get back on the trail. However, the wind, rain and darkness complicated matters. Weaving through the trees was like hiking through a pegboard maze.

Then, like a page from a horror story, we got lost. Actually, we weren't lost, we were just highly uncertain about how to find the trail again. We didn't find the trail where I expected we would. Instead, we found more forest. Deliriously, we stumbled around in the dark looking for the trail that was so familiar to us. In the darkness, nothing looked familiar; just trees and more trees. For a few minutes we wandered aimlessly through the forest.

Remembering my rules about getting lost, I stopped. Soaking wet, with water dripping off my forehead into my eyes, I sat down on a log to clear my mind. I took a few deep breaths, then purged my negative thoughts. I turned my attention to the basic topography of the area; that was the only thing that we could see, anyway. I knew that the trail followed the South St. Vrain Creek from Isabelle Lake to Long Lake. If we had to we could follow the creek down to Long Lake. I decided that the best course of action was to angle up the mountainside, then descend back toward the creek; surely we would have to cross the trail.

It worked! We finally found the trail. We didn't count our blessings right away, but we knew that we were in the clear if we could stay on the trail. It was only a two-mile hike through the forest to the warmth of the car's heater. Without the benefit of moonlight or starlight, we depended heavily on the flashlight to keep us on the trail.

The well-kept trail was a pedestrian highway through the forest. We easily made it back to the trailhead. I never thought that I would be so happy to see a parking lot. After reaching the parking lot I thanked God for keeping our flashlight glowing. We hiked another quarter mile down the paved road to the car. Whether or not I slept was irrelevant. Dry shelter and warmth were my immediate concerns. We were free from the wicked wrath of the unforgiving storm.

We spent the night at the hotel Ford Fairlane. The front and back seat beds were lacking on leg room, but they were warm and dry. Somehow, we even managed to get some sleep that night. I knew I would be stiff in the morning, but that would be worked out when I hiked back up to Lake Isabelle to retrieve our gear the following morning.

The next morning I awoke to the beautiful sight of sunshine. I felt so robust that I decided to let Craig sleep in while I went after our gear. Under the clear blue sky it didn't take me long to hike the two miles up to Lake Isabelle. I retrieved our gear, then carried both backpacks back down the trail. The clear sky and sunshine boosted my spirit and filled me with energy. I could have carried the weight of four backpacks if necessary.

Later that day, bouncing back from our bout with nature, I ran to the top of an 11,400-foot unnamed summit and back down in twenty-four minutes, from a starting altitude of 10,521 feet. That was my greatest alpine running feat to date.

Δ

Mother Nature taught us a good lesson that night. The mountains have a way of keeping mountaineers in line when they get a little out of control. The mountains let you know when you are approaching your limits. All you have to do is listen to the natural signals, which we obviously didn't do on that night of misery. Ignoring nature's warning signs inevitably results in disastrous consequences on any type of mountain adventure.

My memories of our "Night of Misery" will be remembered for a long time to come. Every experience like that is just one more step toward becoming a wise mountaineer.

Our second attempt to make it to Crater Lake failed. If you read "Five Days in the Backcountry," you know that we successfully made it to Crater Lake the following summer.

As previously mentioned, the Indian Peaks Wilderness Area is teaming with adventure possibilities, and the Brainard Lake recreational area is a good starting point for numerous adventures of varying difficulty. From there you can take a variety of day hikes, fishing excursions, overnight backpacking trips and mountain climbs. In the winter it is an ideal place for remote cross country skiing. I encourage you to visit the Indian Peaks. Take several rolls of film with you, and please help keep it a beautiful place for future generations to visit.

Considering my disregard for using good judgment during our "Night of Misery," the following frequently used quote from my mother seems like an appropriate way to end this subchapter. On many occasions, after describing my mountaineering exploits to Mom, she would say, "You idiot, you shouldn't take all of those chances."

Dripping Water Rock

DURING MY ALPINE adventures I often push my courage to the edge and say to myself, "never again." Then, a month later, the magnetic lure of high country adventure draws me right back to the edge. Figuratively, the edge is the limit of my mountaineering ability. Literally, the edge, in some instances, is the edge of a cliff, the boundary between safety and danger.

"Dripping Water Rock" is a short story about an eternal moment. It is my experience of a few minutes on the edge. The adventure occurred on a rock outcropping on a mountainside, above timberline, in the Colorado Rockies. Craig and I started out on an innocent, lackadaisical climb. As often happened, our easygoing climb transformed into a hairy situation. We weren't thrill seeking, just trying to find our limits.

Our experience on Dripping Water Rock on 14 July 1984 put us in the grip of death. That is third on the scale of nearness to death. The scale is as follows, from farthest from death to closest to death: near death, very near death, in the grip of death, and at God's mercy. To put this adventure into perspective, in our descent of Mt. Princeton's Chalk Cliffs we were at God's mercy. When mountaineers are at God's mercy, they have ventured beyond the limits of their abilities or into situations in which the objective dangers exceed all possible safety countermeasures.

It is important for all mountaineers to know their limits, but sometimes, during your early years, it is difficult to recognize your limits before exceeding them. Sometimes your high country adrenalin is flowing so feverishly that it overtakes your fear instincts. That is what happened during our afternoon experience at Dripping Water Rock.

Guess how we happened onto the slippery rock outcropping? Yes, it was while taking one of my infamous shortcuts. Somehow, eighty percent of my shortcuts turn out to be long-cuts.

Our primary objective was to reach the top of an unnamed 11,000-foot peak. After reaching the grassy summit, our energy levels received an extra boost from the high country sunshine that penetrated our skin. The peak was the lower end of a spur that forked off from the Continental Divide. The lure of the sun-washed higher peaks drew us farther up the ridge.

We followed the ridge upward toward the divide over numerous, intermediate high points. Although the divide was a tempting target, it was too late in the afternoon to make a serious run for it. We continued up the ridge, waiting for the mountains to tell us that it was time to start back down.

Above 11,500 feet, the ridge grew narrow and jagged between two glacially formed valleys. The glaciers, cutting from each side, left a hard-rock spine between them. In addition to the tougher terrain, the sky darkened with thunderclouds. It was the warning for which we were waiting. Our final warning came as a gust of wind. We knew it was time to end our day of play and to get off the ridge. I didn't want any part of descending that ridge during a thunderstorm or simple rain shower.

At our position, the sides of the ridge were too exposed to descend safely, so we backtracked down the ridge. After a few minutes of backtracking, the ridge sides lost their threatening appearance and the U-shaped valley below looked beautiful. The valley was grassy, spotted with rocky knolls and highlighted by a network of alpine streams connecting pools. After a couple of hours on the barren, rocky ridge, the alpine valley was very appealing. As a means of getting into the valley faster, I proposed a shortcut down the steepsided ridge.

It wasn't as steep as it was higher up, but it would still be a challenge to descend. It was a hard class-3 mountainside; not too difficult, but not something that could be accomplished while sleep-walking either. We maintained a three-point climbing technique while making the descent.

Then, midway down the mountainside, we got cliffed off by the ravine that we were following. We were going along a trickling

stream in the bottom of the ravine. Unfortunately, it channeled us
right to the edge of a cliff, where the stream became a trickling
waterfall. Without backtracking back up the ravine, there was one
possible way to skirt around the edge of the cliff to get back on
"safe" ground. We would have to traverse a slanted ledge with
questionable surface friction. We suspected that the ledge led to
safety, but we couldn't see beyond a large protruding rock mass. It
was a situation that was on the borderline of requiring a belay. If
we had brought our equipment, we would have set up a belay just
to be safe.

Rather than backclimbing, we decided to try traversing the
ledge. We attacked the ledge using a spread-eagle, full body spread
to maximize the friction force. Our situation quickly transformed
into an ugly bear. Fully committed to the ledge, we traversed
beneath an overhang, still on the sloping ledge. Then, we came to
a section with a trickling stream of water flowing over the overhang, onto the ledge. The water made the rock ledge extremely
slippery; the friction was almost nil. Over the edge of the ledge was
a forty-foot straight rock face that terminated on a steep mountainside. Our position was very uncomfortable. I nervously hugged the
slanted ledge, relying on fingertip handholds and body friction to
keep me from slipping over the edge. At the peak of my discomfort, I reached a point where the water dripped off the overhang,
onto my back. Hence, we began to refer to that place as Dripping
Water Rock. Adding to my psychological discomfort, the sky was
dark with thunderclouds which threatened to burst into a downpour at any moment. Craig was showing similar signs of anguish.
He was frozen to the rock, starting to inch himself out of the
precarious predicament.

Every move portended disaster. I was afraid to move for fear that
I might slip. With the incessant water dripping on my back, I froze
to the rock to regain my composure. I frantically hoped for an easy
way out, but there was none. The only way out was to backtrack.
What were the chances of someone happening by with a rope? I
wondered. Maybe I could just stay there until a rescue team
arrived. Before help would ever arrive, the rain would probably

wash me over the edge anyway. The worst part of my ordeal was that annoying water dripping on my back!

After a few minutes that seemed like hours, I stopped my thoughts from racing toward panic. I had to remain calm. I blanked the dripping water from my mind and focused my concentration on getting back to a safer position on the rock. Moving like a caterpillar, I inched my way off the dangerous ledge. For the next minute my heart pounded vigorously, and sweat dripped off my forehead.

We both made it to safety. We sat for a few minutes allowing our pulses to return to normal. After our experience I saw things in a new light. I was ready to backtrack all the way up to the top of the ridge, if we had to. At least I knew that that route was relatively safe. I decided that a shortcut wasn't so important after all.

We backtracked up the ravine and found a route around Dripping Water Rock, without having to climb back up to the ridge. We still made it down into the beautiful valley with a few minutes of daylight to enjoy. We collapsed on a rock in a Swiss Alp-like setting. We were surrounded by grass and an intricate network of small alpine streams. Steep, towering peaks formed the backdrop, and a U-shaped valley with intermittent finger lakes stretched eastward in the foreground. It was the perfect setting in which to wind down after a trying experience on the mountainside. It was soothing to be able to look back up at Dripping Water Rock from the safety of the valley floor.

Δ

Our experience on that high country afternoon was the topic of several campfire conversations on subsequent hiking trips. Even today, the words "Dripping Water Rock" immediately remind us of the events of that day. It was an experience that will forever hold a special place in our memories. Like files on a computer disk labeled "Rocky Mountain Adventures," my brain also has a special area reserved for adventures.

This adventure, like all of my adventures, is about gaining experience and finding personal limits. Every time mountaineers venture into the world's higher elevations they learn something new about themselves and the mountain environment. All mountaineers, from beginner to advanced, are in a continual learning process. Even the best mountaineer in the world doesn't know everything about mountaineering and the dynamic mountain environment. Every route on every mountain offers unique challenges, even the same route on different days of the year.

Hail Storm on Paiute Peak

A THIN LAYER of hail blanketed the mountain like a coat of snow. Across the valley, the distinctive summit of Mt. Toll was beautifully coated with a thin sheet of hail. It looked like a mountain setting after an early, light snow. However, the peaceful after-appearance of the mountains effectively concealed the period of violence during the course of the hail storm. It was a mid-July storm that approached from the opposite side of Paiute Peak, forcing Craig and me to search for shelter in the rock ocean of the above timberline landscape.

Paiute Peak's 13,058-foot summit is part of the Continental Divide, located west of Mt. Audubon in the northern half of the Indian Peaks Wilderness Area of Colorado. It has a pyramid-shaped summit, with two peaks joined by a col. Its southern neighbors are Mt. Toll and Pawnee Peak. From the east, it rises steeply from a forested valley containing turquoise lakes and briskly flowing creeks.

Our climb started well below the base of the peak in the glacial valley leading up to it. We started below the finger lake, Mitchell Lake. It is about three and a half miles from the Mitchell Lake Parking Area to the summit. Our route followed the well-traveled trail to the picturesque tarn lake, Blue Lake. Blue Lake is a good starting point for climbing Pawnee Peak, Mount Toll, Paiute Peak or Mount Audubon. Even in mid-July eighty percent of Blue Lake is covered with ice sheets. By the way, Blue Lake is an excellent place for alpine picnicking and lazing in the sunshine.

On the clear morning of 15 July 1984, Craig and I started our ascent of Paiute Peak. The air was cool, fresh and pine scented. Higher up, the mountainside snowfields scintillated in the morning sunshine. It was one of those typical, refreshing, mountain mornings that elevated the spirits of everyone fortunate enough to experience it.

Wearing sweatpants, longsleeved shirts and tennis shoes and carrying daypacks, we started toward our objective. We anticipated an easy, leisurely trek to the summit. Hence, our climbing mood was relaxed. We were familiar with the Indian Peaks Wilderness Area and viewed the climb as a day in the backyard. Paiute Peak was one of our objectives in our grander goal of climbing all the Indian Peaks.

We deeply enjoyed every minute we spent in the Indian Peaks Wilderness Area. We were free to express ourselves without worrying about the constraints of societal norms. During the course of our climbing adventures we had time to discuss life, politics, the universe and anything else that surfaced.

Blazing up the mountain at our typical, robust pace, we arrived at the shore of Blue Lake (11,300 feet) by midmorning. We stopped there long enough to savor the alpine panorama, photograph our objective, and pick our summit route. The wide open mixed grass and granite landscape was a setting I could savor forever. Before continuing on, I slowly turned a full circle to enjoy every perspective.

After relaxing in the beautiful setting of Blue Lake, we set out for Paiute Peak's lofty summit. The climbing terrain was primarily composed of tundra-like short grass mixed with smooth, rounded boulders. The climbing was technically no harder than off-trail scrambling. Five minutes into the ascent we were in the full spirit of the climb. As Blue Lake grew smaller, the arete summit of Paiute Peak grew larger. On our ascent, we passed by many prospective glissading snowfields. In a time crunch, glissading could save us valuable time on the descent. We were scrambling up the mountain at a healthy pace.

Then the fairweather cumulus clouds started to transform for the worst. The ubiquitous afternoon thunderclouds started forming sooner than normal. The discouraging part of it was that it wasn't even afternoon yet. If it was a typical Rocky Mountain day we would have started the climb early enough to avoid the threatening thunderclouds, but this was an atypical day. We had hoped to be on and off the summit before the thunderclouds appeared. We would definitely have to hustle to the top and limit our summit stay.

We were off the comfortable tundra and onto the roughness of the boulder-strewn higher elevations. Lightning hadn't struck yet, but the ominous thunderclouds reminded me of lessons that my Outdoor Recreation teacher taught me back in junior high school. He said, "If your hair starts to stand up, haunch down to provide a low profile, but stay on your feet." He also warned us about the dangerous possibility of electric currents flowing through the granite during an electrical storm. Then I remembered a story about a golfer who was struck by lightning. His smoldering shoes were the only remains that the search party could find.

We made it to the summit. We stayed long enough to snap a few photographs, drink some water and eat a snack. By that time the sky was dark with thunderclouds. Before cinching down our daypacks, we pulled our longsleeved shirts out and put them on for an extra layer of warmth. One way or another, we knew we were going to get wet during the descent.

We were well above timberline. A large overhanging rock would be the only shelter that we could hope for, and I didn't notice any of those on the way up. Maybe if we closed our eyes, clicked our heels together and said, "There is no place like a tent," we would instantly appear back at camp. A white flash of lightning followed by a booming blast of thunder bounced us off the summit and launched us into motion. We were about to be rained on, snowed on, or hailed on. It would be difficult to predict. Snow would be nice, rain would be miserable and hail would be a nightmare. We had to get off the mountain as quickly as possible!

Like contestants in a downhill run, we raced down the east side of the summit. It was a dangerous place to be in a hurry, but we were caught between risking a broken ankle or getting toasted by a bolt of lightning. The sky was ready to drop something on us. The air smelled and felt moist. It was about to happen.

We were cringing in anticipation of getting wet. Then, miraculously, we happened across a large boulder with a sheltered overhang. It was like a good will offering from the mountains. Without saying anything, Craig and I hustled under the overhang. A few moments later, the sky burst open with an onslaught of marble-sized hail. Safe beneath the overhang, the otherwise unwelcome hail storm became a spectacular display of nature. We were pinned to the summit until the storm dissipated, so we made the most of the situation.

Our attention was focused on Mt. Toll's prominent peak, south of our position. The hail highlighted Mt. Toll's alpine features like eye shadow on a woman's face. The horizontal rock surfaces turned white, further defining the vertical rock faces.

It was a rare, special experience for which I was thankful; it was an evanescent experience. Like the life of a Day Fly, it would soon be over forever. It was a one-time show of nature. The sun would return, the hail would melt and we would move on. The experience would be remembered but never would be duplicated in all its glory.

After the storm subsided, we resumed our descent. The melting hail made the rocky mountainside very slippery. Remembering the snowfields that we saw on the ascent, we angled toward them. As always, we wanted to foot glissade. I loved the adrenalin rush that always accompanied sliding down a snowfield! It was a good way to add spice to an otherwise uneventful descent. The only serious drawback to many glissades was a rocky bottom; many tempting snowfields have been passed over because of rocky bottoms. Regretfully, some snowfields that should have been passed over were not. Sometimes the temptation to experience a few thrilling moments overrides common sense and the will for self preservation. Many contemporary sport climbers and alpine thrill-seekers live for the thrill of the moment. Fortunately, the snowfield before us wasn't too steep, and it leveled out before ending at the bottom. We would have plenty of time to arrest our glissades before sliding off the snowfield.

On the way back to Blue Lake, we glissaded down every snowfield and patch of snow that we came across. We milked the mountain for every drop of glissading action that we could find.

Δ

My experience on Paiute Peak is a good example of how every recreational experience in the Rocky Mountains is unique. Every climb, hiking trip, backpacking trip and excursion is unique. Even if you are climbing the same mountain, by the same route, you are going to have a unique experience. You could climb the same mountain 100 times, and each climb would have something unique about it. The mountains themselves are continually changing. The Paiute Peak that I climbed then would not be the same as it is today. The variables of nature make mountaineering a dynamic, interesting sport that always poses different challenges to the adventurer.

If you are interested in climbing Paiute Peak, the trailhead is in the Indian Peaks Wilderness Area above Brainard Lake. It is about a three-and-a-half-mile trek from the Mitchell Lake Parking Area. Plan on making a leisurely day's climb. Start early to beat the afternoon thunderstorms (if climbing during the summer) and plan to spend some time at Blue Lake on your way back. If you climb before mid-June, be prepared to cross vast stretches of snow.

Bouldering at Vedauwoo

MY FIRST VISIT to the fascinating rock formations of Vedauwoo was during an antelope hunting trip with my father. I was just a young tyke, about eight years old. We camped overnight at Vedauwoo while enroute to hunting grounds near Medicine Bow, Wyoming. My dad called it Robbers Roost. Consequently, I also called it that until I learned its real name while attending the University of Wyoming. He told me that many of the robbers in the late 1800s used to hide from the good guys in the large rock formations. I don't know whether or not that is true, but it sure helped get my young mind wandering. I kept myself entertained for hours running, climbing and role playing around the amazing rock formations. We revisited Vedauwoo during several other camping and hunting trips, and, for ten years of my life, it was my favorite place in Wyoming.

The Vedauwoo rocks are in southeast Wyoming, thirty-five miles west of Cheyenne and fifteen miles east of Laramie. They are located at the south end of the Laramie range in the Sherman Mountains. The Laramie Range is the northernmost extension of Colorado's Front Range of the Rocky Mountains.

The Vedauwoo rocks are large blocks of weathered Sherman granite primarily composed of crystalline fragments of quartz and feldspar. The higher concentration of feldspar gives the rocks a pinkish tint. They are grouped together in large granite towers formed by stacks of huge rectangular blocks that have been rounded by windblown sand. They provide some of North America's best technical climbs. Although they lack cracks and holds, they provide excellent friction and chimney climbs.

Living only fifteen miles from Vedauwoo while attending the University of Wyoming, I had the privilege of spending many weekends climbing, rappelling and hiking around the rocky wonderland. Vedauwoo provides a welcome outlet for many stressed college students. It is also frequented by technical climbers, family picnickers and campers. Few nice Wyoming days pass without numerous climbers testing their skills on the vertical rock faces.

The focus of this subchapter is bouldering or simply friction climbing without belay or technical climbing equipment. Friction climbing at Vedauwoo could also be appropriately referred to as slab climbing. Basically, it is pure climbing fun without the cumbersomeness of ropes, hardware racks and other climbing gear. On the negative side, it is also done without the safety of ropes, although it doesn't have to be. Anyone shouldn't feel obligated to do any climbing without the safety of a roped belay. Even on moderately sloped boulders or slabs, climbers should be respected if they wish to climb with the added protection of a belay. Frankly, there are many slab climbs out at Vedauwoo that can and have resulted in fatalities. On some rocks the friction is so good that it tempts climbers to boulder up dangerously steep slabs.

There are also many good rappelling locations throughout the Vedauwoo area. There are numerous rock faces that you can set up your rappelling ropes, rappel down and boulder back up to the top. In some places you can rappel down a 120-foot rock face and scramble back up to the top in fifteen to twenty minutes. Those qualities make Vedauwoo an excellent training area for rappelling. There is also a wide selection of rappelling challenges to meet everyone's experience level. There are forty-foot cliffs for beginners and 100-foot overhanging free rappels for more advanced rappelers.

I didn't have the time to devote to climbing that other non-engineering students had, but I still managed to slip away to Vedauwoo fairly regularly. I was a part-time gung-ho climber. Brent, my great friend and engineering study partner, was a highly gung-ho climber. Brent and I spent many weekend days playing follow the leader up and down the rock formations at Vedauwoo. We were both bouldering, scrambling maniacs while out at Vedauwoo. We seemed to have an endless supply of energy that allowed us to run from one climb to the next. We are well-matched climbing partners. We are both very determined and strive to achieve the highest goals; after we start up a rock face, we hate to quit without making it to the top. Sometimes our determination drives us too far, placing our lives at risk.

Both of us were tenacious, hard working, disciplined engineering disciples. We spent the majority of our free time solving problems, cramming for exams, reading and crunching numbers. Engineering is a highly competitive, sometimes stressful, major, but we both enjoyed it. On the weekends most of the students scattered in three directions: the bars, the mountains and the library. The party crowd went to the bars to douse their frustrations with firewater, the outdoor crowd fled to the mountains to purge their frustrations with recreation, and the studious crowd went to the library to increase their frustrations.

Brent and I fled to Vedauwoo to run wild and go berserk! Vedauwoo is a rock climbing wilderness paradise. It is the perfect place to cut loose and act natural. It is possible to wander around in the labyrinth of colossal stone formations for hours without seeing anyone else. It is a great place to escape the formalities of the classroom structure or the social formalities of civilized life.

The Vedauwoo wilderness contains a vast array of natural features to entertain a wide variety of interests. Some of the rock formations are chimneys, crevices, overhangs, tall vertical faces, Indian bathtubs (large, weathered pits in the rock surfaces), teetering boulders, anvils, mushroom-shaped rocks, ledges and natural courtyards surrounded by stone and anvils. Other natural features include a small cave, forested valleys between rock formations, ponds and streams.

My most memorable day of bouldering at Vedauwoo was on a sunny Saturday afternoon toward the end of our college educations. We had been cooped up in the classroom all week. Brent and I were full of potential energy. We were ready to turn that energy into kinetic energy by bouldering and scrambling around at Vedauwoo.

After arriving at Vedauwoo, we took off from the parking area so fast that we almost forgot to shut the car engine off. We stripped our shirts off and trotted toward the nearest rock formation. We automatically started a game of follow the leader. The greater the challenge the better. I followed Brent to the foot of a steep, monolithic slab of solid granite. From our vantage point it looked impossible. While I was staring up at the granite tower in awe, Brent was already crack jamming his way up the first pitch. The only way for me to climb was directly in his fall path so I opted to stay at the bottom to help him find footholds and handholds. He followed a large crack that angled up the rock face. It was easy climbing until he reached the end of the crack, about midway up the climb. At that point, he was about thirty feet above the ground.

Brent's lighter body weight was a definite advantage while rock climbing. He carried about thirty pounds less weight than I. He could squeeze into tighter crevices and control his body weight better than I could.

At the end of the crack, there was no way to continue safely up the rock face. After studying his predicament for a few minutes, he was forced to backtrack down the crack ledge.

While he was downclimbing, I bounded for the next obstacle. I found a steep-sloped face with fractures and small knobs for handholds. It was a good warmup climb. It was only a fifteen-foot pitch. It was a class-4 type of pitch, but it wasn't long enough to warrant a belay. I topped the pitch without any problems.

Closing the gap between us, Brent rambunctiously rambled up the pitch like his life depended on it. While he worked his way up that rock, I scanned the towering rock formation for another short pitch.

There weren't any attractive pitches within eyesight. I waited for Brent, then we descended into a forest separating two large formations. We jogged through the forest obstacles, around the base of the formation in search of another attractive pitch. The pace for the day was established. We jogged from one climb to the next for most of the day.

On the roofs of the rock formations we had to cross crevices between large boulders. In most places it was just a matter of leapfrogging across the crevices and jumping down from one larger boulder onto a smaller one.

We were moving so fast that we didn't have time to get frightened by the risks that we took. We jumped from boulder to boulder, leaped across gaps between boulders, ran up short pitches, skirted along the edges of rock faces, long jumped across wide gaps, and continuously planned our moves a few steps in advance. The only times that fear caught up with us was when we were forced to slow down to think carefully through our climbs.

My most frightening experience that day occurred on a face of the largest formation at Vedauwoo. It is a large dome-shaped mountain of granite. It can be approached from any point around its roughly circular base. Depending on where you start climbing, the difficulty ranges from class-1 to class-6 (hiking to aid climbing). Brent and I chose a very challenging class-3 to class-4 climb.

We attempted to climb a particularly difficult pitch on the south face of the dome. From our vantage point we could see climbers on the challenging east face. The east face contained the best free climbing and aid climbing routes. The pitch that we attempted to climb was on the borderline of requiring a belay.

On the first third of the climb, we picked our way up through a maze of leads and deadend leads. We found plenty of intermediate ledges randomly spaced up the pitch. It was like climbing from one tier to the next on a crude pyramid.

At the top of the first third of the climb, it got hairy. The rock face became steeper and the route finding was harder. Traversing back and forth along a horizontal ledge, we searched for the best route, and the only route that we could find looked extremely risky. It was a crack up a steeply sloped slab. The crack angled about two thirds of the way up the second pitch of the climb, then it abruptly ended. Without climbing to the top of the crack, we couldn't determine whether we could continue climbing above that.

Using an undercling grip on the crack, I climbed up the angling pitch. Climbing up the crack wasn't overly difficult, but the presence of a sheer rock face behind definitely increased the risk. A fall would probably be fatal. Focusing on the task at hand, I climbed the crack without looking over my shoulder. From the top of the crack the climbing looked impossible. There was a ledge to the west, but it was separated by a steep, featureless section of rock. The only way to reach the ledge would be to use a full-body friction climb; there were no holds. After seriously contemplating my situation, I decided to attempt it. From the ledge, I could probably climb on up a vertical fissure to the top of that section.

Lying on my stomach, I inched sideways toward the ledge. Shortly after committing myself to the rock face, it became impossible to continue. There wasn't enough friction to prevent me from slipping. Every time I tried to make another move I slipped. I hugged the rock as tightly as possible. For the moment, I froze lying spread eagle against the rock. Getting back to the comfort of the crack was my new focus of attention. I had problems moving in either direction. My situation was extremely intense. If I slipped, I would fall at least fifty feet.

While frozen against the rock face, I recalled the keys to survival. I took three deep breaths, cleared my mind, relaxed and analyzed my alternatives. I decided to focus all my efforts at backtracking to the crack.

Inch by inch, I worked sideways across the rock. Finally, I made it back to the crack and promptly wedged myself into it. After a few breaths of relaxation, I downclimbed back to the bottom using the undercling technique.

Despite the difficulty that I had, Brent had to try the route for himself. I looked for another, safer route up the rock.

Amazingly, after a few minutes of sweat and intense determination, Brent made it across the friction slab to the ledge. From his position there, he faced another challenging obstacle. He would have to chimney up a vertical fissure to make it to the top. While he started to chimney the fissure, I searched for an easier route.

It took me a long time to find an alternate route to the top. Brent was waiting for me when I finally made it. After my earlier close call, I was just happy to be alive. I would have taken the rest of the day getting to the top if I had to.

We finished our day of bouldering at Vedauwoo by scrambling around on top of the dome. We stayed up there until a thunderstorm chased us off the formation.

Δ

Vedauwoo is a good place for a variety of outdoor recreational activities. At Vedauwoo you can enjoy free climbing, aid climbing, bouldering, camping, hiking, photography, sun bathing, fishing, picnicking, jogging, rappelling, bicycle riding and observing wildlife.

To get there, from Laramie, Wyoming, drive fifteen miles east to the Vedauwoo exit on Interstate 80; from Cheyenne, drive thirty-five miles west to the Vedauwoo exit on Interstate 80. The rock formations are visible from the interstate.

10. Conclusion

The Rocky Mountains and earth's many other natural wonders are gateways to unlimited adventure activities. Your knowledge, appreciation, understanding and enjoyment of these areas will ensure that they are preserved for future generations to enjoy.

I N THE INTRODUCTION I stated four goals to convey to you through my Rocky Mountain adventures. My goals were to (1) entertain you with my adventure tales, (2) tell you the importance of recreation adventure in a person's life, (3) emphasize the importance of preserving parks and recreational areas, and (4) persuade you to make the most of your recreation time. I certainly hope that my goals for you were met.

I certainly enjoyed the time that I spent in the Rockies participating in these adventures. I hope that you have been inspired to enjoy your recreation time more, and to help protect the world's recreational resources.

The demand for recreational resources is increasing with the shift toward a service-oriented society. As technology continues to make life easier, our free time for recreation and other pursuits will continue to increase. As the world population grows beyond five billion, our natural recreational resources will become increasingly invaluable. As the world becomes more crowded, it is imperative that we maintain our recreational resources. By the year 2040 earth's population will be reaching its theoretical maximum. By then, everything will be in great demand. Recreational resources like the Rocky Mountains will serve an important function in the role of maintaining our society. People need recreational areas to relieve stress, to play, to spend time with their families and to vary their activities.

The importance of the mountains extends far beyond their recreational value. During my adventures, I looked beyond the recreational pleasure that I found in the Rockies. Throughout all of my climbing, skiing, running, backpacking, caving, exploring, prospecting and other adventures, I was observing, studying, thinking and learning more about the Rocky Mountains and the environment in general. In addition to the physical satisfaction gained from my adventures, I discovered emotional, intellectual and spiritual contentment. The Rocky Mountains have influenced me in profound ways. I gained new insight to our relationship with our environment. I learned that we can no longer set ourselves apart from nature. No matter how super our technology becomes, we are still going to be dependent upon the health of the world's environment for our survival. Nature's other creatures live in harmony with nature. On the other hand, the intelligent and ignorant humans have the ability to select their relationship with nature. We can either act like a cancer and destroy ourselves along with earth, or we can act like white blood cells to protect the health of our planet.

The recreational value of the Rocky Mountains and other world mountains is only part of the reason that we must preserve them. Our very survival depends on how well we can preserve the mountains and other wilderness areas. The mountains are part of our delicate ecosystem; just like the oceans, rain forests, deserts, grasslands and marshlands, the mountains are a vital part of earth's ecosystem. Earth's health and our longevity are directly linked to how well we can take care of the ecosystem. As we are learning more and more every day, we have to view our actions with a global perspective.

Through my Rocky Mountain adventures, I have opened my eyes to new perspectives on life. All of the time I have spent in the Rockies has positively influenced my philosophy about life.

During my teenage years, the mountains gave me a healthy alternative to the common teenage pitfalls. While many of my peers were drinking alcohol and taking drugs, Craig and I were getting high on Rocky Mountain air. We discussed our frustrations while venturing in the high country. We had many campfire and mountainside discussions about life. One evening, after hiking a portion of the Continental Divide, we sat on a grassy mountainside talking about life while the sun sank behind the peaks. We talked about personal problems and problems that humankind faces. Sometimes our discussion topics were women, world hunger, peace, nuclear war, acid rain, the greenhouse effect, life and death. Thanks to the mountains, our high school peers didn't see much of us on Friday and Saturday nights.

One of the first things that I learned during my adventures was that nature is not partial to any of its creatures. Nature treats everything with equality. When it rains, it rains on everything within the storm's reach; when the sun shines, it shines for everything in its path; when the flowers bloom, they bloom for the benefit of everything around. Survival in the mountains is dependent upon acting according to nature's ways. Since most of us are so dependent upon technological conveniences, we have forgotten our natural ways and must educate ourselves before venturing out into the mountain wilderness.

One of the key qualities that separates me from the sport climbers and sport mountaineers is that I honestly care for the mountains that I enjoy. I don't climb mountains to set records. I climb mountains because I love being in the alpine environment. I don't venture into the mountains to satisfy a psychological need to experience high risk. I venture into the mountains to experience their abundance of natural beauty. The next time you are in the mountains, forest, jungle, swamp, canyonlands, ocean, desert or other wilderness area, I encourage you to take a close look at nature. Observe the beauty and listen to nature's message.

In the appendix, I've included an essay titled "Harmony." It summarizes my feelings about humankind and nature. It contains the essence of the secret to our survival. We must relearn how to live in harmony with nature, rather than trying to set ourselves apart from nature. Our ignorance and disregard for the natural environment have already caused permanent damage to our only refuge within a vast, cold expanse of space. We need to alter our attitudes toward our existence and the environment. If we don't keep our home clean, who will?

I can't keep from getting emotional about the health of our planet, especially the mountains. I value highly my Rocky Mountain adventure experiences. I have to wonder whether or not your children and mine will have the same opportunities to enjoy earth's recreational resources. They won't have the opportunity if our generation destroys it.

Energy is a very critical factor that directly influences the health of our environment. The ways that we have produced and consumed energy have caused most of the environmental problems that we have today. Exhaust from combustion engines gets into the atmosphere, then falls back to earth as acid rain. Even the world's highest mountains have measurable quantities of nitric acid in the snow and water systems. Misuse of nuclear power has resulted in harmful radioactive fallout and nuclear waste products that stay active for thousands of years. Wasting energy by producing too many disposable items is creating solid waste problems in the form of too much garbage to dispose. There are many examples of how energy is being abused, resulting in damage to the environment. The sooner that we can convert to using renewable energy sources such as wind, solar, geothermal and nuclear fusion, the sooner the environment will be able to start recovering.

As you can tell, my concern for the environment goes much deeper than just concern for the mountain environment. Besides seeing pollution in the mountains, I have also been to polluted beaches; I've seen lakes and rivers that had to be closed because they were so badly polluted; I've seen the devastating impact of strip mining operations; I've seen the damage caused by oil spills;

and I've breathed the brown air of Los Angeles, Denver, Fort Worth, Oklahoma City, St. Louis, and so on. I'm not just a mountaineer turned environmentalist because I have to drink from mountain springs that contain nitric acid. I am a recreational mountaineer working as a civil engineer. I've lived in Colorado, Wyoming and, while writing this book I lived in Atlanta, Georgia. I have firsthand experience in many different environments. Yes, I am very concerned about my favorite recreational area, the Rocky Mountains, but I also know that just trying to preserve the mountains will not solve the problem. No matter how hard we try to keep the mountains clean, we can't stop the nitric acid from falling from the sky until we stop using our gasoline combustion engines. If the pollutants can get into the atmosphere, they're bound to fall eventually on the mountains with the precipitation.

As an engineer and mountaineer, I plan to do everything I can to protect our environment and especially the mountains that I ineffably enjoy. I am an advocate of using solar energy for buildings. During five years in Atlanta, I conserved 2,900 gallons of gasoline by riding the rapid transit system to and from work. I ride my bicycle and walk as much as possible. I minimize my consumption of water and electricity. I save recyclable products. And, as an engineer, I strive to find more efficient ways to use earth's resources to benefit humankind. I urge you to also save energy to preserve our environment and the Rocky Mountains so that future generations have the same opportunities for adventure that I had.

I hope to write another adventure collection to be titled "Great Mountain Adventures of the World." Mount McKinley would be a nice first step in that direction. For now, I have to get away from this computer. I've spent too much of my recreation time writing about my recreation time.

The mountains are beckoning me. I have been away from them for too long. I must go. I have mountains to climb, ski slopes to ski down, forests to run through, lakes to backpack to, caves to explore, ghost towns to visit, gold to find and high adventure to seek!

Appendix

Harmony: An Essay on Our Home, Earth

LIVING IN HARMONY with nature is the only way to assure a healthy, long existence on earth. We must all learn to accept earth as our home. As the world population increases, our home, planet earth, must support more and more people. Earth is a limited planet with limited resources. We must nurture renewable resources to assure a sustainable future. We must use our intelligence to achieve a harmonious relationship with our environment, our home, earth.

Earth is home. Our home has over five billion humans in it. Unlike moving from one family dwelling to the next, or from one town to another, it will be a long time before we will be capable of moving to another planet. By 2015, our home will have eight billion humans in it; we cannot afford to contaminate our home, because we need every available resource to support earth's growing population. We must safeguard our water supplies and efficiently cultivate the limited farmland we have. Earth's resources should be valued like our best-kept personal resources.

Appendix

Earth, like our own homes, has limited resources. Eventually we will exhaust all of earth's nonrenewable resources, such as petroleum, coal and natural gas. For energy, we have to switch to renewable energy alternatives, such as solar, nuclear fusion, wind, tidal and more efficient hydroelectric plants. In addition to having alternative energy sources, we must also conserve and use our energy more efficiently. Every time we throw something in the trash, we are throwing away energy. Newspapers, bottles, wrappers, containers, boxes, etc., all require energy to produce, distribute and then to dispose of. We need to increase our use of reusable and recyclable products. I was appalled by the marketing of disposable cameras and contact lenses. The disposable camera is the epitome of our wasteful society. Instead of using our intelligence to feed the forces of entropy, we should use it to develop a more energy conscious, harmonious relationship with our environment, our home, earth.

Intelligence is the primary difference that urges us to separate ourselves from the rest of the natural world. But, are we really that much different from the other living creatures on earth? Should we set ourselves apart from nature? No, I believe not. Whether or not you believe the biblical or the scientific viewpoint toward our existence, the fact is we are dependent upon earth (and nature) for survival. Our intelligence gives us the power to manipulate our environment for better or worse. We have the intelligence to prolong our existence or to terminate prematurely our existence. The dinosaurs and most of the other species that ever existed during earth's five billion year history didn't have the intelligence to avert their extinction. Maybe we don't either. Of course, even if we do achieve world peace and harmony with nature, we still cannot completely control our survival. Ice ages will still come and go, large meteorites and other large astral bodies will still strike earth from time to time and the solar system will eventually die. But, by avoiding self-destruction and caring for our home, we will have the time that we need to solve our immediate and long-term challenges of survival. To survive, we must combine our intelligence to develop a harmonious relationship with earth for the mutual benefit of everyone.

As more and more people tax the resources of our home, we must focus our intelligence toward using our resources more wisely and toward developing the technology of renewable energy sources. The time is rapidly approaching in which we will have to quit wasting energy resources for destructive purposes, such as making war machines, so that we can improve the methods of feeding, sheltering and caring for earth's population. Humankind must pull together to share, conserve and use wisely earth's limited resources. Everyone must be taught that humankind lives together under one roof, earth's atmosphere. If someone smokes a cigarette in your livingroom, it disperses through the air into other rooms in the house. If pollution is put into the atmosphere by one country, it spreads to other countries. Most importantly, we must combine our most valuable ability to develop a harmonious relationship with our environment, our home, earth. That ability is our intelligence.

Δ

If you are wondering how all of this relates to my Rocky Mountain Adventure Collection, I will explain my logic. Without the Rocky Mountains I would not have the setting for my adventures. The Rocky Mountains and all of the world's mountains are critical parts of earth's ecological system; they must be preserved. Along with the mountains, we must also preserve and safeguard earth's lakes, rivers, deserts, marshes, oceans, forests, jungles, canyonlands, swamps, beaches, etc. It just so happens that many of the areas that are so environmentally important are also recreationally important. While preserving these recreationally important areas, we will also be helping to preserve our environment and consequently our own survival. I exhort everyone to help preserve our recreation areas, and to seek a harmonious relationship with nature.

Glossary

aid climbing: class-6 rock climbs that require the aid of ropes and other technical climbing equipment.

arete: a sharp, crested mountain ridge between two cirques.

bear: slang, a difficult, intense action requiring concentrated effort.

bear brush: slang, see krummholz.

belay: a method of providing a safety rope controlled by an anchored person (belayer) for climbers climbing steep rock faces or otherwise dangerous slopes.

bloody bear: slang, three times as difficult as a bear.

bouldering: scrambling up and over large rock slabs and boulders.

bushwhack: to clear a path through thick woods, especially by chopping bushes and low branches.

cairn: a human-made heap of stones piled up as a memorial or landmark; typically found on summits.

cake: slang, a simple task; requiring little effort.

cirque: a deep, steep-walled basin, shaped like a bowl, formed by glacial activity; the depression that remains at the head of an extinct glacier.

cleft: a fissure or crack.

climb ratings: a system of numbers, letters and sometimes adjectives used to rate the difficulty of climbs. The system used in this text is the Yosemite Decimal System:

1—hiking
2—off-trail scrambling
3—climbing; rope for beginners
4—belayed climbing
5—leader places protection
6—aid climbing

Class-5 climbs are also broken down into decimal ratings that range from 5.0 to 5.14. A 5.0 climb would be up a rock face with ample footholds and handholds. A 5.14 climb would be up an almost impossible smooth-surfaced overhang.

col: a pass or depression in a mountain range.

couloir: a steep gorge or gully on a mountainside.

crag: a steep, rugged rock or cliff.

enchainements: two to five mountaineering feats accomplished one after the other.

extreme skiing: skiing on slopes so steep that if you fall, you die.

false summit: a knoll or mound on a mountainside that appears to be the summit during an ascent.

finger lake: an elongated lake, originally formed in a glacial trough.

fool's gold: iron pyrite; a yellowish-colored metal that is often mistaken for gold.

ford: to cross a creek or river by wading.

fourteeners: mountain peaks between 14,000 feet (4,267 meters) and 14,999 feet (4,572 meters) in elevation.

free climbing: climbing a rock face or mountainside without the direct aid of ropes and other climbing equipment; ropes, carbiners, harnesses and leaders are used only to arrest a fall.

friction climbing: traveling up a steep rock surface by using the friction between feet, hands, body and the rock.

glissading: sliding down a snow-covered slope without the aid of skis or sleds, usually on your feet, stomach, back or seat.

ghost town: the remnants of an abandoned town.
grew hair: slang, a situation or climb became difficult or intense.
gung-ho: an intrepid, "go for the gusto" type of attitude.

hairy: slang, a difficult or dangerous situation; a bear.
hairy bear: slang, a very difficult situation, twice as difficult as a bear.
hanging trough: tributary glacial trough with a floor higher than the main trough that it intersects. This geologic feature frequently contains scenic waterfalls and cascades.
hard-core: slang, a serious, tenaciously determined attitude.
hoarfrost or surface hoar: light, feathery snow crystals that sparkle in sunlight, typically formed after a clear cold night.
horn: a sharp pointed peak formed by three or more intersecting cirques, such as the famous Matterhorn of the Swiss Alps.

krummholz: elfin wood. Short bushy evergreen brushes typically found near timberline.

labyrinth: extremely complex or tortuous in character; maze-like.

mogul: a small, rounded bump or hill of snow on a ski slope.
mother lode: the big, rich gold or silver vein sought after by miners.
Murphy's Law: If anything can go wrong, it will go wrong.

pinnacles: spires, sharp, jagged, cone-like formations, topped with pointed peaks.
pitch: one segment of a climb, typically less than 150 feet, and marked by belay positions.
placer deposit: an accumulation of gold flour, dust, gravel and nuggets originally deposited by flowing water; typically found at the banks of old river systems.
potential: slang, having attractive attributes for further exploration or effort.

Rocky Mountain High: a feeling of elation experienced at Rocky Mountain altitudes and caused by the lower amounts of oxygen in the higher air.
Rocky Mountain Smile: an unintentional smile produced by the

great satisfaction of being in the Rocky Mountain environment, typically experienced with a Rocky Mountain High.

roust: wake-up term used to get climbing partners out of the tent in the morning.

scree: a heap of small stones or rocky debris; small talus.

screeing: the activity of sliding down scree; glissading down a scree slope.

slab climbing: similar to bouldering and friction climbing.

spur: a ridge or lesser elevation that extends laterally from a mountain or mountain range.

steepness scale:

    0–30 degree incline: gentle

    31–45 degree: moderate

    46–60 degree: steep

    61–80 degree: extremely steep

    81–90 degree: vertical

subpeak: a lesser peak near a larger peak that does not meet the distance separation and elevation difference to be considered a stand-alone peak.

talus: a slope formed by an accumulation of rock debris, typically formed by the weathering and breakdown of a cliff.

tarn: a beautifully-colored alpine lake residing in the bowl of a cirque.

thirteeners: mountain peaks with elevations between 13,000 feet (3,962 meters) and 13,999 feet (4,267 meters).

timberline: the elevation above which the climate is too harsh for trees to grow; the terrain above timberline is similar to tundra terrain found in extremely northern latitudes.

Tommyknocker: little, two-foot-tall sprites, believed to be the ghosts of dead miners.

topographic map or topo: a map that shows geological features and elevation contours of a certain quadrant.

wild-haired: slang, a crazy and often dangerous idea or suggestion.

Share the adventure with a friend—
Books make excellent gifts!

✂

Please send me
Rocky Mountain Adventure Collection

____ copies @ $12.95 each =   _____
California sales tax (7.75%)(California residents only) +   _____
Shipping ($2.00 per order)   +   2.00_____
TOTAL   = $_____

Name _____

Address _____

City/State/Zip _____

❏ My check is enclosed

❏ Please bill my MasterCard/Visa

Number _____

Expires _____

Return to:
FITHIAN PRESS
Post Office Box 1525
Santa Barbara, CA 93102

Or order by phone toll-free: (800) 662-8351

If you enjoyed this book, you'll also enjoy . . .

Alone in the Sierra by Marcel 'Pete' Fraser $8.00

What does a hiker think about as he lugs a heavy pack up a steep Sierran slope? Fraser mentions no place names, but gives us a uniquely intimate account of what the wilderness experience is really like. 80 pages, paperback.

Malibu by Michael Banks $6.95

A paean to the unspoiled California coast–its beaches, hills, and arroyos. Banks, a former financier, extols the virtues of the simpler life and natural surroundings, drawing on the philosophy of the ages, including the wisdom of the native Chumash Indians. Unlike any other book about Malibu–or any place else! 160 pages, paperback.

Please send me:

___ copies of Alone in the Sierra @ $8.00 = _____
___ copies of Malibu @ $6.95 = + _____
Subtotal + _____
California sales tax (7.75%)(Calif. residents only) + _____
Shipping ($2.00 per order) + ___2.00___
TOTAL =$ _____

Name _____

Address _____

City/State/Zip _____

❏ My check is enclosed

❏ Please bill my MasterCard/Visa

Number _____

Expires _____

Return to:
FITHIAN PRESS
Post Office Box 1525
Santa Barbara, CA 93102

Or order by phone toll-free: (800) 662-8351